Primera Edición
© *2007 Guillermo J. Morell-Chardon*
All rights reserved
Editorial MOCHA
Houston Texas
Cover Photo: © *Ricardo Pacheco 2009*

To: My wife, the Motherland and God, my oasis in the desert of reality.

CHAPTER 1:
[[Sunday A.M., Jobo's Beach Just Before Sunrise]]

The drive from Rincon had been an uneventful one. The forecast was for mildly rough seas and some rain during the evening. Winter, if you could call this a winter, was his favorite part of the year.

As a former surfer, turned martial artist by life's circumstances, Jose could appreciate the changes in the tides and the ten to fifteen feet tides that came with the season.

But he was not there to surf, he came to train. He trained rigorously every day for a month in order to go to the international competitions. He had a regiment that consisted of weight, resistance, aerobics, forms and speed. At 25 he was one of the youngest Tae Kwan Do practitioners in the island to achieve a 3rd degree black belt. He was shooting for silver in Houston's competition. With the "other Jose" as he called the two times Gold Olympic medalist from Houston in the competition the only realistic hope was silver

He will start with two hundred push-ups and fifty complete repetitions of abdominals. Five miles run and practicing all his twenty-two forms, until he could not stand it anymore fallowed this.

Jose was a good man. He was trying to make of his situation the best. He had a plan, he had a chance but it was rough to train, have a full time job and also teach 6 classes a week in his dojo in Rincon.

And on top of all these, the Christmas holidays were here. Christmas in the island was also an endurance sport. The holidays lasted more than one month. This was usually associated with weight gain of 10-15 lbs and monetary losses in the millions.
On the other hand this season united the country in one single purpose, in one Single Spirit, "brotherhood of men", etc. Every drunken man was a courageous patriot and every drunken woman a willing

whore.

It was no coincidence the most islanders were born in September and August. His birthday was September 3. The Metropolis permitted these minor infractions with the promise of selling to the 3.5 million islanders everything they could desire but did not really needed.
The payment will come eventually in sweat and tears and in the blood and guts that the men of this island have spilled in every war the Empire have designed. Most of these wars had no rime or reason.

"We had not sold our souls to the Devil, we had mortgaged it to the almighty dollar"...he whimpered as he completed the first series of abdominal repetitions. There is no hope for his country as long as its men laid on their knees, begging like lepers for crumbs, our manhood loss and perverted.

The Empire was not a benign Republic, "the beacon of light in a world of darkness", like they liked to call themselves, was ruthless and unforgiving toward its enemies. His uncle had been recently executed by FBI Swat team style and his wife seriously injured.

What was his crime? Thirty years ago he had rubbed a bank in order to finance the Island Front For the Liberation "los macheteros". All of them had been clean, brilliant jobs. He was captured and escaped from a maximum security jail in the capital, where he "had taken" several vehicles until he reached the island 10 years ago.
One night "the federales" decided that they had waited enough. They would execute the enemy of the state. He did not begged for his own life, he begged for the life of his wife and 5-year-old granddaughter. After he was shot he was denied medical care and he simply bled to death. That was 6 month ago and as a result "muni-

tions and personal" had been deployed and a major uprising was schedule to explode "any day now and the Federal Bureau of Investigations building in the island's capital will be demolished and every "petit yanqui" with a badge will be disposed appropriately"-claim the group's new directive.

His last words will never know he was not a man of words; he was a man of action. His last act was to write the name of his loving wife of 30 years, which she shared with the granddaughter, Titiana: "…You will live to avenge my death and only then will be there will be

All these were written in his own blood, on the floor, photographed by the forensic experts and leaked to the press.

Jose kept thinking about those memories as he continued his push up:
"One hundred and one...one hundred and two..." In the distance, sounding like a whisper almost like the echo of his own soul he herd the cry for help:
"...For God's sake, for the love of Christ..." He strained his eyesight and was able to see, with the first ray of sunlight hitting the green waters of the Atlantic the enormous white promontory and the head floating in the waves.

"…Aquí cabrón..." He sounded exhausted.
He probably had a partial opening of his parachute and in addition to the trauma of the fall, plus fighting the current here he may be in his last efforts..." He took his hunting knife and his trusty silver Brazilian dart gun and his acupuncture needles full of curare and place in his Playero© fanny pack, grabbed his surf board and started sliding towards the promontory, at good speed. He shouted: "…Maricón, aguanta, I am going to save your sorry ass..."

At a distance, a flat boat slowly and painfully progressed towards the beach in minimal speed, unnoticed by either man on the beach...

[[JOBO Beach 10,000 feet 30 min before:]]

Jerry Vaelga was his name. Mafia drug mule was his game. He was the middleman, the first one in the venerated capitalist chain of middlemen that made it possible for good and services to arrive to the consumers. It was his racket.

His life has been completely loss for years. His father, Adolfo Vaelga, was a brute that beat his mother senseless and raped everything in his way, his own children, the paraplegic aunt, and the Jehovah's Witness missionaries.... He was feared by the whole town of Añasco, including the police, the mayor and the priest...

Gerry had started using heroin when he realized his only escape from that reality was either to die at the hands of this brute or to kill himself from an overdose.

His best friend in the world was Ana Maria Cabrera- Sampayo. "La Sampayo" had slept with every male in her Junior Class at the Morel-Campos High. Anita, as he afectionally call her, was the heir apparent to the west Coast Cartel in Cabo Rojo. They kept the lowest profile...

One night "Anita" decided to experiment with Jerry's psyche. Jerry was always a willing subject "it's amazing what men will do for a little sex", she use to tease Jerry before that fateful night. She mixed cocaine, LSD and PCP together and kept some Qualude at hand to bring him down. She injected the mix straight line...

Everything seemed to be under control until his father arrived home. Drunk as usual and ready for "action". It became clear that the object of his "affections" that night was Ana. He proceeded to pull her clothing off...and that was the last thing he ever did in his life...Jerry later would say that night he became a man...his "first blood", the first time he had ever killed anythingvertebrate.

He had the strength and the valor (i.e. lack of inhibitions) of 10 men.
He ripped one of the legs of the old rocking chair and in a single movement broke his father's nose and face. All desire escaped from his father's face, revenge and hate substituted.... But before he could say anything Jerry swung back and hit his chest braking half his ribs...His father's face was of desperation as he realized his minutes were counted... the next swing broke his chest wall in the left side.

His father lay in a pool of his own blood he did no try to fight back, he had no strength, as his left lung had collapsed. His only option was to crawl out of his house. Before he had a chance he felt the knee of his son in the back and Ana's bra on his neck.

As Jerry squeezed harder and harder his father started making fun of his strength "… You squeeze like a girl, Maricón…" Ana had been in shock, but reacted by squeezing with Jerry with all their might until his father stopped jerking. His father's last thoughts: "...I should have killed this bugger while I had a chance…"

The next day Jerry waked up to find him surrounded by the town and state police, including the state homicide police. The last thing he remembered was strangling his father. He had the worst headache of his life. Ana was not there and he panicked he realized that he was nude, covered by a blanket, covered in his father's blood and excrement. His father had been gutted and bled, like a Christmas Pig. His blood and excrement were used as ink and his many crimes were chronicled in the white walls of the house, inside and out.

A young homicide sergeant, Frank Molina, look at the languid teenager in disbelieve: "…Son did you kill your father by yourself?

He was a big man...!"
"...Yes, I did as you say, and I am proud of it, and if I had another chance I would do it again, and again and again...!" said Jerry
"... Son, Where is his penis...?"
"...Garbage disposal..."
"...His brain and heart...?"
"...I fed the rest to the pigs, his priced pigs; they will not suffer any longer, either..."

Ana begged his father to intercede. With his best lawyer and the town priest they convinced the jury of the obvious that Jerry had acted while insane (the toxicology blood screen disappeared under mysterious circumstances) After 6 months in a state hospital the island Governor was convinced of pardoning Jerry with the condition that he left the island.

With Ana's father's blessing, he joined the army during dessert storm and retired during Iraqi Freedom. He was the most condecorated soldier during that period of time. Not only was he a "big hero" that was permitted to go back to the island but also he established a network of heroin producers in Afghanistan with refineries and the monies stolen from Sadam's palaces he could finance the weapons needed.

As he jumped he did not suspected that his brother in law had planned his assassination. He carried $30 million dollars in cash plus 300 million dollars in heroin and cocaine. He opened his parachute and realized it had been sabotaged. He opened the auxiliary parachute but it was too small to hold his weight and money and drugs. He opened the parachutes to the money and drugs duffle bags. He assumed extreme gliding positions and hope for the best.

He hit the water with a big splash. His body was on fire, he had broken an arm, and otherwise he was in shock, probably some internal bleeding. On the beach he could see someone exercising, if he could call his attention, he could help him get to the beach. Then his carrier would transport him to Rincon where they would get together to plan the final assault to the Cabrera-Sampayo compound to liberate ANA.

He could see the surfboard gliding towards him. He took his gun out to take control of the situation, however Jose disarmed him. In the process he broke his trigger finger. Before Jerry could attempt to say anything Jose had an accupuncture needle with curare in his forehead and Jerry was out.

With much difficulty Jose took the whole cargo to the beach.

Ignacio Baron has not always been a fisherman. As a mater of fact he feared the sea. It had been the tomb of his grandfather, who had raised him after both his parents were killed in a drive-by shooting. Both his parents were clean as a whistle, were on the wrong place at the wrong time and they were collateral damage of a drug war between the Cantillos and the Jimenez clans who competed for the capital's territory.

After the burial, Don Ignacio Baron Serrano, originally from "Las Canarias"took him under his wings and thought him everything he could about the sea and about being a man. About honor, about loyalty, about God. "Only an idiot does not fear God or the sea. "… Sometimes, Ignacito , they are one and the same, that is God and the sea… ", his grandpa used to say...

Grandpa died transporting illegal aliens across the Mona Straight. The sea did not killed him ,it was firepower from a Black Hawk Helicopter patrolling the area The ironic thing is that he did not do it for money. He patrolled the Mona Canal one night a month to pick up the bodies of the casualties and to pick up survivors. The rest of the month he worked as a fisherman. , that night a month he became a Mennonite Minister looking for lost sheep in the blue-green pastures of the Atlantic Ocean

After that he joined the army where he met Jerry. That night he was betraying everything he held dear for a "fistful of dollars" He will be sure Jerry's death would be as painless as possible. He will pick up the cargo, disposed of the body afterward, he will marry Jerry's wife and kill all her enemies. He will control the west coast family. Jerry Vaelga, the great war hero would be remembered for a short period of time. "I have always desired Ana, and before she became a one man woman, before Jerry swept her off her feet, she had been mine.". Now she only had eyes for Jerry.

One night, before Don Ignacio passed away, he had waked up to the cries of desperation of his grandchild. the cries of unfulfilled desires of pleasure and pain "Ounce you had one the Sampayos, the Sampayos had you"...grandfather used to say. He had been Ana's grandmother's lover and after 30 years he did not know how he could forget" that amazing specimen of femalehood"

His boat, a flat-bottom high-speed hydrofoil was approaching the beach. Gun in hand ready for the "coupe de grace". This was a little complicated. He could see that Jerry was in bad shape but also that he was not alone. Somebody, of great strength had rescued him. He will have to kill both. In love and war everything is fair. He would have to approach the beach and disembark as the vibration from his boat made it very difficult to kill them...

Jose realized that he was in great danger. A non-official hydrofoil with an armed man, an unconscious half drawn man who was requesting his help from the other side of a 45-barrel. He had to act quickly and ask questions later. He took his ceremonial silver tranquilizer dart pipe, three curare laced darts and three Shuriken.

Ignacio approached the beach in neutral. He had enough momentum o disembark kill those two "hijos de perra", get the merchandise and get the hell out of there before the coast guard, border patrol or local police intercepted him. No time to dispose the cadavers. Jerry will get his "heroes funeral" at the national cemetery...

Jose aimed the first shuriken toward the hand with the gun. Instead, he hit the oil line to the motor causing failure of the motor, with a dramatic jerk that distracted Ignacio long enough for him to blow two darts in succession. One hit the forehead, the other the hand of the weapon, his right hand...

"...I guess I was not counting on this crap..." Ignacio lost first strength in his right hand, to the point he could not hold his gun. "... Shit I guess I am lucky that Shuriken hit the boat and not me...either you are amazing or amazingly bad..."
He felt as all his muscles relaxed, the hydrofoil hit the beach he flew face down in the beach. He heard the hydrofoil been keyed off. "...Son of a gun, he even has time to prevent an explosion and keep the keys ,so nobody could escape..." He could not turn around he was going to drawn in one inch of sea water. Then he felt the needles, three in succession: two in his neck at opposite sides of mid neck.

His head was turned around. "... I will memorize that face and I will personally kill this SOB for what he had done today…"
But when he turned around Jose had converted his winter wool hat into a ski mask and placed the third accupuncture-curare needle deep between his eyes.
"The Buddha's Peace Triangle ..." He remembered from his martial arts training in the army, a very ancient acupuncture technique which was fabled to have been discovered by the Buddha himself, which rendered the victim paralyzed, for several minutes and semi-comatose until the third needle was removed, the one neutralizing the "third eye". One needle for Ying, other for Yang and the other

for the third eye. He witnessed the operation again with Jerry and passed out.

Jerry in the meantime, admired Jose's flawless technique. His last thoughts were: "... Darn, this guy is good..."

Jose who was a religious man by nature kneeled in the sand , gave thanks for still been alive, for his opportunity for training under the great Filipino accu-ninja master Bernardo Ayala while he was stationed in the Philippines. And for all his training.

What to do next? The both had tried to kill him; it was poetic justice that they were both at his mercy. Years of training and discipline had thought him to respect the sanctity of life, even scum-life like these two.

Curiosity took the best of him and he checked the contents of the two duffle bags. One was full of white packages...Heroin? Cocaine? No matter he was not turning into a dealer now...He emptied the duffle bag in the sand and moved the two limp bodies away from the beach, filling their pockets with bags.

The second bag had two satellite phones and hundreds, maybe thousands of banking cards each in a glad plastic bag with the banking code typewritten in a small paper. "...Jackpot...!" "...As God is my witness, will never be poor again..."

He grabbed the duffle bag. Placed in his car. He took a pair of handcuffs and handcuff the two "sleeping beauties" together .He picked up the cell phones a got in his car. He drove away; the sun was hitting the beach.

He opened the phone. "....Coast Guard Please..." ....Yes I like to report illegal smuggling at Jobo beach...No, no joke. Ill be waiting...Hope there is a reward...!"

He opened the other phone:" operator gives me the state police" I like to report a double murder at Jobo Beach.... Yes I'll be waiting." He disconnected both phone batteries and put them in the globe compartments. "...I wish I could stay around and see the faces of those two when the police arrive...!!!"

CHAPTER 2
Town Plaza: Rincón 6:30 A.M.

Gilberto Goya, "direct descendant" from the luminous Spanish painter opened his Barber Shop with his usual ritual. He would go to the corner bakery buy a pound of buttered local French Bread that will last his whole day and two cups of coffee.

He would sweep the floor of his five feet by fifteen feet kingdom. His brother, who had been a partner for 60 years had died 6 months earlier. He had never taken any care of himself and unlike Gilberto, never exercised.

Gilberto was a long distance runner who has competed in BOSTON, NEW YORK, TOKIO, MOSCOW, BELFAST, PARIS ROME, and ISTAMBUL... over the last thirty years. He had the Guiness© book of world record citation for the most marathons ran in the most diverse number of countries.

The whole walls were covered from top to bottom, except for his mirror, with pictures of all his marathons, all his ancestors from the 1880's Mayorca to present. The Goya genealogy was taped to those walls.

At least Juoquin died never to be seen again. Grandma Goya refused to meet her ancestors and remained in Rincón, which was her version of purgatory, because she was "still needed here on earth".
She appeared in her funeral photo ahead of the coffin in her most exquisite *mantilla*. Expert had come from around the world and testified to the authenticity of this photo.
As usual he left the second cup of coffee, for *abuela,* in the mantle where his Kenyan Marathon Medal for fourth place rested. A photo in the Nairobi stadium showed the ghost of *abuela*, among the 60,000 spectators.

Actually, the 'specter spectator" as the family fondly called *Abuela was in every family photo.*

As usual the old lady materialized an took her cup of coffee "There is no descent cup of coffee in purgatory, I hope there is in heaven..." as usual Gilberto pretended to ignore the old geese. She will usually get infuriated and punish him with a bad spell of cough, rheumatism or a seizure. Today she made him tickle so violently that he fell on the floor, without control and peed on himself.

"...Oracle of the lord!" She said, dead serious
"...Don't tell me you are a prophet...?" Asked him exasperated and sarcastically.
She proceeded to open hand smack him in the back of the head, so hard he loss vision for a couple of seconds.
"...Technically speaking dead spirits are dead spirits so they can not be prophets, you moron! I can see the near future...!!!
"...OK, should we get exited, oh seer of the near future...?" Asked him while doing a mocking genuflexion
"...The living is in very great danger!! There will be a blood bath in this town like it has never seen before. Men with heavy weapons and no consciences, hate and contempt, but no love; adrenaline but no compassion..."
"...Should we activate the Samaritan Brotherhood...?"
"...Most of the Brotherhood is too old and weak, the average age is 68, and is no match for the children of Satan that are preparing for the kill..." "We need new blood..., conviction...resolve ...and fear of God Almighty ...and faith, deep faith!!!"
"...I know the man, but he is not a Christian..."
"...Son Good is Good, Evil is Evil, God is Love and Love is God. Its time to visit our Buddhist friend and give him a chance to stop Evil..."
"I hope upon hope this will be the case..."
"...Me too, me too son, me too....your universe is rapidly deteri-

orating into chaos...and I fear because I can feel Evil strengthening in our midst ..."
As Gilberto locked the Barbershop, Ana Rosa's ghost fallowed him.

Sitting across the plaza sat Brother Ignatio Blancforte. He was a sturdy Italian man originally from the North. He has been trained as a mystic; God had given quite a career in the Catholic Church. He was the official Vatican exorcist and the Holy Father's personal confessor. In his youth he had competed in the Olympics doing archery and in the winter Olympic he got gold medal for ski shooting.
After that he had an epiphany when ,not unlike Paul, he had a vision of Jesus Christ revealing himself to him. He gave up a career in sports endorsements or the joy of serving his vision of that God. I was a roller coaster ride being both the Vatican Exorcist and the confessor of his Holiness

Over 30 years he had fought evils and demons, heretics and ghosts. During his first week he met the ghost of Michelangelo. Because of his disdain for the Catholic Church, the medieval pope had not only excommunicated the painter in life but also barred his tormented soul from entering Heaven or Purgatory. The calculation was to send him to Hell. He believed, in spite of his flaming homosexuality, that with the interception of the Holy Mother that he will not go to Hell.

And so it was centuries after his death, he was still in ghost Limbo. Ignacious needed a spectacular exorcism. Michelangelo will give him a sample of his power. After so many centuries the ghost's power were formidable. Earthquakes, seizures blood lettings, strokes, violent hallucinations, gut worms of prehistoric proportions were endured by Ignatio during that first month.

One day during a violent seizure the solution came to him in a dream. He remembers the order of the Holly Sepulcher. This order kept all the material objects that were ever in contact with the *holly blood of the True Christ.*

He knew the curator of the Holly Collection, Padre Pereira, a Brazilian that looked more like Pelé, than like **_Martin de Porres_** the first Afro-Antillean American, to be recognized by the Vatican as saint.

"...What you need to get to get rid of the Michelangelo, master, is the spear of Christ, that wound's blood will get rid of Michelangelo; for good buy and good riddance!!!

"...At least theoretically, my friend! If this works, just remember your dear friend, Padre Pereira when you get to the top. I need the Spear back by midnight, if not I will get forty minus one lashes, you know the game..."

That night he hid behind one of the support columns. When Michelangelo's ghost passed his back- stabbed him. At first nothing happened , then a great fear froze Ignaitos's heart , not because he had defeated the ghost, but because on the peaceful smile the painter had, he realized that he had not send him to Hell, but rather had it made it possible for him to enter Heaven, against the Church's wishes. There was a rip of light on air and the painter, effortlessly floated towards the light .He disappeared into the rip, which closed with a great thunder. He meticulously put the spear away and later lied on his report that the Spear had gone with Michelangelo. Of course the painter has gone to Hell.

In 30 years that was the only ghost he had send to Heaven, all others had gone directly to Hell.

Now in Rincon's Plaza, in his backpack he played with the spear getting ready for the kill. He walked towards the ghost of *abuela*. As he ran for the kill, he was swept away and thrown on the floor nonceremoniously by the still athletic Padre Pereira.

"...You need to learn Aikido asshole ..."

"...Pereira, she is going away...". He protested.

"…She needs to get away, the future of this town and this land depend on her..."

"…He will escape, she needs to go back to hell, where she escaped..."

"…Senile old fool , you still have not learned , *some people stay behind for the greater good, not because of the selfish desire to hang up, like Michelangelo* did ..".

"…He went to Hell that night...."

"…Bull shit ! I fallowed you to the Chapel that night, I want you to return the spear to me now...

"…But..."

"…No buts, I will brake your sorry neck, and this is no empty treat…"

Reluctantly Ignatio realized that for now he was defeated, that he could not overcome this younger man, with years of training in martial arts.

"…Keep a close eye on me because at the first chance, I will kill you..."

"…Another back stab? If you try something I will kill you without a second thought...."

Defeated for now, Ignatiou fallowed Pereira to the town square pizzeria: "Three Brothers"

Gilberto and abuela continued their uphill walk to the end of the plaza.

They past the public school with pictures of old governors, dead and alive (all thieves, dead and alive). It was the holidays, so no voices emanated from the school.

"…Gilberto, you know what has kept me around for so long…?"

"…Not really, abuela ..., (as to pull her leg) Fear of punishment for lascivious thoughts…?"

"…Very funny…!" She proceeded to smack him hard in the back of the head.

"…Abuela, cut it out, You are going to hurt me, remember I am older than you, after all…!"

"…You are a wimp! Just like most men. If you grab them by their manhood the rest of the body will fallow…"

"…For God's sake, now stop quoting Richard Nixon…!!"

"…You ungrateful and pompous ass, I will quote whoever I please. To set the record straight Nixon wanted to grab your balls, my proposal may be" a prima facie", much more acceptable to most men..."

"…OK, tell me why you still her... I am all ears…"

"…Is the children, the future. The little voices in the school yard, their songs, their laugher. There is no laugher without children, there is no future without children there can be no gods without men to adore them..."

"…So you did everything for the children...?"

"…Yes 80 years in Limbo, protecting my family, this town, this island, and in spite of my efforts there is calamity brewing in the air. We need help and we need it now, there is Evil in the air…!"

"…Do you mean Satan…?"

"…NOT YET! But lest say that there is a convention of demons and there is a pretty good chance He is going to be the key note speaker...!"

As they passed the Playero© store the Green House became evident. This was classical nineteenth century architecture. Two stories high, huge porch. Had been abandoned for years that is until recently, when the Buddhists moved in. Most buyers abandoned the idea of buying the house ounce they realized that it was haunted. Ghost roamed this place like it was Union Station. An Apocalyptic cult had committed mass suicide in 1898 after the American Invasion. They feared that the Puritans would punish severely their bisexual, polygamous, hedonistic, Baal -worshiping ways , like they had done in the mainland where they had send the New Babylonians scattering toward the islands of the Northern Pacific , Hawaii , the Florida Keys and the Caribbean.

But the Llama did not fear the dead. He had moved to take over this place and rid it of these evil spirits while waiting for the Great Struggle against Evil. Every re-incarnation had such struggle and for the first time ever he was really organized.

He and his disciple had organized a "Circle of Light" .They had been fasting in a circle for three days, chanting reciting in unison the 101 names of the Buddha. . Finally the rip in the fiber of time had appeared, and the 20 devil-ghosts one by one were sucked out into the Seventh Hell. The cries of pain and fear where deafening even for *abuela.*

The Llama stood up after officially breaking the circle. He looked at Gilberto, and then concentrated on abuela: "Madam you are too late. You will have to wait until our next circle.

"…So he can see you…?"
"…Of course, the Llama and I go back..."
"…Of course everything was platonic..."
"…Of course said Abuela with a smile..., you were always a gentleman…"
"…Ginebra, what can this humble monk do for you, we tried before to send you to Your Heaven without success. Your mission is not completed yet ..."

"…Your Holiness, we need your help, the Storm of Evil is brewing and I can not do this alone..."

"…You are not alone; we have been told to come to Rincón, rapidly and to clean this house. We completed face one. Everybody willing to help is welcome here, "mi Casa Verde es tu Casa Verde"
"We will need holly weapons and warm bodies…"
"…Ginebra, the Blood of Christ and the Blood of the Buddha

are here in Rincon for the first time together in more than 2000 years.... Do you know than the Holly Inquisitor and the keeper of the Holly Sepulcher are here...?"

"...Yes, I felt his presence, one wants to kill me, the other to save me..."

"...We need an army of believers to defeat the invading hoards... we can take care of the demons, but we need to defeat the terrestrial armies of dead, before innocent blood gets spilled. Again...!"

At the Three Brother's Pizza and creole restaurant Igntcio and Pereira went through their breakfast, local French Bread toast on butter (*pan de agua*)and passion fruit juice with cappuccino.

"...Not bad, for fifty cents you can get a cappuccino as good as any in Rome..."

"...Ignatous, you are such a cultural slob...Open your eyes ...these people are in real trouble. Rome sent me to stop ghost hunting...they need you to start demon hunting....Exorcising ...Cooperating with the Llama..."

"I don't believe you...John Paul II would never have order such as thing..."

"...Perhaps not him, but he is not here with us, Ratzinger is, and he feels that is to our best interest to cooperate with the Llama ..." He took a folded document out of his travelers side pack; it had the seal of the new Pope.

Ignatous opened, recognizing the authenticity of the seal, he trembled with rage and owe.

The message was simple and yet had the power of a ton of rocks: "***to the carrier of this letter you owe complete loyalty and submission, in the name of our LORD and Mine, on penalty of eternal damnation, in the name of the Holly Trinity, AMEN***"

"...You know this does not change anything between us...."

"...On the contrary, dear Ignatio it changes *everything between us*"

His large ego defeated, Ignatiou threw himself to the floor and

kiss Pereira's feet: " I am your slave...*for now...*"
"...You are *my* slave until you die, or you will die *__Forever__*...!"
He should had return the stupid spear when he had a chance.

CHAPTER 3
[[JOBO BEACH 8:00A.M.]]

Frank Moreno has been in the West Coast Homicide Division for 20 years. Recently he had been transferred to vice. For the last six months he had patiently studied the methods of distribution, drug lord's dynamics, the hierarchy of the families, the turf wars. His philosophy was that given enough rope and time, these monsters will eventually do something stupid.

He knew about the money and drug dropping areas in which mules would risk their lives for a couple of thousands , while the drug lord amassed his millions with little personal sacrifice or risk.

When he arrived, he could barely believe his eyes. Two of Sampayo's henchmen with enough evidence to convince any jury in the world to of their guilt. This is too good to be true. But I guess you deserve a brake ounce in a while, if you behave.

He had seen everything, but nothing prepared them for the show that was the most brilliant tableau. He approached the two men, took their weapons and pulled the acupuncture needles out. Immediately their breathing accelerated and they became fully awake.

"…Good morning ladies, which of you is going to spill the beans…?" He looked Jerry an immediately recognized him as the scarred and scared young man who wrote with his father's guts his many sins on the wall. Years of military service had made that man into formidable opponent.

"…I need to go back to the gym darn it, my six year old niece has more muscles than me..." the lieutenant mused.

The other man was even sturdier. He had the physic of a professional assassin

Something did not add up."…Why would a professional assassin great a mule, unless **the mule was the target** ...!" he continued in his mussing while he studied the assassin in detail. He made a great circle around the still confused and flabbergasted men.

He thought: "…Then the whole transaction went sour when the third party, a shorter man **neutralized the assassin and his intended pray... without any visible damage and without long term consequences..."** This was extraordinary…!"

He finally spoke directing his words to Jerry directly. "…Jerry...you were born again today at least three times....I suspect that you don't have a friend in the world...your family is probably in great danger...we can offer protection...we can arrest them and take them away...the mainland is BIG and we can have FBI involved , before you now you will Jimmy Alvarez-Real State Broker..."

"…Can you believe this crap ..."said the assassin," ...he plants all this evidence here...,has not arrested us ,we are legitimate businessman...Jerry here wanted a parachute ride with my hydrofoil and we lay in the beach exhausted...the next thing...he plants the evidence and he is trying to separate us ..."

"…Pig, what is your name, asked Jerry? You look familiar..."

"…I am Frank Moreno, lieutenant Moreno, I am here to help you…but you need to treat me with respect or I promise you and Mr. Muscles here a very rough time..."

Ignacio interrupted. He could not let Jerry out of his sight. He still had a dagger in his boots; he could silence him for good. If he could not have Ana, neither will Jerry. "You have no evidence..." He went for it with his free hand, the tip of the dagger came out of the boot and he was going for the kill when Jerry broke every finger on the handcuffed hand with his free hand and dislocated the assassin's shoulder using his handcuffed shoulder. In the meantime the assassin's nose had been re-arranged and the lieutenant's Reebock© sole was in his face.

"...Jerry, who prepared your parachute today...?" Asked the policeman.

"...He did...", pointing with contempt at the bloody, unconscious mass Ignacio had become. "..He insisted as a matter of fact... in the Rangers he always did it..."

"...Does he have a reason to betray you ....apparently you were army buddies...?"

"...Money, drugs, self preservation...he always had the "hots" for my wife, whatever reason he is not going anywhere soon...that was a nasty kick..."

"...Whether or not he survives is not of my concern..." said the lieutenant. "Sampayo wanted you dead badly and was willing to deal with this "future brother in law"

"...I was planning to kill Sampayo and rescue my family, destroy the labs and move to Upper Wisconsin..."

"...WE may be able to do that with very limited risk for you and your family   But you have to trust me...I want the least bloodshed, specially of innocent civilians..."

"I don't want my kids to suffer...I will fully cooperate with you!"

"To establish trust, Jerry, you have to earn it ...I want to ask you some questions and I want the truth as an answers, if I smell any bullshit, the deal is off..."

"I'll be truthful and trustworthy..."

"Who was the third man?

"...Not a friend, although he saved my life twice...he had a mask...was short ...was light...typical *criollo in color* ...was **very fast**... had martial art pants with ITF-Olympic sticker...but the most amazing thing was how he used "**Buddha's Circle of Peace** ".This is a ninja techniques who renders the opponent completely defenseless and puts them in a reversible coma...He could have killed us instead he showed mercy and chose life..."

"...I feel more admiration than hatred ..." said Moreno, opening the handcuffs and cuffing the second wrist in between the assassin's left leg causing an audible grunt of pain..."

"...No hatred for you either, I remember you from the terrible night I killed my father..."

"...Your father was a pig which deserved to die, without death penalty in the island, and his athlethic physic he would have been the king of jail, he dominant male ...you were jury, witness and executioner...don't feel bad with what you did to the bastard..."

"...You were kind and by God, you were very young... I guess years don't go in vain...."

"...Hold that thought, said the Jerrt, I want to introduce you Helmut Moreno, my brother..."

Helmut was younger and more athletic. He had joined the reserve and learned photography with the editor of Star &Stripes. Now he worked for the murder seeking reporting *El Vocero* newspaper

"...Hey big bro, what's up…?"

"...I need to fake these people's deaths..."

"...Consider it done ....I will do magic here ..." After introducing himself as Moreno's brother he asked Jerry to lay o the floor. He was younger and sturdier than the detective but his peaceful greenish brown eyes were unmistakably also his brother's. Out of his back pack he took a spanking new Martha Stewart © white sheath, non-fitted Queen. He learned this tricks in the first Iraq war when he was a reporter for *Star and Stripes.* " You have presented a human face of the enemy, when the enemy is in pieces you construct the enemy, I recommend Queen White sheaths, people don't feel good about burned remains in craters, but they can relate to bloody sheath!" His editor used to say.

"...In addition you can make a Toga, annoy your African-American friends with a KKK uniform and get laid- is universal outside and inside the US, specially in Asia and Africa, a clean white Queen size white sheath is the most powerful aphrodisiac ... of course you will need to leave the sheath behind as a token of your appreciation for services well rendered, when you leave..." Captain Jablonski used to say.

He opened the sheath and covered both men, the assassin still unconscious.

He placed both empty guns on top of the sheaths for dramatic effect. Then he took a bottle of soy sauce and filled a water gun. He proceeded to splash soy sauce all over the white sheath. "...in black and white photos is the best blood..." he took out his digital camera and took pictures from every angle, with one or two appendages out of the sheath for dramatic effect. After he reviewed them, he sat in his computer, wrote the first page headline and the short paragraph:

Sampayo Drug Gang Killed in Showdown With ATF, FBI and

Local Police:

The story mentioned Jerry and Ignacio by name, made allusions of the grotesque appearance of the corpses and promised another Internal Affairs Investigation. Please with himself he e-mail the article to his editor, which promptly change the first page for the fabricated headline and was there for the Late Edition that night and the next day edition

He came back , uncovered both men . Jerry was amused .He was officially dead!! The assassin waked up , but another kick in the face knocked him out, this time from Helmut . His Addidas© flower adorned the other cheek .

Jerry looked at the two greening brothers , who gave each other high fives and danced over the Ignacio's limp body: "...ok boys , you really need to stop this practice ,you are enjoying your work way too much..."

"...*Sargento Garcia ,* take the unconscious piece of trash an take him to the regional hospital as John Doe,bandage him up, keep him cool and isolated, rip off the phones from the wall , 5th floor at least and 24 hr surveillance. I will_____ ***personally kill you if he escapes , or word gets out that he is   still alive***,Comprende...?"

"...*Capiche* ": what do I do with the other cadaver...?"

"...The other "cadaver" is my concern and only my concern. Call Figueroa, from TACTICAL OPERATIONS and get a tea m assembled in the Doctor's Beach house at Puntas del Mar. Also... everybody in plain clothes. We also need the speed boat and 10 sets of bows and arrows...rapelling equipment ...French Bread...Roasted Chicken from Don Teo....Toilet Paper..."

"...Consider it done *Comandante*..."

Garcia was a muscular six-footer who owned his life and his job to Moreno. The lieutenant trusted him; in these parts that was the best letter of recommendation possible. He picked up Ignacio like a bag of trash over his shoulder and dumps him in the back of his patrol car. He sped away and with his typical nauseating driving guaranteed that the prisoner would loose anything that he had in his stomach.

Helmut looked at his brother with great pride. "...So what is the plan...?"

"...*The* plan is that you get back to the capital, tell everybody that will listen to the "how savagely" we **_executed_** these criminals. How appalling it was...stir the IA people, the Mafia, the liberal senators etc. etc. I want this man death to cause an uproar...In addition check with the sports department in *El Vocero* who has represented the island in the Olympic in the last three Olympics *in Tae Kwan Do* .Blueberry© the i nformation to me.

"... OK, Mr. Paratrooper, this is the deal. I go and get an order from the Judge to arrest your wife and the   kids with the excuse of identifying your body. If we get any static we back off and assault to-morr   ow night. Silent deadly and swift..."

"…And hence the bows and arrows…?"

"…Also the reason to check who was your rescuer. I suspect he is pretty good with a bow and a Bo, I suspect that will find out soon." He looked at Jerry for a long time, in silence.

"…Yes lieutenant you can trust me. Upper Wisconsin with all the money of my wife will be comfortable. You know that my brother in law ordered my assassination, he also killed my father-in law's…"

"…How? I reviewed the available evidence and he died after a work out at his private gym…"

"…That was death by Gatorade©. He spiked the beverage with antifreeze and he was poisoned. I fear for my wife's life now that I am "dead" nothing can stop him from killing my wife and the kids…"

"…That is exactly why we need to arrest your wife and kids, because they are no longer useful to him, they are as good as dead. Lets go, we need to get a Judge order to arrest your family and join the Task Force at Puntas..."
"…What are our chances of success…?"
"…Much better than the prospects of failure …" Said the lieutenant. With that he got in his unmarked car with Jerry and sped towards the Aguadilla Court House to get a subpoena. Both prayed in silence that it was not to late for Ana and the kids..."

Rincon Scuffle 30 Morell-Chardon

CHAPTER 4:
[[Hedonistic Escape Resort: Añasco Beach 8:30 AM]]

Perla Goldman started her morning riding. She had started at sunrise and both she and the stallion she rode had broken out quite a sweat. She liked riding early in the morning, as most of the guests frolicked until sunrise and went to bed at that time.

Breakfast at the resort was served at 2:00 PM, Lunch at 6:30 and the 1:00 AM buffet. Of course there was an open Bar which was staffed by two gorgeous *nativas,* whose sex appeal emanated from what they hid, rather than what they showed.

The sex workers had gone home for the night. "Las vampiras "(the Vampires) they were called because their peculiar sleep habits. They were locals, Venezuelans, Cubans, and Brazilians. They were "clean"& "certified" by the state. Guests would pay $3,000 a night, which did not include the girl.

Perla was the hotel administrator. She was only 26 but thanks to a Yale MBA she had landed this cozy job and had made this sex-resort the most profitable for the company in the world. The owner, a Frenchman by the name of Guillerm Zola owned 30 such resorts around the world, trash-burning crematoriums which recycled most materials in addition to generating cheap electricity. Water bottling and water desalinization plants completed Zola's recipe for growing money.

Of course Zola had links with both the Russian and Sicilian Mafias. He was a "hands on" guy and anything that lost money or made him large amounts required his undivided attention. Perla had made quite an impression on Mousier Zola. Half British and half Jewish she was a woman of outstanding beauty.

She could pass as Hispanic, Jewish, Palestinian and Central European. Her long hair, straight and black went down to her thighs when out of her ponytail. The MOSSAD had recruited her when she was thirteen. She was fresh and knew nothing outside the kibbutz.

Her first handler was a woman. A lesbian that had survived the camps and who not only trained her as a spy but had trained her to satisfy men and women. "Remember Perla, if you keep The Pigs happy, you will live another day..." She will tell Perla while gently caressing her number tattoo in the right arm.

In college she was approached by M6, who found her name in a database they recovered from an El AL wreck. With the British she learned disciple of purpose....

Her thoughts were rudely interrupted by the protesting hyperventilation of her stallion, which had collapsed in sand after a very spirited final ride.

She cautiously dismounted her animal while tenderly kissing his forehead.
She tenderly looked into those blue eyes she knew so well and said:
"...Darling if you were so close, you should have slowed me down..."

Zola covered with sweat and sand could barely focus his vision, "le petite morte" today felt like high grade coronary. His prostate was not contracting, it was in status eppilepticus.
"...Perla you must be a witch, I am telling you one of these days you will kill me..."
Perla thought to herself: "... Not unless you try to kill me first, not unless I have direct orders and NEVER if you propose to marry you. This PIG was happy enough!" She finally mumbled: "...Why don't you stay with me today, I will clean you up, shave you feed you and get you ready for action..."

"...Perla, God, you are insatiable! I would love to stay. I have business to attend. I will finalize the sale of the Colossus Sugar Cane Refinery to convert it to a Zola Limited Electrical Cooperative. We will save 6-7 millions a year to the west coast municipalities , provide 100 new jobs an will make "boucue de argeant" from the electricity sales . Plus will have several mayors in our pocket, which means more resorts, more water bottling plants and less environmental boloney...

"...Are you riding whales today ...?" She hated when he went whale riding. That was one of his passions , he had given up extreme surfing for whale riding. This was the proper season. He had done it several times here and across the Pacific .He learned from an Eskimo girl and had 200 rides to her name.
"...That is the general idea...not a scratch so far, actually those humpbacks are much gentler than some Olympic skaters I've been with, specially the Russians..."

She placed his hand on her nude buttocks, looked into his eyes and declared:
"... You will not get any of this in the grave.., so don't get killed by the whales or the Russians..."
"…You are nothing but a whore..." He said graving her buttocks with both hands
She caressed her own ribs and breasts and declared:
"…**With a body like this, what else can I be ...?**

He was tempted to stay, but the whaling season was coming to an end and he will miss possibly the last chance in his life to do this. "...Thanks for the invitation, but I will pass ....tomorrow is another day…"

He ran to his private mansion to take a shower and looked back at her beautiful sand-covered body and thought to himself: "...I hope I am never forced to kill her, if I do it will be a fast painless death..."

She saw him running towers the house and thought to herself: "...I hope I am not ever forced to kill him...I will be a slow agonizing death...after a prolonged lovemaking session..."

He picked up his phone and started speaking in French: "...Yes the sale is almost final...I will be a great hiding place for our nuclear device, during construction, we will assemble the missiles and we will be able to strike North and South America, destroying the oil reserves, the refining infrastructure...everything in the name of Allah, and Mohammed his true prophet, the sale of the Iranian and North Korean missile is final and will be delivered as factory pre-fabricated structure panels for Zola's industries..."

"...Well done brother, Allah wishes will prevail..." declared Osama, hiding in Granada two continents away. He hanged up.

Perla had bugged his cell phone months ago. She had hit the jackpot. While he bathed she used the secure internet line and downloaded the call and sent to her handlers in London and Tel-Aviv. "...Fly, little dove fly away...!" She said gesticulating like liberating a pigeon.

Captain Fallange was brought back from his ADDidish daydreaming in the Manchester Intelligence Quarters my the "...you got mail.." in his computer. Similar to the National Security Agency , but much thrifty in its budget ,the British spy on friends and foe. He opened the file .To his horror , he played it over and over again , he place the recording in the voice recognition computer program and confirmed Zola and Ben Laden as the speakers . Without thinking twice, he forwarded the file and evaluation to his counterpart in the NSA and to his station chief. "... Just in case the bureaucrats have second thoughts, there it goes..."He forwarded to the British Chief of Staff, the American Chief of Staff and the NATO Commander also an American. "… the cat is out of the bag…the wall of stupidity has fallen..."

At Tel Aviv Commander Middleman received Perla's file. "...So Ben-Laden is in Europe somewhere, or Africa , or in Asia ...but not in Pakistan because we monitor everything that comes out of Pakistan and that call was not generated there..."

Eli, his nephew, was a skinny Hasidic looking young man, who at nineteen, was Middleman's master hacker. Seldom did his uncle showed so much agitation.
"...Eli get into the NSA databank, let's see if you and the boys here can triangulate the location of Ben Laden..."

The young man jumped into action and got to the NSA data bank. At the NSA they detected Eli's signature. Robert Jericho, who played HALO© on a regular basis with his counterpart was in charge of security. Eli was using his HALO© signature. This meant he **wanted** to be detected. He was requesting help; security was at risk so he used an unsecured channel!

Robert called Captain Mark Garza, and explained the situation. They unloaded the file and herd the recording. They could not believe their luck!
"...Robert sent this to our counterparts at the FBI, National Security and the Pentagon...sends the whole recording and all the data that we have to help the MOSSAD with its triangulation, secure channel, for his eyes only..."
'...Which means that Middleman will have the data in 15 seconds flat....?'
'...Exactly, my young apprentice, do not miss-underestimate the Jewish sideof the force...'

Middleman looked at his young protegé and so the smile of triumph.

"...Uncle, we got the file and a *"good luck"* added from my friend Jericho..."

"...Can you trust him, son...?"

"...with a name like Jericho what is not to trust..."

"..Jewish..?"

"...One eighth, Jewish enough for the crematorium, is Jewish enough for me..." He said looking at a black-and- white picture of a uncle very young officer, Ben Gurion and Moshe Dayan in the entrance of the Holocaust Museum in Tel Aviv about four hundred meters from the main entrance to their compound. They had sold the city planners their building as the parking for the museum, impressive parking indeed. Over the enlarged picture, written in Dayan's own blood in Hebrew, the words "NEVER AGAIN"

"...You worry me nephew...you seem to be in love with this computer, need to get out more, get laid to a JAP or nice local girl..."

"...You won't let me date Ruth...!"

"...Well if we stop OBL and or eliminate him you can marry Ruth, if you want...its time to screw the Arabs, for now live my daughter alone…"

Eli smiled, he was already living with Ruth, if OBL's plan came to fruition they will be happy they did not wait , the whole world economy will collapse .We will be a big universal dessert with Mulas as referee of every thought and every behavior...enough to make you puke...'

Middleman on his own was smiling and thinking: "…This little prick...if he was not so useful I would have kick his ass, getting Ruth pregnant at seventeen. He thought they could hide this from ...ME! But my wife is ready to be a grandma, she will drive them both crazy and for the rest of their lives she will remind them both of their transgression...priceless..!"

Two continents away, Perla watch as Zola got on his orange Landrover©) and rode away. He was going to close the deal at Coloso and to ride a whale for probably the last time. She was exhausted but happy. Sleepless nights have given fruits. She knew he cover could be compromised, so she had to procure a escape, a refuge to escape from Zola and his associates. She will go to Rincón and rent a room at the local guesthouse, take a well-deserved nap and be there ready when Zola came back to the Mansion.

"...I feel lucky, I may even buy a lottery ticket..." She thought as she walked away.

CHAPTER 5
[[Town of Rincón 9:00 AM]]

Jose, after many back roads had arrived at his Dojo. There were two things he was very proud of .One was his relationship with his stranged wife, Martha, and his Tae Kan Do education. He had joined the Navy at 16 with a falsified document and was stationed in the orient, where he had learned most of his martial arts. He had the privilege, also of learning acupuncture with the great masters and was able to combine both disciplines.

Today his knowledge has saved his life. He had defeated two considerable adversaries with mostly his wits and training, they were at his mercy but he opted not to go for the kill. Something inside him suggested that this was not the proper time for this.

Actually, is there ever a proper time to kill? A proper cause? The early Christian thinkers had debated this same issue and came with the concept of a "just war" The great Aikido masters came with the concept of respect for life, including your worst enemy, at all costs. In this school of thought not fighting is the best possible course of action and a great victory is when you either are able make friends with your enemy or when you can neutralize him (or her) without causing any irreparable damage to their bodies.

Bruising their egos, on the other hand was permitted and at this point of time there were two much bruised egos at Jobo Beach He entered his beloved dojo, the White Crain ITF Tae Kwan Do School. He had checked the balance on some of those debit cards, $20,000 on all, and you could take $500 at a time. He had $10,000 in his backpack. He entered the darkness and in the floor he saw his father.

He was sleeping on the floor. He looked out the window and saw Mr. Goya taking to himself as usual. A Buddhist monk fallowed him closely. They were crossing the public square. He noticed something peculiar. These two men were casting three shadows!

Maybe what they said about Goya was true, that he had a specter fallowing him around. The monk looked familiar for some reason….

His father tenderly calling him interrupted his meditations:
"…Jose brings me some *pan de agua and a pocillo,* your mother kick me out again…I have not eating since yesterday, and I am starving…'

"…Dad we need to talk, I am in some big do-do…I almost got killed today by two men, which I stopped cold…I think one recognized the Olympic silver star insignia in my pants…it won't be long before they find out who am I…this was a Mafia hit with lots of money and drugs involved… lots of resources…maybe I should go to the police and give them the money and hope they can protect us…"

"…How much money are we taking about …?"
"…One hundred million dollars give or take a few…."
"…The integrity of the police in this town I compromised, I would not trust anybody…specially when that amount of money is involved…the more money is involved the lesser human life is worth…these people are thieves and highway robbers! Trust no one. With the possible exception of your mother…"
"…Should we get armed...?"

"…No you don't get armed unless you are certain that you are willing to pull that triggers…the wonderful thin about trigger, the wonderful thing about triggers , there is only one, there is only one ,yes…'
"…You are crazy, crazy as a fox…!"

At the other side of the Rincón Public Square both Goyas and the Llama entered Manuel's Diner and Sport Bar. They all took a table and asked for some beers.

The owner, Mr.Manuel, was a transplanted Irishman ho had move there to escape the world and his past. He immersed his past and his pain in the best Irish Single Malt.

By the age of 35, he was already an E-bay© multi-millionaire with no inventory he moved materials from ASIA around the world; he had out-Dell the competition. After that was a matter of investing in the right companies and "Viola" a billionaire at 40.

He never thought that his quest for social justice will be cause of his family's demise. Manuel decided to give back to the masses whose sweat and tears had made him rich.

In July 2001 he was in Pakistan, opening a school for the child laborers who made his favorite soccer ball. His family had accompanied him in this occasion. The school had an indoor stadium so that the children who made the balls could play with their product.

In the midst of the festivities four Al-Quaida© operatives entered the gymnasium disguised as DSL© deliverymen. They placed a box full of C-4, nails, broken glasses and cluster bombs in each corner. The boxes said in Arabic "fireworks" Manuel were in the latrine when it was pushed by the impact of the explosion several yards away. When he came to be, he ran into the gym only to find total destruction, there was no recognizable body.

Then he heard for the first time, months before 911 the name of Osama Ben Ladin. He saw two men, one Arabic and the other French-looking laughing merrily and comparing note on the extent of the destruction. Manuel had rudimentary knowledge of Arabic but his French was pretty good.

"...Osama I think this was a well executed operation...as professional as any against the Soviets...any survivors....witnesses… ?"

"..You saw the results, there were no witnesses ..."

Manuel reacted by diving behind some rocks before been detected. The two men continued their conversation:

"...Zola, how are the plans for the dirty bombs coming along…?"

"....Spring...maybe Summer of 2008-2009 , after our declaration of war in New York ,depending on how effective or violent is the American reaction..."

Manuel crawl toward his Land Rover© ,in his storage compartment was his cross bow . He made his inventory of death . He had to stop this monsters before they attacked again elsewhere . Ok six men 20 arrows , 5 seconds per arrow. It was possible to beat the odds .

One by one in the silence of the feathers he took the four DSL drivers out . One arrow to neutralize the person's ability to walk ,second arrow to head or heart. Zola and Ben Laden noted the silence around them. Neither was ready for Manuel who jumped at their presence to a shot all his remaining arrow at the two men.

They collapsed immediately...their clothes impregnated with their cursed blood. He felt on his knees ...sobbing like a child "..everything is gone, my family my past ,over forever...I have nothing to remember my loved ones ., no tomb ,no tombstone ...I can no go back to my house in Ireland

...too many memories...at least I would not have the poison of revenge in my heart ,as these murderers have been dealt with... I have to escape as soon as possible ...I am sure that their friends will miss them..."

He was brought back to his preset reality by the sound of machine guns at a distance. Five converted Toyota© Trucks, *a la Mogadishu* approached the area .He picked up his crossbow and remaining arrows and a box of C4. With a coldness and calculation previously unknown to him ,he mounted the C4 in the remaining arrows and waited until the trucks were 200 yards away. The impact of the first explosion caused the second truck to roll over . The second arrow hit the gas tank." Walking torches of hate ran in every direction... like *victimless homicide bomber* ...Hell here and hell in the next life..." he thought Death an Destruction took a toll on Manuel, he collapsed on his knees and cried like a baby , he was alone in the world, everything that he had held dear had disappeared in a flash , only thing left was death and destruction and the smell of burned flesh filled the air.

Then he saw at a distance a cloud of dust.'.. More SUV's !..I need to run..'

He ran and climbed his SAHARA- Discovery© and drove like he was running from the Devil himself. The mortar fire was lagging behind him, three or four meters behind. However ,his driving skills, not his fighting, saved the day. His pursuers could not handle speed and one by one they flipped over and neutralized themselves . He drove like a madman until he reached the Indian border .He was glad that the terrorists did not have an air force because his orange and green car stock out like seal blood in the snow. Even though there is nothing heroic about leveling a village from a miles away, flying a $500,000 bomb-to-be requires guts: killing woman and children to teach a lesson that our god or prophet is superior is not heroic at all. Its akin to being a Nazi ,it's a low-tech gas chamber.

Much like the national socialist, they will exterminate *everybody they can* two hundred at a time, a Holocaust in the altar of radical Islam . Given a chance to have an atomic bomb they would not hesitate against using one in the name of God , which I doubted any of them had the pleasure of knowing in person or by revelation. The homicide bomber at the moment he detonated his bomb did not meet **his famed seventy virgins** he falls in the void of nothingness , the absence of The True God , Eternal Sadness and there is **no end to that , in the same hell as Hitler, Stalin and Mao.** He had a Islamic mentor for a year , like Mother Theresa and the Dali Llama, which he had met , exuded Peace .

The Holy Koran he read did not condoned killing children for *any cause , and there was no mention of **any virgin as a reward***. Traditional Islam is mystic in nature , defines God ,which in the desserts of Arabia tends to be more difficult to find than in the Iguazu Falls ,and teaches to honor and adore HIM and guides you through your journey through life.

The Devil himself, who The Prophet mentions with some regularity not as an abstract concept, but as a living Entity worth stoning, has hijacked the religion. Every innocent child that dies only satisfies Satan.

Modern man has forgotten the Devil but the He has not forgotten modern man .

When 911 happened and he realized that those two demons had survived his arrows , he was profoundly depressed for a week. He sold his business , moved to Rincon to wait for the Nuclear Holocaust. He was a broken man whose only joy in life was to talk religion ,philosophy and politics with his inebriated customers , which made more sense that a lot of the world l leaders. His favorite patron was Mr. Goya , who "knew everything" and had 'seen everything' from the crystal ball advantage of his barbershop. He cold not see *Abuela ,* but he believed she existed , he had seen her shadow too.

"...I understand that you are quite and archer...?" Inquired the

Llama.

"... *I* have some arrows in my lifetime , Irish champion 1990-1996 both in bow and cross bow...son of William Tell the Irish Press would say..."

"...what do you know about Zen Archery...?"Asked the Llama

"... Is a form of meditation in which you learn to intercept arrows that are coming at full speed. Extremely difficult, require extreme concentration and ability...only the masters can do it..."

"...I am surprised of your fond of knowledge ...".Said the Lama

"...I met a Zen archer on my voyages through Japan when I was in High school...it was amazing...!"

"...Fallow me..." He walked to the plaza. "…Bring your best bow...".Everybody sat a the gazebo on one side of the plaza , 300 feet away was the wall of the Catholic church. Midway at your right was the Three Brothers Pizza at the extreme left Goya's Barber Shop. The monk walked to the church wall and waited for Manuel.

At the White Crane both men looked with interest at the orange clothed monk. Jose walked out of his Dojo , fallowed by his drunken father . He was transfixed.At the Pizzeria the two priest looked with most interest. Ignatous had training in archery and so did Pereira.

"...Son ...",said the Llama "... Use the bow first..." The first arrow flew in his direction , as it was about to hit his target the Llama stopped it by holding it and moving out of the way from the body of the arrow before it hit the Llama. This scene was repeated over and over again . Sixteen arrows and not one do any damage. He casually walked to the gazebo with all sixteen arrows.

| Rincon Scuffle | 45 | Morell-Chardon |

CHAPTER 6
[[Mayaguez Medical Center 3:00PM]]

Sargento Garcia received the urgent page to call his old friend Mr. Goya. After Frank told him to make Ignacio disappear, he went to the only person that he could trust, his ex-wife Maricela Paganini. She was an Argentinian transplant, a woman of uncommon beauty, uncommon intelligence and very uncommon fortune.

The have met when her Mercedes was car jacked. Her niece was in the car still in her car seat. She was begging the car-jacker to let her untie her niece, even offered him money.

Garcia was filling his personal car with gas in the next pump out the field of vision of the criminal. He took a construction mallet-hammer out of his trunk. The sociopath was losing his patience and pointed his gun towards her with the intention to shoot. Garcia, whose biceps were as large as a torpedo aimed his hammer towards the bumper sensor for the air bag, raised the hammer and hit the sensor with all his might.

The criminal had no chance, by the time he saw him it was too late, the bag had deployed braking his neck and killing him instantly as he was sitting sideways aiming at the woman. After that he took care of the whole situation, which went quite smoothly. Her car, her niece and the good doctor made it home in one piece within an hour after the incident. She was relieved and very thankful.

She was forty-two, had a CV as long as the Gospels and was the medical director of the trauma regional hospital .She was an eminence in trauma . She had never met a man she wanted as much at this man , not only was he a beautiful man but a very good man and he had not undressed her with his eyes , like most men she encountered , on the contrary he had been a gentleman. He wanted to get pregnant so badly and with this man she could have a family.

Their romance was short and passionate. She sends him a thank you note with an airline ticket and the name of the hotel she had picked for him. He had never been in Paris so he accepted graciously

. After a long flight ,and fights with taxi drivers and obnoxious traffic policeman he finally made to his hotel. When he arrived at his suite , Maricela was waiting for him dressed solely with her beautiful smile .

He was glad that the balcony had a beautiful view of the Eiffel Tower ,because that was the only landmark he did not miss. They were married in Notre Dame, in a small chapel . No prenuptial. That week she was pregnant of their first child.

Although Garcia believed in equality among the sexes in rights and privileges, he also believed that woman will raise the children , at least until they started kindergarten . Maricela thought that her job was too important and that a nanny, under her close supervision, will take up the responsibility of day-to-day care . In addition , Garcia could quit his job and she will give him a salary to be her bodyguard and personal stud.

Garcia loved his job. For him it was the greatest adrenalin rush. He needed that job to stay alive. After one year of trial he decides to go back to full time employment with Frank. He signed a prenuptial agreement and the divorce papers and left his house never to return, never re-invited. After a long conversation over the phone with Frank she realized that she had insulted his sense of masculinity and independence. But it was too late to ask for forgiveness. The worst thing is that she was still deeply in love , and so was him, but with severe pain in his soul.

After phoning her ,she was expecting him to be in need of bandaging ,or a bullet extraction. She was so relieved that was not the case that she asked then and there for forgiveness . Which he fallowed by the same request.

"…Sargento ,I never filled the divorce papers or the prenuptial…"

"…I know , I checked…when I tried to get a loan they informed that I was still married to you.., of course the loan was approved…"

"… I love you so much... Marcos is in Kinder, such a beautiful child … We could have another child , I am close to ovulation , lets go baby, lets go to the call room and maybe we will make a beautiful girl: my looks, your strengths, your goodness and my brains...she will be happy you can move back with us. Marcos will love it..."

"...We do have some urgent business however; my prisoner is in need to disappear for a while especially from the lawyers and his boss who will like to eliminate him before he has a chance to talk ..."

She examined the face of the unconscious brute Adidas© on one cheek, Puma© in the other. "...Whose handy work ...?"

"..Moreno and Helmut..." he said rather sheepishly and conceited way

"...The great Frank Moreno, the guardian of universal rights, war hero of the first Iraqi War, and "the other person in your life"..."

"...We had no other choice..., don't you believe me, love…"

"...I do...the x-ray actually do not show any fracture , CT scan shows a small contusions on each side , nothing major he will live..."

They heard the commotion in the hallway, like packages falling on the floor.

The sound was echoed down the hall ,getting closer to the door. Instinctively Garcia hid his wife in the broom closet , and threw himself under the bed adjacent to Ignacio's . Three men , in trench coats entered the room , they were carrying Barrette© with silencers . The semi-automatic carried 14 shots, he had a forty-five, which had 6 shots: score so far was 42 vs. 6 . He made a mental inventory of his available assets ,gun , and two skinning knives. Not good.

'... Ignacio, this is Ramon Bravo , I am really sorry but I have no choice...If Sampayo discover what we were planning he will kill us all and our families too...we already killed two policeman ,one security guard and one doctor, there is no turning back. Getting ready to shoot , with their back to Garcia, they raised their guns in unison. That was the cue , Garcia crawled under the adjacent bed , hunting knives pointing backward and forty- five in his chest…"

With enormous strength he lacerated the calf muscles from knee down making a clean butcher cut through the length of the muscle and landing the knife in the dorsal surface of the feet. Pain was excruciating. He picked up the gun from his chest and blew the two kneecaps on the third person and forced him to the floor ,disarming him . He was in agony.

"…Gentlemen we need to stop here before someone really get hurt…"

The two men with calf surgeries recovered their wits , and one raised his gun , which was the last thing in life he ever did as he found himself with a whole in his chest , heart and left lung, making him collapse instantly dead.

The second one ran towards the door with much difficulty, he turned around , raise his gun against Garcia who jumped out of the line of fire into the floor emptying whatever was left Bravo's gun in the criminal's chest and head. He died in a blink of an eye.

The next thing he felt was a piano wire around his neck. Instinctively he let both guns fall in the floor and he blocked the closing of the noose with his open palms, taking control again. He started fighting to get the noose out of his neck and eventually remove himself from the danger.

He started moving around in circles until Jose Bravo dropped down on the floor ,using an Aikido technique Bravo was stunted but not neutralized . He made a gesture and went for the spare gun in his ankle. This was counter by Garcia picking a glass saline bottle from the side table and breaking the object on Bravos head .The assassin went limp, had mockingly seizure and expired.

Cautiously he checked him for pulse. None was detected. He proceeded to check the other two, dead as dead can be. He picked up his knifes, a sterile drape with saline to clean and dry them. He walked to the broom closet ad unlocked his wife. He was intact.

"...I see that you still use the Russian Commando Knifes I gave you for your birthday...!"

"..Is the gift that keeps up giving, durable, eternal sharp, throw able...in beautiful ebony or white for those Siberian jobs that we all love so much...Titanium..!"

"...You **are** a sick poppy...what is the final score, darling...?"

"...Inside here 3-0, please check Mr. Ignatous there, I don't think that he was hit by any stray bullet, but please confirm status. Keep four point restraints at all times. Also confirm the other three are dead..., please.

"...I love when you talk military to me: and four point restraints ... **Ah! Kinky...!**"

He picked the four guns, checked for bullets and went out the door to meet not only death and destruction, but also the wrong side of a M16. He immediately recognized Mario Truxillio. Third generation Italian, built like a linebacker, Sargent in the SWAT team. They both lower their guns.

"... And now another episode of Sargent to Sargent, in which a mere Sargent that can never get promoted bitch about their lot..." said Garcia mockingly.

"..Man what the Hell happened here there is dead people all over the place, 3 civilians, 4 policemen I thought that we faked this guy's death with the help of the Master of the Scene, Mr. Helmut Moreno..."

"...Probably they were on Jobo's and fallowed us here ..., I suspect they have a driver or guard in the building..."

"...They had one, he has been acidified, there is nothing neutral...he is part of the lobby's permanent collection, a surrealistic de-coppach in the large mural of the palm in the hurricane ...he made the classic mistake: he had an ear ring with a SWAT team uniform...old Captain Garrido would had exploded if any of his boys ever used an earring ..I pass the guy, he realized that he had been discovered, he goes for his 45 which is in the Velcro holster, in the meantime I raise my shotgun and he flew, he was so close that the bullet proof vest did not protected him, probably a heart concussion..."

"... I will nominate you for the Dick Chaney Award...talking about concussions , our prisoner had two , I have three bodies in there...could you check them out to be sure they are dead and help the lady doctor inside..."

"...Talking about lady doctors, the Guevara twins blueberried me, they want some sweat Italian hunk to service them, they made reservations at the Royal Rincón©, private pool, Don Perignon, private Chef 24/7 "...I am not selfish , I will share the twins with you..."

"...Much obliged, but I have an operation with Frank in Añasco, I have to be available, we are meeting at my wife's condo in Puntas del Mar..."

"...You mean you ex-wife…?"

"..No, my wife, after forcing me out of the house, she never filed the divorce papers or the prenuptial...furthermore I swear to God, the woman is in heat..."

"...You mean horny...?"

"...No, I mean in heat, she wants to reproduce not to have necessarily Earth Shattering Sex; she wants to reproduce..."

"...What do you want..?"

"... Earth Shattering Sex, of course!!! I do recognize that given the overall danger of the present situation, given the body count here, there is a chance that I might not make it out of this one alive, so it will be nice that my wife has something that will make her happy and that she can remember me with, we love each other very much and the new child would be very cool..".."

As they spoke guys from homicide, SWAT and regular island police started congregating at the site. They contacted the cleaning company and the foresnsic experts.

His wife exited the room: "...Your friend there, after realizing you saved his sorry but wants to sing like a bird: locations, distributions, numbers, white slavery. You name it, he knows it...". She noted Truxillio, acknowledged his existence and smiled. "...The man that keeps my Pediatrics department satisfied not only the Guevarra twins, but every young sweet ass that rotate through our hospital..."

"...That is me...!" He said proudly.

"...Are you ever going back to medical school, you were one of the best..."

"...I decided a long time ago that I will be a "kept man" and keep all those doctors happy..., not that I will become one..."

"...Talking about keeping your doctor happy, Mr. Garcia I expect you in my office in 15 minutes, I want to show you a copy of the medical report on the arrest of Mr. Ignacio, I will need your signature..."

She went ahead and got in the elevator. Garcia looked at Truxillio, he returned his look. "...Man , what a fine specimen of the species ...'

"...You mean, what a fine piece off fine Argentinean Derriere...I need you to take care of the shop while I take care of my wife...'

"...No problem, go ahead and enjoy..."

"...Good luck with the Twins..." They high-fived each other, and left to do their duties.

García arrived at the doctor's office to find her ready for action, dressed only with a rose and a smile. Garcia closed the door behind him, locking it and joined his wife on the desk.

"...Relax, everything will work up just right, I am a professional ..You know...Keep an eye on the goal and keep the time..." She said.

"...I hope there is at least for local anesthesia..." He said

"...When I finish with you, big boy, you will be begging for mercy, not lidocaine..."

CHAPTER 7
[[Rincon Beach: 3:30 PM]]

Frank Moreno looked at the horizon for the water sprouts. Originally from this area he had seen many whale migrations. Humpback whales migrated from Greenland and the Eastern border of the United States to mate in the warmer, emerald waters of the Caribbean and the Southern Atlantic. Rincón was in the juncture of both bodies of water.

In his youth, because of the unique combination of a superb physic, natural Latino good looks, a boat he designed and built, and the capacity to swim like a champ he became one of the most looked after guides. He was the darling of Greenpeace© and of the French Cetacean Society©. He was 19 and not a worry in the world.

Then he met his match, Marie .She was the daughter of Madame Rene Eiffel, the "Jane Gooddall" of the Cetacean world. Two weeks short of 18, she was one of the most outstanding woman he had ever met. Not only was she gorgeous, she was hot! Five feet and eight inches, 135 lbs of untamed and unmitigated, tireless and titanic lust, even her perspiration was erotic.

"...Frank, my dear...whales have an intimate song by which the bull invites the females to mate. It is both a beautiful and melancholic song, fallowed by a dance of surprising erotism and agility for such a massive and primitive creature..." They were in his boat in the Desecheo Canal by the moonlight.

She sounded like a young, very excited, Jacque Costaue. She threw the microphones overboard and turns the tape recorder on. She had connected recorder to the boat's sound system and she turned it on. She started a dance that at first was like a beautiful ballet and rapidly progressed into a bountiful strip tease. Soon she rested on cushions stark naked. Frank joined the festivities with a dance of his own, leaving on only his Speedo© . Marie was good to herself and the invited Frank to join the festivities.

By mere accident they turned on an auxiliary recorder, which recorded Marie's own mating songs and Frank's Grand Finale. They were exhausted in each other's arm sharing a cigarette. He realized that their session has been recorded and suggested to Marie to return the favor to the whales and play back to them their love song. She found it amusing and sexy, suggesting to her young lover that after that, they should continue their activities on shore at the beach, for a second round. She looked at the control panel and found the playback control. The microphones, which consisted of one foot square block boxes, also had speaker capabilities.

At first nothing much happened, other than some awkward moments in which they found each other sound hysterically funny; out of context they had lost their erotic meaning, belonging more or less in the theater of the absurd. (That is why pornography is so successful but not porno-phony.) Then they realized their mistake.

The bull interpreted the recording as a challenge song from another male. He attacked the boat furiously with his head. Frank put on his bathing trunk and grabbed Marie. They had no power, no motor to attempt escaping the brute's fury and one lifesaver. Marie managed to place the lower part of her bikini on before the brute stroke again , this time with the massive dorsal fin ,sending both flying .The merciless killer, satisfied that he had destroyed his competitor returned to his amorous pursue , leaving the scene of the crime.

Frank managed to hold on to Marie's limp body and float to the beach where he realized that she was not unconscious, but dead. He examined her from head to toe, no evident trauma, no bleeding, and no portal of entry. He suspected that either she had a broken neck or a heart attack or contusion. Nearby some teenagers were enjoying a bonfire on the beach, near the Rincon Lighthouse, at the surfing beach. He walked to them asked for help, and after explaining where Marie was, then, he passed out.

Three days passed before he regained consciousness. He was in the hospital and he had a cast in his right leg and arm, bandages in his back and front, a chest tube in his right lung and the most excruciating headache he ever experience.

Light bothered the hell out of him and sound was unbearable. He opened his eyes and saw this stunning blonde slaving over a nasty looking deep scraping wound on his right foot. Her nametag read "Maricela". She was singing a Menudo© song in a very pretty falsetto.

She turned around and realized he was awake. She smiled, stopping her song
"...I am Dr. Maricela Pagganini, your intern....", She hastily got out of bed, where she has been sitting while she changed his bandages. "...Please don't mention I was sitting in your bed, my staff is neurotic about "appearances of impropriety", and has suspended even "full fledged doctors" because they sat on the patient's bed during rounds. Please sir does not mention this even in passing...I had a horrible call and had to rest my sorry behind...".

Frank, who was happily stoned out of his mind with a combination of inconceivable pain, the presence of opiates, plus the smell of her perfume mixed with her 36-hour sweat, started giggling without control.
"...Make yourself at home, grab a chair, a gentleman never tells...". He almost had died, Marie was probably dead, he had a morning erection which was trying actively to conceal and a poor soul was worrying herself to death about appearances of impropriety.
"...By the way there is nothing sorry about your behind! Can

you tell me what has happened in the last three days, I have been out of the loop, you know…?"

"…There was a boating accident…a whale attacked your boat…several times …not very common …you were catapulted out… you managed to save yourself and carry the body of your girlfriend to shore …over a carpet of sea urchins (an thus your feet wounds and infection) and notify people where her body laid in case something could be done…as far as I am concerned you area hero…"

"…This accident was all my fault, we managed to piss the whale because of my stupidity,.. it was not for me that woman would be alive…"

"…A hero, wrote Churchill, is defined not on his failures, but what he does when even God seems to be plotting against him, how he rises to the occasion and is able to prevail against all odds. You don't have to act heroic to be a hero, must true heroes don't…"

"..How about Marie, what happened to her…?"

"…Autopsy report show significant head concussions, a tear of the internal carotid in the right, with bleeding, massive pericardial effusion and heart concussion, she was bearing a baby approximately two months old, she had evidence of recent coitus with sperm present in her vagina…no signs of struggle , probably consensual. No alcohol or drugs in either your or her body, cool an clean…"

"…VERY CONSENSUAL…! I have "known her" four months …that was my son…" He said and started crying bitterly, like a drunk.

"…The mother was livid, he wanted you arrested for kidnapping, rape and homicide…the judge, who is a relative of yours…determined that given the physical evidence present, that none of the charges were of merit and convince her to take her body back to France for burial, like a good Christian, and to be happy that you never abandoned her daughter even when you realized she was probably dead, and that she had at least a body to burry, thanks to you…"

"…Did she leave for France…?"

"...Yes, but she came here one day, sobbing, saying that she was truly sorry and ashamed, asking for forgiveness. She left the money she owned you for the boat, the three months as a guide: about $5,000 with a letter to be opened when you turn twenty one and one ticket to Paris to visit her at the institute. All that is in the Manila envelope in your night table..."

Those memories were as vivid today as they were then. Believe it or not he never dated that stunning intern; he even introduced her to Garcia. They swept each other away. They had a stormy but very loving relation. He envied them in his solitude. After Marie, and Rene later, he had never had any real relation; he swam though a sea of one night stands, each leaving him emptier than the previous and with no hope of redemption.

He even dated Uncle Jaime's daughter. She did not want his love, she wanted a sperm donor. Her name was Charlie, she was a flaming bi-sexual, who had settle with Monique and wanted a sperm donor for both.

After several months both were pregnant with baby boys. They offered him to stay and to marry one for the appearances. He realized that he would always be a parasite in that relationship, that he will loose over time the emotional commitment to that relationship and that it was better for the boys to be war orphans and be raised by the "sisters"

Not even the tempting promise of a weekly threesome appealed to him. He was "Uncle Frank, the policeman" who was always, strangely enough, around for every special occasion and milestone, with love, male support and bonding. "...Someday I will be promoted from sperm donor to full -fledged Daddy with all privileges and responsibilities of the post..."

He had the evening edition of his brother's newspaper. The fake cadavers were in the front page. They have collected the court order signed by Uncle Jaime, who never had failed him. The venerated old fool was instrumental in him getting his job at the police after serving in the army. The subpoena for Ms. Sampayo was in his pocket. Jerry was under lock and key for the moment. He will avoid seen his wife until the passage to upper Wisconsin had been warranted for him and his family. With his wife safe he would be a more cooperative witness against not only the Sampayos, but hopefully against the other drug families in the island.

He was going to summon his people when he noticed it at a distance. It was a personal airplane, one motor pushing the frame, which was made of balloon like compartments. He started going down in a spiral towards the area where the whales had been spotted. He glided effortlessly towards the whales, his motor off. Perfect landing, harness in hand, loss the glider with the push of a button and ran towards the head of the animal, opened the harness and prepare him to ride.

The whale was oblivious to Mousier Zola until he opened the cans of jalapeno mace smoke, one for the massive mouth, and the other for the dorsal spout. That wakes up the massive brute. He was in pain. Zola then pulls the brides with all his might, showing who the master was. Now there was no coming back. If the whale had been ridden before, it would comply submerge at full speed and jump out of the water in all his might. It would repeat the operation 2-3 times until the rider got tired or seasick and would let the brute go. If the whale was a neophyte anything could happen. Usually it involved dorsal fin splashing and very deep diving possible decompression and death of both whale and rider.

Lucky for Zola this whale had been ridden. The magnificent animal just went with the flow, without need of any more positive reinforcement the whale navigated in and out of the water until Zola was too tired to continue. He was also nauseated. He took the harness release and jump in the water swimming until he reached the beach. There waiting for him were three muscular men, who helped him out and gave him 10 mg of Zofran and 6 oz. of ethanol intravenously to control nausea and cramps. Photographs were taken and e-mailed to all major news outlets .The title was: '...Zola rides again, with the "world record" time for endurance written in the photo. He was his best promoter!

An assistant gave him the phone, he speed dialed: "...Osama, the city council approved the "trash refinery"...I need your people to get all the equipment here by Friday, to start construction and I want my son back. You will have the capacity to destroy the Americas and I want my son here Friday without a scratch..."

"...That was the deal...I am a man of my word...you will see your son Friday
 Alive and kicking, but if you betray us he will die..."
 "...I have nobody else to betray..."

Half a world away Eli had decoded the phone, recorded the message, forward it to his friends in British Intelligence and the NSA. He gave Middleman a report.
 "...Do we know where he is…?"
 "…Granada. The president of Iran is going there for a meeting of OPEC..."
 "...Can we take them prisoners..?"
 "..Very unlikely, but we can neutralize them..."
 "...Do we have location of the call? We could rescue Zola's son and would be a bargaining chip..."
 "...We have three agents in the area, the Perez brothers, they have been triangulating all morning...No luck so far..."
 "...It would be nice to capture the Iranian president to formulate

the last details of the air attacks on the nuclear facilities in Iran, with the least possible collateral damage..." Said Middleman "...Since we are making enemies for generations, let's made the minimum number...when is the air raid…?"

"...According to plan we have 600 bunker busting bombs, 30 F19@ to escort the bombers, five of those have nuclear capabilities ...just in case conventional weapons don't work. The second squadron will destroy all long range missiles...every target has been catalogued and coded...we are as ready as it can be..."

"...Never again! Eli...you have my blessing, call high command on Friday ALLAH will have plenty of visitors we will send him... Neutralize OBL and capture that crazy Iranian bastard..."

"...Consider it done uncle...consider it done..."

"...Uncle do we have any good archers in the island.., other than Goldman..?"

"..Yes, Yuri Singleman, retired there, lives in the capital, he must be in his 50's. He was 20 at Munich.

He hunted down, literally, two third of the terrorists over the next 15 years. Methodical, patient, that is Yuri…"

"...Permission to contact Goldman with info..."

"...Granted, use secure channel priority one, we will provide info to Goldman..."

Yuri Singleman was banker for the Bank of Nova Scotia at the capital 2 blocks from the docks .He was Vice-President for International Banking. His main responsibility, as he understood it, was the financing all MOSSAD operations in the Western Hemisphere. Money was diverted from shipping transportation charges in tankers with Panamanian and Costa Rican companies who were owned by the Israeli government. Weapons selling to Turkey and the Kurds, Pakistan and India, Cyprus and Greece: this maintained a balance of power in many areas of the world. You sell weapons to both sides, same level of technology, nobody wins. Human cost was very high both in terms of death and destruction. He understood the cost equation well; one brother and two cousins lost in Munich one sister in Lebanon, uncles and grandparents in the ovens. He was tired of burying kin and had lost all the sympathy towards his neighbor's pain.

At the time his phone rang, he was taking photos of the Al Qauida cargo vessel docking into port, "EL AMAL". Middleman himself had e-mailed him with the arrival time and cargo manifesto. There was a two-ton discrepancy between inventory and actual cargo. Zola had bought the old nuclear reactor site in Rincon, near the lighthouse, with the excuse of converting it to a museum and donating it back to the town.

Two tons of unaccounted for plutonium rods plus explosives could make a very effective dirty bomb or worst. There was also in the manifesto thirty Spitfires©, not the cars but the airplane! Damage to the infract structure could be tremendous if the were armed with at least dirty bombs, if not real chain reaction based bombs!

He got close enough to detect radiation of significant nature from a concealed Geiger counter in his attache case. No question this was the ship, and no question this represented real danger. He walked back towards his office , as he turned the corner he realized he was been fallowed ,two middle eastern men, 180 lbs each, five-six ,armed with silenced guns perhaps , early twenties.

He was the target. How has my cover been compromised so badly? After all these years he had face death for God and Israel, he was going to be eliminated by amateurs. This was not fair. Not only was his life at risk but that of millions. For the first time since Munich he prayed with faith, with all his heart. Then it came to him.

He continued uphill, ignoring the entrance to his office building. The two men were perplexed, apparently the have not counted on this scenario. There were policemen every 10 yards; this was the tourist area, where all the antique and jewelry shops were located. They would have to fallow a wait until the proper opportunity arrived.

He continued walking until he arrived at a shop across from the Catholic Cathedral. It was an antique shop, one of those were you need a special card to enter. The banks provided these cards to their exclusive clients so they could shop without carrying cash and at the same time were able to enter at will to these shops. He carried a card for a very good client. He was going to deliver it at the docks, but at the last minute the client changed his mind. He was heading to the office to deliver it there.

The two men were twenty yards away, as he placed the card in the reader. Which unlocked the door? He moves into the shop with minimum opening of the door. He used both arms and his right leg in a front snap kick to close and lock the massive door. It locked! Card in hand he approached Ferdinand Marquez, the Filipino who owned the shop, an old friend and sparing partner.

Mr. Marquez was about five feet four. Thin and muscular, looked like an old version of Bruce Lee. He was glued to the monitor, amused. At the other side of the door were the two men, trying to force it open.
"...Welcome Yuri...I guess your client is not coming, are those two bozos friends of yours..?"
"...Is he the last one today…?"
"...Yes...look at that..." He pointed at the monitor in amusement. The two men fired the pistols at the lock with no effect whatsoever.
"...Given enough time they probably kill themselves..." Added Yuri.
"... Ferdinand, call my office and advise my client that we had technical difficulties with the security lock and to stay put in my office and I will take him to lunch...'"Ferdinad complied with his re-

quest and relayed the message that Kin Ferguson III ,"heir to the Ferguson wireless empire", would wait for him at the Japanese Steak House..."

They both turned their attention to the two clowns outside. A very corpulent man with a big attache case has joined them. He opened the attache case to reveal 4 nice packages of C4 and some detonators.
"...How much C4, do you reckon...?" asked Ferdinand, starting to look nervous.
"...Sixty, maybe seventy grams...don't worry they are inexperience so the won't use all , they will start with one third of a bar... not enough to damage the 4 inch bullet proof plastic door...they will go up until they are able to blow it open...'
"...So what is the plan, Mr. Yuri...?" Asked Ferdinand.
"...I was hoping for one from you, but I feel one coming in now..." An explosion interrupted him that shakes the building but did not opened the door. He looked around. They were in an antique weapon store. The most modern weapon was a crossbow and a mosquet. The walls were covered with 4-5 century old Tang, Katana, traditional Samurai Swords, looking as new as the day they were built, testimony to the great Japanese swordsmanship. There were also Kamas, Nunchaku, Tonfa, Sai, Kwando and even Mulan fans.
"...I would like to buy the mosquet, do you have powder ...?"
"...I have a box of shot gun pellets but no shot gun, I also have several boxes of flying stars, as I have a competition in Añasco this coming weekend, will give those for free...I will even add a lighter for the same price..."

They jumped into action. Prepare the mosquet, which were small cannon. They pointed towards the door opening, emptied the powder at the bottom of the cannon, fallowed by all the pellets, the throwing star, and 2 boxes of thumbtacks. They prepared the wick.

"...I feel like this might work..." He was interrupted by a second explosion, stronger but still unable to brake the door.
"...Amateurs…! "

"...The next will make the door collapse from the hinges...they will use too much explosive next time ...."Said Ferdinand. "…Will have 2 seconds to shoot this monstrosity...I will like a bit more insurance...get the bow and arrows , you activate the cannon and I will start shooting , then you join me..."

"...Insurance. Not a bad idea...".Graving two sets of bow and arrows he armed himself and his friend...they looked at the monitor, the men were putting the last details on the charges...they moved on the side s of the wall and detonated.

"…One, two, three said the friends in unison…"

They fired the wick as the three men entered the shop with blazing guns; there was blood everywhere and cries of pain. The three men were on the floor in pain, shooting stars and tags everywhere. Any attempt to fire the guns was answered by an arrow to the head or heart. From the car the driver went in with a sawed shotgun and a grenade. The first arrow hit him in the left eye, the second and third in the heart, fourth, fifth and sixth in the belly. He pull the grenade pin, but could not release the grenade, he was dead before he reached the floor. The friends repined the grenade. They breath again in relief.

"…Well my friend, I have a ship to blow, care to join me..?"

"…I will be delighted, do we have to improvise…?"

"…No, we have the proper equipment in port ..." He stopped hearing the police and ambulances. "…I have no time to explain, I have thins to do..." They looked outside. The Mercedes was functional. "...Lets take a ride..." They jumped in and speeded away. His cell phone ringed .It was Ms Goldman.

"…Mr. Yuri, are you doing anything tomorrow...I am Pearl Goldman, I am sure that Eli talked to you about me, I am calling to invite you to a bow and arrow tournament, I heard you are very good, but so are all people here you need to come and practice with us...."

"...I will be delighted to join you in your spirited competition; can I bring a friend...?"

"...Of course, the more the merrier, can he shot...?"

'...He is probably as good as me or better..." He winked at his friend, who was driving. "...We will be there tomorrow, we have a project we have to finish tonight, then will head your way...."

"...I will blueberry you our address, it will be in Rincon. Over and out...."

They sped away; the police had not attempted to pursue them. They were busy with the fire and the wounded.

"...Where to? I know you have a mission...I overheard after that we are going to Rincón for an archery tournament, are you nuts...?"

"...We are going to the Isla Grande airport. I have some equipment we have to have ready for tonight...I understand that the ships are coming to harbor, there will be great confusion ...and we will blow El AMAL out of the face of the earth..."

"...How about the radioactive cargo...?"

"...We are going to steal it before blowing it out, it will be in Israel by Tuesday..."

"...I thought you already had the bomb..."

"..We have ten, never used any, we are considering Iran..."

'...What will happen if you fail to steal the plutonium and cant sink the boat..."

"...Millions of lives will be at stake..."

"...Well, count me in, I have always being a sucker for saving millions of lives, its almost a vice with me..,".

They arrive at the airport. They drove to hangar 11A. There it was a amphibian airplane, capable of landing anywhere. I n addition two Israeli fighter jets.

"...Tomorrow is the air show. During the commotion we steal the plutonium , during the end of the show, the drone plane will get out of control and impact the ship where it is carrying the explosives for our grand final .Will regret first the loss of life and then will mourn the death of our "great pilot", a great war hero etc., etc. Nobody will know the real truth..."

"...Sounds like a plan to me but remember the words of the immortal Lennon:

"Life is what happens to you when you are making other plans"

"…He also said: "I am the egg man and you are the Walrus", so will you stop quoting Lennon because most of what he said had no real meaning or usefulness..."

"…OK boss, let's get this puppy potty trained, let's get this baby off the ground, let's send these guys to smell the daisies..."

"…The pilot will come out of this hangar. He has two air-to-air missiles we can use to blow the El Amal out of the waster, if the drone scenario does not pan out. He has made dozens of practice rounds, only the Blue Angels had made more practice round. They are plan C. The British have two mirages available to us, they blueberry me a little while ago: plan D…"

"…How about plan A, what about the drone….?"

"…Let me introduce to you the master drone operator, imported exclusively from his previous engagement in Pakistan, via Afghanistan and Iraq , no other than Ferdinand Marquez II. Aaaaahhhh! The crowds cannot contain themselves!!! The young Captain is in charge of the division of deadly video players. Rumors are that he inherited his eye to hand coordination from his mother, a former Olympic Volley Ball player, and his libido from his father…!"

"….Commander Yuri! Sir! An honor and a privilege! Thank you

for this opportunity. Thanks for letting David play with me, I have not seen your son in years and he has been a great asset, he had been debugging the programs like he invented them…"

"…I do have the patents for the war game programs, you know? If we are successful I will give you the latest version and the military upgrade, it has GPS, infrared and ultraviolet scanners capability, all whistles and bells…."

"…Oh! Excuse ME! Pardon me for breathing on YOUR oxygen. You must fart higher than your butt! Said the young Marquez, looking at the roof of the hangar, smiling…"

"…Thanks for the reality check, Captain Marquez: Hum! Did you get your rank from a Pop-Tart © box or from a Fruit-Loop© box…?"

"…Actually I found it in your sisters' panties…." They looked at each other measuring each other, probably they had the same military experience and martial arts training, neither of them wanted a real confrontation , because they both will get hurt. They both started laughing loudly.

"…Some things do not change…" Said Marquez.

"…Ditto, by the way my sister still talks about your first date together…, you caused quite an impressions…"

"…I caused a deep impression on several occasions that night…she was quite impressed…"Said Marquez smiling, reminiscing....

Rincon Scuffle 69 Morell-Chardon

Chapter 8
[[Punta de Rincón Resort]]

Garcia knew well the guarded entrance to Puntas de Rincon. Before he joined the police force he had worked as a mason, building most of the frontal concrete wall in addition to the guard post. That was years before he met Maricela. Naturally when he realized how loaded his wife to be was, he suggested buying an apartment. Instead she bought four and made one available to the police.

He saluted the guard in military fashion, which he responded to with great emotion. Jimenez had been with his platoon in Iraq. He had lost one leg to friendly fire. A leg for a life, not a bad deal if you think about it. Jimenez was walking towards a land mine turned explosive device when the lieutenant detected him, shot him in the calf to force him to stop (he had one of those darn MP3 on and could not hear shit). Jimenez fell backwards (away from the device). Between him and the lieutenant, they dragged Jimenez away from the explosive device, which should have detonated with all the vibration. Three "insurgents" came out of nowhere to finish the job. They passed an unexploded device. The lieutenant turned around and in a fashion true to form shot the device with his 45, single shot, which detonated the device and kill the three men ,after placing them in short orbits. Jimenez got a medal of honor, bronze star, the lieutenant place three more scratches on his helmet (203 since Fellujah). Jimenez was able to go back home, while they stay another 12 month. They learned Arabic so that they read the wanted posters offering money for their capture. In a sense it could be considered amusing, if not for the extra risk the poster brought to them.

He drove towards the beach where he noticed the lieutenant, Zola with his posse. They were getting back in their fancy boats. He looked back in his sardonic way, offered them some Champagne and gave them a double birdie, fallowed by escaping at full throttle.

"…What is this guy's problem…?" Asked Frank suspiciously.

"…To much money fallowed by no common sense..." Said Garcia

"…Maybe he is just trying to grab our attention. Did you noticed that all the member of his entourage are Middle Eastern types? Don't you find it peculiar that a French magnate would no have a single French bodyguard or assistant…?'

"…You are implying that the man is a prisoner in a golden cage? But what would have caused him to become so vulnerable? And where is Mousier Tibbue, his mentor, uncle and advisor…?"

"…Also, where is Zola Jr., the heir apparent to the fortune, who usually whale rides with his father…?"

"…We need to stop reading the tabloids, we know way too much about this guy. Zola is acting very erratic, his two most important people who represent his past and the future and who he loves dearly are missing in action and only these rug burners surround him. Garcia, do you still correspond with Eli…?"

"…Yes I play HALO© every weekend through the net and the guy from the NSA…"

"…Get in the net and ask him to contact you through your satellite phone. I am telling you, been the kept stud of a rich woman is something else…!"

"…You just have satellite phone envy! My satellite phone has much more reach and penetration than your stupid old digital…!"

"…Is not the reach, is how fast you can speed dial! Call Eli, explain our little scenario here and ask for free curve sides consult through your incripted phone. In the meantime, I am going to the dedication gala of the Colossus recycling plant to take pictures of the rug burners to e-mail to Eli so that he can illuminate us…"

"…If by illumination you mean checking into the MOSSAD data base's Identity Recognition Program, he can probably be quite enlightening..."

As they spoke Frank received a Blueberry© massage: "…Boss,

only two men can claim those competition patches 1-Jaime Hernandez 2-Jose Lopez…"

"…Garcia what do you know about Jose Lopez?…"

"…***The Jose Lopez….?*** He used to teach at the academy when he was only 16. He joined the navy and was station in the Philippines where he learned from the "Esgrima" masters and from the great accu-ninjas. Is he our man…?"

"…Most likely. Where is his dojo…?"

"…Since you are such a fan, why don't you go and question him…?"

"…If by questioning him, you mean arrest him, me and what army…?"

"…Garcia I have seen you fight eight armed Iraqis with your empty hand and teeth…"

"…I was drunk, it was dark, and they were stupid…This is Jose Lopez…!"

"…The taller they are the harder they fall…"

"…I am taller! Maybe I should just chit-chat with the man; he has a reputation of being a very personable…good guy…"

"…Garcia I don't want you to date him, only to talk to him! Well, Have it your way, big guy. Ask if he will help us rescue Ms. Sampayo…"

"…In exchange for what, he already has millions of dollars…"

"…He may need our help, sooner or later…"

"…OK, I will attempt to establish diplomatic relations with Mr. Lopez while you play spy at the Collosus complex. Anyway Mr. Goya wanted to give .me a haircut which I am truly overdue…"

They parted ways. Garcia continued on the phone with Eli, who he had placed "on hold":

"… Are the boys in "the club" planning any operatives in the island…?"

On the other side of the world, Middleman was overhearing the conversation and looking at the roof in unmitigated disgust. He picked up the other line and introduced himself:

"…I am Mr. Middleman, who are you..?"

"…Commander Middleman, what an honor. I am Ernesto Garcia, present at this moment to serve you and God, not necessarily in that order..."

"…What is the deal down there, son?' He made a mental image of the absurdity of the situation and the willingness of this man to help them from 8000 miles away…"

"…My superior, who is a very astute man, has the theory that Zola is in under unbearable pressure, his whole organization has been infiltrated by middle eastern men, probably Al Qauida , and his mentor and confident, Mr. Tibbeau has disappeared into thin air…!"

"…How long did it take him to deduce this…?"

"…I would like to hire your superior. Is he Jewish? Mr. Tibbeau's body was found in a car junkyard in the outskirts of Granada. In his pocket he carried a bloody handkerchief, which was not his blood-type but that of Zola's son..."

"…The plot thickens! My boss is going to obtain pictures of all the entourage so you can help us with the ID's, maybe by association you can get the whereabouts of Zola's son…"

Middleman hesitated, but the cat was already out of the bag: "…Zola's son might be in the island, he wrote "El Amal" in his own blood in the handkerchief. First we thought that he was just giving us information about the vessel that would bring radioactive material for nuclear bombs. The signature is from the Iranian reactor. We need to get the plutonium, destroy the ship and return the enriched plutonium back to its home reactor, destroy the reactor with a bomb of its own signature. Ups! An accident…!"

"…Mighty elegant. Can we coordinate a rescue of Zola's son, let your guys steal the plutonium, blow "El Amal" & Iran to smitherings. We need Zola's son as leverage to convince the father that is safe to abandon the Arabs..."

"...Excellent! We will wait anxiously for your incripted e-mail. The answer to your question is yes. Will contact Silverman to co-ordinate the attack with your boys is going to be tomorrow 9:00 am .If possible you should rescue Zola tonight or early morning..."

"...Understood, commander and thanks...."

He hanged the phone. He was almost at the plaza. He was glad that the affair with his wife had been a "quickee". He was going to need all his wits and energy to pull this one. It was 5:30 PM when he parked at the plaza and entered Goya's barbershop. The old man was shaving the head of a Buddhist monk, he paused to great Garcia:

"...Hi *mijo*, nice to see you again, how is work? How is that **hembra** of yours...?"

"...On both accounts everything is going fine, I came here to interview Mr. Lopez...we will need his assistance...do you think he will be cooperative...?"

The monk interrupted: "...Man be careful with that shaver, I have to postpone my next re-incarnation until at least next Saturday. Hi my name is Lung... I am the director of the Green House Center for Meditation and Affirmative Buddhism. Lots of titles, no money. I am afraid Mr. Lopez was actually expecting you, and he is sitting closer to the door...."

Lopez stood. He was a non-impressive man that could do quite impressive things. They studied each other in silence. They were measuring each other as potential adversaries, like you would do in a competition. Finally they bowed to each other in respect. Garcia spoke first:

"...It is a great honor to be in your presence Mr. Lopez. I will be honored if you join us tonight to rescue two sets of hostages. Your unsurpassed abilities as accu-ninja will be useful..."

"...Mr. Garcia, it is my privilege to extend my hand in friendship. Is not any day that you meet **the grappler of Baghdad...**you are a legend, you are the man..."

"...No, you are the man, Mr. Lopez, or should I say Sensei Lopez..."

Sitting across from Jose was Perla Goldman. When she spoke, all men became quiet, mesmerized by the sweet tone of her voice. She stood and spoke: "...Gentleman, I am sorry to interrupt your romance but we need to place the situation on the table. Mr. Grappler here has asked us to loan our champion for several hours, what are you willing to give us in return? We need two warm bodies for a little battle against the forces of evil that we are organizing. We need you and Frank Moreno. We need you in top physical condition and trained in Zen Archery by Friday..."

"...And who is going to train us, in such short time? This disciple requires years of experience...!"

"...I will..." Said the Buddhist monk, smiling, not a hair in his scalp: "...Time my friend is a concept of the crazy western counties, time is as precious or as worthless as you make It. Ounce you understand this you can bend the fiber of time and make it last as much as necessary, to learn new things and skills, to make passionate love for hours, every learning process becomes easy...!"

"...Are this your agents? I know you have recently come into a great amount of money..."
"...Rumors, gossip, envious people with bad karma, highway robbers, mass murderers, Devil worshipers, people without sources, full of bad intentions...About 200 millions..."
"...So let me get this straight , you will help , do anything we

need in the next 24 hrs in exchange for us showing up for your little theme party on Saturday...?"

"...Is not just Saturday, you need to practice 10 hrs a day for the next three days in order to be able to develop enough proficiency with the bow and arrow not have any friendly fire deaths and to be able to kill as many as these evil people as possible, all of them preferably, including the son of the Devil..." said the monk.

"...I always thought that Buddhist did not believe in violence and murder. That ever life was precious etc..."

"...These entities we are going to be fighting are more "evil incarnate", than precious life, human or otherwise..." Said the monk.

"...Aren't you bending the rules to confirm the hypothesis..."

"...I can sleep very well at night, no moral dilemmas, no existential metaphysical questions, happiness with the acceptance of personal responsibility...inaction and apathy in this case can be more lethal than a spear..."

Ms. Goldman interjected: "...Lopez has to be returned tomorrow in one piece; part of the deal you have with Middleman will depend on the good faith you demonstrate towards this man, we need both you and Moreno for Saturday's activity..."

"...Understood. I will be sure that both me and the lieutenant are available to your service..." He said sardonically.

His phone rang, it was Eli, acknowledging receiving the photos from Moreno and confirming their suspicion "...Mr. Garcia, all the handlers and bodyguards are Al Quaida , some date back to the Soviet invasion of Afghanistan..."

"...We analyzed 22 photos. Your boss is an excellent photographer, by the way...anyway our experts are 90% certain that Zola is under duress and that he might not even be aware of the death of Messier Tibbeau. The main operative is Mohamed Rajul, the butcher of Kabul. Taliban regional commander who was in charge of the national stadium turned concentration camp. His record consists of 23,000 deaths in 3 months. About 30% woman and children. Ruthless and pitiless he is, with an agenda of death and destruction plus world domination. Our analysts believe he would be able to trigger an atomic disaster even if mutual destruction is assured, he will try to escape if he can, but he has a bad case of "suicide bomber envy" that may need fulfillment. Of all The Al Quaida commanders he is one of the few which actually believes all the rhetoric, seventy virgins and all…"

"…This issue about the seventy virgins sounds like a very painful proposition, in addition is virginity recyclable? ...I mean if the whole idea is to have sex with seventy two virgins through all eternity, you are going to run out of virgins in 2-3 months tops…Then what?...Think about that, the whole scenario becomes unsustainable after a short period of time…" Said Garcia

"…Now, on the other hand if you have seventy two whores, the scenario makes sense and can be sustainable for eternity…" Said Middleman, tongue in cheek and very serious, upon overhearing the conversation.

"…And, of course, uncle you have hit the nail in the head, that scenario would be a whole new ball game. We have contacted Silverman regarding the issues with Al Quaida and Zola's Son and he will be expecting you around 11:30 PM His team consist of 15 MOSSAD, average experience of 12 years plus four pilots from the INA that can land an F18 on a roach…"

Garcia responded: "…We will bring 10 men, including my boss, his boss, me, Jose Lopez , two demolition experts..."
"…Not the Jose Lopez, the Accu-Ninja from Mindanao..."
"…Well, actually I am not Filipino, I am from this Island, and I trained with Robert Chang and Jaime Escudier in Manila. I made my

fame in the Battle of Mindanao..."

"...Where he "neutralized" two hundred members of Abu Sayaff..." Said Middleman in a note of sincere admiration for the young Lopez.

The Buddhist monk interjected: "... He anaesthetized without evidence of permanent damage two hundred hard-core terrorists. If that is not elegant, I don't know what is, and on the anniversary of the Matanza de Moros! By contrast, in 1906, the Christian soldiers both native Filipino and Americans massacred 1000 Muslims. That was not elegant at all...Buddha's Circle of Peace is a wonderful thing...!"

"...I need curare, I ran out of it..."
Garcia responded: "...My wife can get us Pancuronium from the regional hospital in 40 minutes..."
"...I need needles..." Said Jose trying to get himself out of such high expectations.
"...We got a whole new batch, which arrived in the mail yesterday..." Said Mr. Manuel
"...So it is settled, now you are officially members of MOSSAD ..." Said Middleman: "...were shooting down communications from Israel, good luck to you all, God's speed..."

At that moment Frank parked at the plaza. Maricela drove through giving a box of curare to Frank driving away on way to the beach home. The rest of his team surrounded Frank. He entered the barbershop. Garcia was getting the end of the haircut, when he saw his boss.

"...Garcia, are we ready. Have you signed Mr. Lopez for our team...?"

"...Believe me he is not coming cheap, I hope you can take a leave of absence, because we are going to learn to use the bow and arrow in a ZEN fashion.

"...OK, let's get this baby off the ground..." Said Moreno.

The massive man paced the balcony sweating like a pig. He hated meeting with Angel Sampayo.

"…It was ironic that this servant of the Devil had Angel as the first name…" He spoke in almost imperceptible voice to his tie

He reviewed in his mind those themes that were considered taboo in his client's house. He had seen longstanding loyal lackeys summarily executed on the spot for mentioning any of these issues. The Fact that he belonged to a high powered law firm and that he has significant press coverage was no guarantee that his disappearance could not be easily arranged , he knew it was a mater of a couple of phone calls and presto, he was gone. Not even his mother will remember him

The biggest no-no was the mention of his neck scar. He used turtlenecks even in the death of summer to hide the shame of his scar. He was around 16 when he was abducted. First they kill both his bodyguards. That was a terrible blow to him as both men has raised, trained and loved him like a son.

Actually they were the only parents that he had ever known, as his father, even though he was his first born, had shown more interest and invested more time with his Paso Fino horses than with the boy.

Both men had suffered torture in the hands of the Bravos de Boston gang with such brutality that Angel went absolutely insane. The photograph they sent his father with the ransom demand depicted Angel in the floor of the warehouse, nude in semi-fetal position, covered in the blood and feces of his bodyguards who hanged from the roof, heads down carotids slit, like pigs about to be processed.

"…And after seen the picture, that son of a hyena refused to pay the ransom…" Thought the lawyer, may he rot in Hell…!"

He transferred the family to Miami and declared war on the gang. Every gang member and every first degree relative assassinated. When they arrived at the warehouse, Angel was hanging from a noose, executed as the last act of defiance/desperation from a coursed nation (the Bravos).

He was sill warm when they got there. They brought a doctor with them who performed CPR and brought him back. But Angel was never the same. There was no resemblance of humanity, not a glimpse of compassion, just pure evil and disdain. His death did not become him.

Above everything he had developed a virulent hate for his father. His father had refused to negotiate for his life on the base it was not good business practice. His vendetta was because he had lost two reliable and loyal employees, not because his son was been tortured and abused.

Angel had been in Hell. Four minutes in Hell had been enough. He actually sold his soul to the Devil. In exchange, he will be high in the leadership ladder of demons, not an inmate, not a capo, but a Mengele, making decisions of who, how much pain will be inflicted and what type of degradation would be inflicted on the victims! In addition he will impregnate the DeMello, the whore of Babylon with the seed of the Devil and the fruit of that union will reign over the planet for a millennia, a dressed rehearsal for Hell.

Mr. Gayle Carson has been the main council for the old Sampayo. Now for Angel. He had positioned his company to control business deals that will make them extremely wealthy but will give the Sampayos virtual monopolies over the control of the ports in all the Americas, and eventually the world. With this they could corrupt the whole world, move drugs, sex slaves, money at will. And everything would be "legal".

The only remaining issue was Ana's fate, and of course the darn nephews.

"…Gayle, I need your help to finalize the transfer of my sister's assets to the company…she was the old man's favorite, you know. While I hanged by the neck, the bitch was getting serviced in Miami by the Jerry: *el muy pendejo...*" Said Angel.

"…Here is where I can get into quick sand in a hurry…" Thought Mr. Corson.

"…He has mentioned the hanging, the sister and his defunct brother-in-law. If am not careful my head will roll…." Finally he ventured: "…Talking about the Devil, your brother in law's photo was in the front page of "EL Vocero", he died like a pig…."

"…He died like an omelet, after falling from 10,000 feet there was not much left…" Said Angel with glee.

"…Be as it may, we have the issue to resolve about your sister..."

"…With the death of Jerry, may he rot in Hell, my sister is not an issue, we can dispose of her, we could make her useful and sacrifice her on Friday's ceremony, when the son of the Devil will be begotten and the beginning of the new millennium will start…!"

They heard a bell and send two arm guards to investigate. There were 26 guards in the premises, armed to the teeth. His enemies did not dare to attack, especially after they have realized that he was far more malignant than his father and way more unstable.

After several minutes in which the lawyer made some small talk about the weather, Frank Moreno, and Sargento Garcia, escorted by the two guards entered the courtyard. In the shadows Lopez started his cleaning job. They did not have the time to guarantee the safety of the hostages and of the guards, so instead of giving the guards the Buddha's circle of peace, instead they would receive the Dragon's Breath. This consisted of 2 needles precisely place in the C3-C4 and C6-C7 spaces: total paralysis and death in 5-6 minutes, unable to speak, unable to shout, unable to breath. *The silent death,* six minutes of pain fallowed by an eternity of death.

"...Mr. Sampayo, I am Lieutenant Moreno from homicide..." (Three guards neutralized in the roof) This is Sargento Garcia...." Frank extended his hand to great him, Mr. Corson did instead.

"...I am Gayle Corson, Mr. Sampayo's main counsel to what do we owe the honor or your visit at this ungodly hour...?" (Hanging from the roof, Jose breath's neutralized the next three)'

"...Well Mr. Carson, I have a subpoena for Mrs. Sampayo and her two children to come and identify the body of her late husband..."

"...You must be kidding, there is nothing to identify..." Said Angel

"...On the contrary, the gentleman in question died of a bullet wound to the heart and not from the fall. (Six more neutralized on the third floor balcony)"...

"...That is totally bogus..." Said Corson

"...I am here to escort Mrs. Sampayo to the district Morgue for ID of her late husband; I have the proper forms, as you can see everything here is by the book..." (Jose in the second floor neutralized six more goons)

Mr. Corson looked at the forms in detail. They were legit but he had to buy some time. He made a mental note to get rid of that judge, one way or another.

"...This forms are falsified, I know personally this judge, he would never agree to this FISA injunction. I am going to ask you to leave the premises, or will expel you by force, this is private property..."

"...Believe me I have better things to do than waste my time here. I would appreciate your full cooperation. There is no reason for this to become a confrontation. At the end of the day we can all go home tonight alive (Three more neutralized in the first floor). This judge is my uncle and "father-in-law". This is as legitimate as it can be…please surrender Ms. Sampayo…"

Angel, not used since his death to be resisted was fascinated and exasperated. There is nothing more dangerous than a man who cannot be bought, a man that can be destroyed, but not defeated, won but not bought. This has gone too far it was time for a final confrontation. Tonight Ana and the bastard children will join Jerry in Hell, escorted by these two coppers. (By now, the breath of the dragon has neutralized all the first floor guards; only the two guards flanking Meriano and Garcia remained alive. Jose positioned himself at shooting distance with his silver dart gun at hand, darts laced with pancuroneum)

"…Corson, get Ana and the kids. I guess they will be leaving us in the company of these gentlemen…I hope there is no hard feelings, I hope you understand that a man in my position have no choice but to impart discipline, respect and over all fear…" He made a pre-conceived signal to order the men in the balcony to shoot at will. No reaction from the galleries. The signal was re-implemented for the benefit of the two remaining guards. The guards understood the signal, upholstered their guns. This was fallowed by a very rapid disarming and fracturing of their trigger fingers and two tranquillizer darts on each one from Jose's gun.

Corson arrived with Ana and the two children at gunpoint. It was not the first time he was placed by the Sampayos into a situation in which he could be disbarred. He had a very bad feeling about the whole situation. Angel and the two cops were at a double Mexican stand off. The guards were in the floor immobile and there was no response from any of the other guards.

"…I don't like this at all…" Corson said to himself, he calked his gun when he heard it. It came from his left side, like a whisper. A mosquito bite fallowed by complete loss of body tone, his knees could no longer support him, he fell forward, still gun in hand, he watched in horror as the gun that was about to shoot Ana started pointing in his direction as he fell. Then the sum of all his fears at that point, the blast of the gun and the hot bullet, Bunsen burner-hot, entering his chest wall, then nothing.

Ana-jumped into action. She grabbed the gun and placed in his brother's occiput. Garcia promptly disarmed him. Before the first fist could land in his face, Jose in full Ninja uniform appeared out of the shadows.

"…Enough death for today, you can not harm Angel; the prophecy will not be fulfilled…" Said Jose. He promptly placed three needles I the Buddha's Circle of Peace configuration and Angel was paralyzed but still breathing.

"…You are still alive because you have a destiny to fulfill. We will live instructions in you so that your maid can liberate you in the morning, see you on Saturday…!" With this, they all left the Sampayo compound in Anasco, leaving behind a trail of death and destruction, Jose had serous misgivings about what he had done, but understood that there was very little choice.

Angel made mental note, like if dictating to his secretary: "…Get rid of the Ninja…" The ungrateful bitch was getting away and he had nothing that will prevent them from escaping their execution! All these months of planning for nothing grabbed from his control by second rate policemen: Garcia and Moreno. He repeated those names like a bad mantra, one time after another, as to not forget them, while he planned his revenge.

Outside, a Black Hawk helicopter awaited them. When the door opened Jerry was there, waiting for his family. He hugged them and helped them in. He waved them good- by and closed the door behind them. He approached Jose, bowed and informed the Master: "…You have saved everything I hold dear, I am forever in your debt…"

José took off his mask, bowed back and said: "…My dear friend, one week of commitment will suffice. I have pay dearly in blood for your family's life and freedom. Don't let them waste this precious gift..."

As the Black Hawk disappeared in the distance, Jerry's tears escaped his eyes: "…Master those lives will never be wasted, I will guarantee these kids will grow in honor and strength…"

"…May God hear your words, and may we all survive this terrible week…" Said José.

"…Amen…", accented Garcia and Moreno as they got into their Expedition on the way to the capital. The night was just starting.

CHAPTER 9
[[Black Hawk Helicopter, Atlantic Ocean: Midnight]]

Ana looked at the island from the distance since her father's death she has been a virtual prisoner in her own house. In spite of all his faults, her father was an honorable man. You can argue until the second coming of Christ, weather or not his business deserved to be called honorable or not.

She knew Jerry would rescue them. Her heart broke when she saw his picture in "EL VOCERO". She also suspected that with Jerry out of the way, her life was not worth a cent to Angel and that her time in Earth will be counted in hours, not days. As he closed the helicopter's door he had signed to her in SASL "…I LOVE YOU and I WILL BE BACK FOR YOU…"

As the helicopter ascended she saw him bow to the man in the Ninja uniform and more remarkable still, the Ninja had unmasked and bowed back at him. He understood the terrible price that had been pay for their liberty. Her husband was promised to this little man so he had lost his liberty pursuing theirs.

This was a DEA helicopter. "The enemy", as her father used to call these guys. There were two pilots and two crewmen, well actually a crew-woman and a crewman. They were all connected by radio through the helmets. The woman passed the extra helmet to Ana.

Ana thanked her in sing language, which was standard communications for helicopter pilots. Then she added that the boys were fluent in SASL also, so be careful with what they say. The woman smiled back, gesturing; "… So no sexual innuendo in front of the kids…" By now the two pre-adolescents were making a racket.

"…Where are we headed, Miss.?"

"…My name is Captain Morgan…I understand your situation, I specialize in relocations of witnesses. We are flying to Grenada, from there we will fly to an unknown destination (she started to sign-Switzerland) where we will board the kids and prepare you for a life of seclusion and relative safety…"

Of course you will have full access to any bank account your father may have hidden from the IRS. In the meantime we will give you rental money, pay for the first semester of tuition and provide you with a contact to help you in case of emergency. You are not to contact anybody, especially your husband. Will provide information as we go, on a need to know basis. Do you speak any of the languages…?"

"…I am fluent in German, Italian and French, as of secret bank accounts, there is none, my brother raided them when my father died." She lied as she tried to remember the numbers, tattooed backwards in the base of her ample breasts.

She will need a mirror in the bank!

"…We will be in Grenada in about thirty minutes…the DC10 will leave in one hour and you should be arriving in Spain in about 8hrs, from there a flight to the Swiss capital probably two hours…" Said Captain Morgan.

"…I have a confession to make now that the kids have gone to sleep. In Iraq I was hospital transport. I was involved in rescuing the wounded. Jerry was a platoon leader there. Your husband is one of the most handsome men and most gallant men I ever met. God, I wanted him so much! On one occasion I bribed an Iraqi worker five hundred dollars to let me in the shower while your husband was there…"

"…Does this story have a point? Whatever happened in that shower is business between you and my husband…"

"…Nothing happened, when I entered the shower he was in they're relieving himself, in the other hand a photo of you in a tight string bikini. He smiled and said: I am honored but you are 15 years too late. I was so embarrassed! And so incredibly horny! That night an Iraqi worker went home $500.00 richer and with a smile in his face..."

"...Thanks for sharing your erotic adventures with my husband in Iraq. Coming back to reality for a couple of minutes, how come we are getting this VIP treatment...?"

"...Your husband has agreed to eliminate your brother and dismantle the Sampayo's empire..."

"...Do you realize that my family just controlled 25% of the entire drug trafficking in the island? Do you realize that the vacuum you will leave behind will be filled within weeks with eager investors, both natives, American and Columbians...?"

"...Not unless if the other two cartels destroy each other in a gang war. Wednesday, World War III will happen in Nemesio Canales-the housing project. Both parties have been arming themselves and selling weapons to "Los Macheteros" who were planning to disrupt the festivities of Barbosa's birthday. More than a thousand stoned to their gills and armed to their teeth with old vendettas, equal a blood bath. Too bad "los macheteros", trying to gallantly avenge the death of their charismatic leader, will be stuck in the cross fire, 'darn too bad'

"...At least the will go in a flash of glory..." Said Ana, while thinking to herself that no armed resistance will be present to keep at bay the whims of the political will of the patricians from the metropolis, or to resist the advancers of the Russian, Israeli or Italian Mafia. Any chance the island had of a long term political solution will be gone and a civil war would explode sooner or later. They will have to be stopped, but how?

"...When is this great event happening...?"

"...Wednesday night, 9:00PM, we are trying to minimize civilian casualties, but collateral damage is expected to be high…"

Ana realized they were landing. They have arrived at Grenada. As promised a passenger plane was waiting for them at the tarmac. The transfer of the three passages took less than 5 minutes and they had strip priority. They were air-bound in less than twenty minutes, in route to Spain.

Morgan sat with them, trying to catch some Z's, her holstered 45, hanging between her breasts. For a split second she chuckled, realizing that the most powerful weapons this woman had was not made of metal, but of flesh and bone. Any man, except her husband, (she chuckled again) would surrender to her charms any day, but may actively resist her revolver.

"…Someday you will realize that a woman's body is the most powerful weapon in the world, men can be saved or eternally condemned in your arms, you can make a man to show the best or worst of his persona. With such incredible power comes grave responsibility, thus should not be abused…!"

Her two sons, were peacefully sleeping, the night engulfed the plane. There were no other passengers. The plane was flying due east towards Europe.

Morgan was sound asleep. She must have been exhausted. In 48 hrs there was going to be a massacre and she needed to prevent it. She could have to communicate with her husband somehow. This was a senseless loss of life that would benefit no one, and would only harm the future of the island.

She took out her cell phone put in computer mode and sent e-mail to her husband; hopefully he will get a message. She will try gain later and again in Spain or as soon as she was in Swiss soil. An uncle of hers had a small hotel in Zurich that catered to prostitutes and druggies; maybe she will be able to contact her husband from there.

She wrote: "…Gang war in 48 hrs in Canales, macheteros also to be killed, please stop." After sending the message, she turned around only to find Morgan's palm in her face: "…Surrender your phone, you lunatic, from now on you are no longer the Sampayo princess but rather my bitch…"

She threw the phone in the floor and smashes it with a hammer: "…From now on you are *"incomunicado, comprende…?"*

"…Don't you ever touch me again, or I swear to God, I will rip out your uterus through your but! If you touch any of my sons, I will pull your uterus through your nose. Comprende…?"

"…That is anatomically impossible…" Said Morgan with a sneaker.

"…Tempt me and you will find out how possible it is. The fact that my husband sold his soul to you all for my life does not mean you can do we us as you please with me or mine. I will defend those two angels with my last drop of blood. There are crimes that do not deserve any compassion; these are crimes so horrendous that the only deserving punishment should be crucifixion. Don't mess with me, you little bitch, I can run in circles around you…"

"…OK, enough of this crap, go back to your chair, and leave me alone..."

Ana complied, hoping upon hope that her message will somehow reach her husband in time enough to stop the bloodshed.

CHAPTER 10
[[Middle of the Atlantic, Israeli AWAK plane 1:30 AM]]

High above the Atlantic an Israeli AWAK captured the e-mail
"…What do we do with this information? It came from the vicinity, 100-200 miles at most, American Plane signals…"
"…E-mail a copy to military intelligence and other to MOSSAD, someone will figure it out…"

Eli received the e-mail from the AWAK and called Garcia. They have been driving towards the capital in their Expedition© when he received the call. He placed the call in speakerphone.
"...Garcia, here..."
"…This is your friend Eli..."
"…Honey you can not live without me, you cheap slut…"
"…I have an e-mail that one of our AWAKS intercepted over the Atlantic. I make reference to one of your housing projects so I assume you will be interested, I will send you a text message…"
"…Sweaty, thanks a lot…We will keep you posted in the Zola affair, over and out…"
Garcia received the message and read it.
"…That sounds like Ana…" Jerry said.
Moreno sighted, the DEA was playing God again, he thought.
"…Guys, the DEA has betrayed us. We cannot trust anybody, except for the MOSSAD. That leaves us in a very precarious situation. If all the gangs and the Macheteros are destroyed, a political vacuum will ensue which will be filled with innocent blood. We need to stop this…"
Jose, who had been taking a nap, spoke: "…We need to speak with the leaders of the macheteros so that they do not show up to the fight. Please let me barrow the hone and I will warn them…"
Jerry spoke: "…I know the numbers for the two opposing gang leaders; we can abort the meetings…"
"…OK, go ahead, use Garcia's phone; no problem…"

Jose marked the phone and after ringing 12 times a woman answered on the other end:

"…Buenas, mi amor…"

"…About last night, I am so sorry I was too fast, baby…" Said Jose while Moreno looked at the roof, smiling.

"…For this time I will forgive you, are you coming back tonight, my love…?"

"…No, I am working overtime for the police commissioner. I was calling because the activity you have on Wednesday is not kosher, the DEA is getting involved, and they want to play too rough…"

"…OK honey, will take that into consideration, will wear protection, and avoid any rough spots…"

"…Best to your family..."

Jose smiled and passed the phone.

Jerry picked it up and in a more direct fashion, explained the situation to the two gang-lords in a three-way call. They agreed to a fight moratorium until things settled down. Hopefully clear heads will prevail, and bloodshed will be avoided. In 48 hrs most gang members would have received the news.

Frank had serious issues at this point. He had a man he could trust without questions with his life and two potential traitors. He had to place these issues over the table, put everything in the open.

"…Mr. Lopez, are you still active in "los macheteros"…?"

Jose looked at him intensely: "…Not active, but as you can see, I keep my contacts. We had our philosophical differences and we decided to divorce amenably. I promise you that you have my complete loyalty…"

The lieutenant decided to let hell loose. He took two guns from the glove compartment and gave one to each man. Jerry Vaelga received it with lust. It felt like an old girlfriend, ready for action.

"…Mr. Vaelga, it is loaded you know…What about you, can I

trust you…?"

"…My loyalty is to Mr. Lopez here, I owe him my life and my family's life and liberty. If you trust him, you have to trust me too…."

Garcia interrupted: "…Boss, this is the last toll plaza prior to the port, will be there in *Puerto Nuevo* in about 15-20 minutes. Anybody hungry…?"

All agreed the will stop for a snack, at Garcia's choice. It will also be a piss stop.

Then Frank, put all his concentration on Lopez. He had received the gun with a mixture of disdain and anger. He will push the envelope one more time:

"…Mr. Lopez, can you shoot…?" He stared directly in his eyes, while Lopez without flinching, dismantle the gun and save it in the front section of his backpack.

"…I was able to shoot a man between the eyes at 600 yards with a Beretta…"

"…Was that when you were in "the macheteros"…?"

"…. Was that when you shot Pedro Vargas-Lopez? Is that the reason you left the terrorist organization?

"…Yes Mr. Moreno, that was the main reason I left the island freedom fighters. They have moved from destroying military targets to hostage taking for profit. (He started crying bitterly) I was living with the head of the organization, the woman you heard in my phone call. The state double-crossed us, and sent Captain Lopez to liberate the hostages with a group from the riot police. I was ordered to shoot my hostage dead. As I was aiming to fallow the order, your friend, in the most heroic feat I have seen jumped in front of the hostage and took my three bullets for her! He died before he hit the floor…"

"…What were his last words, Mr. Lopez…?"

"…I forgive nephew, run away from these peoples, fast and away…" Then he fell and expired.

"…Was he your uncle…?"

Lopez just cried for several minutes the added: "…Yes that is why I see guns with disdain, I prefer more primitive weapons whose margin of error is much larger, an where developing skills can make a difference.

Garcia interrupted: "…Boss sometimes you can be a prick, there is no reason to torture this man like this…"

"…There is a reason, Captain Lopez was a good friend of mine, and this criminal showed no sign of repentance and never apologized to the widow…"

"…In that all mighty Buana, you are incorrect. Not a day passes in which I don't wish I could bring uncle Pedro back. As of Aunt Gloria, unlike you have been able to see the bigger picture, and forgives me…"

"…And what is the bigger picture…?" Moreno inquired, with great sarcasm.

"…The bigger picture is he died like a hero, doing what he believed was the correct thing to do. He became immortal with his death; he will be remembered way after you and me are gone. Furthermore his death was the catalyst that forced me to live the life of a practicing Christian. My aunt realized that I was like the prodigal son, lost everything and came back to the brotherhood of men. I was there at her death bed and she forgave me, I think you could learn from her…"

"…Touché…"…I think he has proven himself to us on several occasions, is time to let bygones be bygones and to start from scratch…" Jerry said.

"… I agree with him…" Said Garcia. "…I don't know about you, but I am starving. We have arrived at "La Ceiba". A good Cuban sandwich and a coffee and we will be ready for a stake-out…" He picked up the phone and informed Silverman of their location, giving an expected arrival time. He claims we are on schedule as long as we get there around 2:30 AM; it's now 1:30AM. We can even take a short nap.

They all got out of the car in unison. Jose, who probably had the fullest bladder, went first. The rest of the guys closely fallowed him. As soon as he entered the room he realized something was wrong. He got the impression that the others perceived it too.

He could not put his finger on it the first time around. Perhaps, it was the smell of burned bread. Apprentice bread makers, as a matter of pride, will not let the bread burn. Perhaps was the nervousness and inappropriate behavior of the sandwich maker or the overdressed cashier. In addition, he thought he heard women's voices begging for mercy.

Then José heard the caulking of a shotgun, which waked him from his sleep depravation based stupor. He jumped over he counter and missed the shotgun volley behind him. He realized that he had fallen on the death cashier's body. His three companions were shooting at the impostor general direction.

Then he heard it behind him. A tall slender man, quite muscular in nature, with a squirm of infallibility was coming down the stairs caulking the bullet cartridge of his UZI©. Jose took two Shuriken stars from his side bag. By the time the man reached the stair's rest two stars were flying and lodging in both carotid arteries. He began to bleed profusely. He started to get dizzy and collapsed on his knees then forwards down the stairs. The racquet produced by the crash of the body made the cashier turn on that direction and started shooting, killing the sandwich maker who was in the line of fire.

Suddenly, a car crashed through the front door causing the can foods to fly all over the place. The driver took out his gun and started to shoot. José's three companions answer in unison. First shot instinctively aimed at the head (Just in case he was bulletproof), second to the heart. Every impact made the body dance in a macabre electro buggy, giving it a sub-realistic flare.

Jose realized that the "cashier" was the only remaining danger, as he crawled towards him above the lifeless body of the sandwich maker. He had run out of gunshot shells. He was going for the Beretta on his ankle to shoot his way out of this situation.

Suddenly Jose jumped into action. He disarmed the big gorilla of a man, breaking his trigger finger in the process. The man, who was not used to have his will resisted in any shape or form, and less by an "inferior being", was at first surprised and amused. Then he became mad with rage.

It happened so fast that Jose had no time to retrieve the revolver from the floor.

The man jumped on him like an avalanche. Jose reacted with pure instinct.

José double punched to the ribs and karate chop to the liver. In his mind he was looking for the painful, but not lethal."…Two ribs and a lacerated liver most hurt…" He thought.

The man's rage, however, increased with pain. He grabbed Jose in a bear hug from bellow and squeezed. Jose, whose arms were free, was in agony now. He grabbed the cashier's eyes and pressed down with his thumbs. The man continued to press harder. Jose jumped up and back using the man's own legs as a base. He retrieved both arms sideways and hit the man's temples with all his might with open hands with the base of the wrists. The effect was devastating. The man looked into his eyes in disbelief. His strength was gone and he had the most incredible headache of his life. Jose was free. With a swift full punch to the neck he collapsed the trachea. The man turned blue, his eyes rolled back. He had an impressive seizure and collapsed, dead.

Behind him he heard the voice of Moreno saying: "…Garcia, take mental note: remind me not to fight Mr. Lopez barehanded. The score is Jose two the rest of us one. Mr. Vaelga goes upstairs and check for survivors, Garcia, check in the back, in the warehouse. Also turn off the ovens. Mr. Lopez, call 911 and get some food to go, we are going to have a stake-out at Pier 9 and will need some nourishment…"

Garcia was the first one to come back.
"…All quiet, no bodies or perpetrators lieutenant. Plenty of sugar donuts…"
"…We got 5 lbs of bread, two pounds of cheese, two pounds of ham and six liters of Pepsi©', 911 has been called situation explained, they will send the coroner…"

Then they heard the distinct noise of human vomiting above them, they realized that Jerry has not come back from the second floor, and became impatient thinking the worst. As Jose went up the stairs Jerry went down the stairs crying.

"…Status report, Mr. Vaelga…", ordered Mr. Moreno. But Frank knew that Jerry saw something so sinister and evil that he was speechless.

Five minutes after Mr. Lopez came down the stairs, pale like a Klan Hood.
"…Status report, Mr. Lopez, please…"
"…Two white girls, twins, about sixteen, brutally raped and executed gang style…"
"…You mean this whole massacre here was an initiation rite…?" Asked Jerry

"…Five innocent people died so they could be gangsters…?" Asked Jose

"…Two children and three adults died so that these men could fulfill their drug crazed ideals of "manhood and chivalry. Those who claim that dugs are a "victimless crime" should take a guided tour of this little hell. They would never take a hit or smoke a pipe in their lives again…!" Said Frank

Jose grabbed his food cargo, picked up his shuriken, cleaning the stars with a bottle of eucalyptus based rubbing alcohol (Which the poor cashier probably kept around to treat her rheumatism) and made a gesture to the other to leave the place in sign language and exited the store. The others complied. They got in the car and he started braking bread and making improvised sandwiches with the slices of mortadella and American cheese, in a sub-realistic ritualistic communion.

Chapter 11
[[Rincón Town Plaza, 2:00 AM]]

The Rincon town square, like every other plaza on the Island, had a Catholic church, the City Hall, bank, at least one bakery (in this case two), restaurants, surfer shop, beauty shop /barber shop. Larger town had series of fountains, in this only one. This plaza also had two pizza parlors, and one Chinese restaurant.

The sidewalks have never been finished. Lawsuits and counter lawsuits had been exchanged like canon fire between two countries. And while waiting for the construction company to go on chapter 11(as to save the government from any of his obligations), nothing ever happened, and two years after the completion of the project, nothing had been finished! It has been lost in the antiquity of the legal briefs whose responsibility it was to finish the sidewalks and the truth laid in the labyrinths of legal papers.

Perla Goldman dressed in Buddhist monk habit, which did very little to hide her voluptuous figure, sprinted from the 'Green House' to the Catholic Church. There were obstacles everywhere from the unfinished construction, which slowed her down a bit. She was exhausted from hours of practice with the bow and arrow. She was worried. Jose and the local police have not contacted them. She did not know the status on her lover, and archenemy, Mr. Zola. And on top of all that she had the pesky ghost of *abuela* fallowing her along, inquiring her regarding her life, her work and her relation to Mr. Zola.

"…God I wish I can silence you! You are worst than a Jewish Mother! You are driving me nuts…!"

Abuela simply fallowed her along. She will imitate her every manerisms, every gesture, and was enjoying herself immensely driving her crazy.

"…You take yourself too serious, too uptight, if I did not know better I would say you are in serious need of a good session with Mr. Zola. And besides, all mothers are Jewish mothers in training…"

Perla entered the courtyard of the Catholic temple without much preamble or discussions with the ghost. She opened the side door and as a consummate spy walked in complete silence. She reached the area of the church between the altar and the first line of pews.

Perla did not know what to say. Laying o the floor, providing the perimeter of a square were Pereira, Ignacious, Mr. Manuel and the Llama. They were nude except for a loincloth, resembling the Amazonian natives garment. In the center of the square, incense burned, elevating frankincense to the heavens. They were all reciting a mantra; "…The Devine is eternal, all that happens is His Will, only through Him we can find fulfillment…"

Perla looked at *abuela,* who was rolling I mock laughter on the floor. The master spy stood up and walked into the center of the square. She addressed the four men who were concentrating on the rising smoke and chanting their mantra.

She addressed the group: "…Gentlemen, this most be the ultimate homoerotic encounter, but I am sorry to inform you that "The Devine" is a She not a Him. We have been looking for you all in a couple of hours it will be sunrise and you have not rested a bit. You need to practice your Zen Archery and perfect your workings as a team…" *Abuela was* enjoying herself immensely.

The four men were not amused. They stood up and assumed lotus positions. Mr. Manuel spoke first: "…This is a Zen exercise, we grow closer spiritually and in space considerations, building confidence and camaraderie among men, making it possible to trust each other with each other lives. Is an old ritual of holy warriors getting ready for the final cosmic battle…"?

Abuela interjected: "…The more you talk, the more I am convinced this is a homoerotic exercise…" She was grinning showing all her teeth.

"…Be as it may…" Said Pereira, "…We are getting ready for battle, do we have any news on Mr. Lopez's group…?"

"…Not a peep…" Perla said. "…They have not tried to contact us at al, but in a sense is not surprising, given the nature of their mission…"

"…The nature of our mission transcends and makes other missions secondary. This is a fight not for a piece of land or riches or breading rights or water, ours is a quest of the Devine, I don't mean that cult classic, of course. Evil does exist. I have been working most of my life attempting to keep it at bay, to slow it down. Only the True Devine can defeat it. My dear friend the Llama can argue metaphysically that these labels are meaningless and that the Devine is in everyone of us that pre-destination and free will are also labels and that we need to let our Devine come out by peeling all the layers of our existential onion. But after all this has been said, he is *here with us* teaching us not only the way to the inner Self, but also Zen Archery…" said Ignacious.

"…I have never seen you so exited about anything since you conned the Spear of Destiny from our procession at the depository. Maybe this has been a homoerotic experience for you after all..." Said Pereira.

"…Nice speech…" Said the Llama. "…You are confusing Buddhism with Hinduism, albeit the fact that in this case I turn to agree with their basic premises…"

Abuela, somewhat exasperated added: "...You need to rest, Lopez and Company will be back and the rest of the group will need to practice for the next couple of days. But is imperative, meditation or no meditation that your aim gets better and that those Zen passes don't kill any of our people. I want to go home to the Light..." She said crying.

Chapter 12
[[Sampayo Compound, Añasco: 5:00 AM]]

In Añasco, the cleaning ladies arrived at the Sampayo's compound. They were there on a Sunday morning because that night there was a scheduled dinner party in which Mr. Sampayo was going to consolidate his power over the family and announce the "untimely death" of his beloved sisters, husband, and kids. It would have been his coronation. He now was paralyzed in his own courtyard surrounded by the bloody corpses of his "Praetorian Guard". He was at the mercy of the good will of these woman, who he had used and abuse through must of his adult life.

The first one to enter was Gabriela Santini. She was the supervisor. Rumors were that after the death of his mother at childbirth, Gabriela had become his father's mistress. His father was a private person and treated this woman with respect. When he was liberated from his abductors, Mrs. Gabriela had healed him back to health, at least his physical. His spiritual wounds started healing when he gave his father the "special Gatorade". His death was slow and painful and he had enjoyed every minute of it.

She entered the courtyard and started to cry without consolation. Sampayo remembered that one of his men was related to this woman. His last name was Sampi. She continued to cry in deep howls of sorrow.

"...Why him? Dear Lord, why him? My son, my only blood...!" She tore her shirt open in sign of desperation and pain. "...The remaining hope for this town was my son, the son of the Great Sampayo and her humble servant, Gabriela, now there is no hope, there is no future...."

She continued checking the bodies for some familiar resemblances, until she met Sampayo. Much to his surprise, in spite of her loss she did not show animosity towards him, on the contrary, she saw him with eyes of pity and love. She found Jose's note and took off the accu-needles as directed by his instructions.

Slowly he raised himself from the floor, inspecting in detail the scene of the crime. It was amazing; three men had destroyed his army of collaborators in about half an hour and had speared his life so a prophecy may be fulfilled.

Gabriella cleaned his face with a clean wet rag. He felt the love emanating from this woman that had all the reasons in the world to deeply hate him. It was too late for him. There was no hope for love. He had been in Hell and met Satan himself and had made the commitment to be his loyal servant and to help bring his son to Earth. There had to be a loophole, after all the Beelzebub himself had invented lawyers and was responsible for 90% of the infernal tax code. There had to be a way to escape his destiny and eternal damnation. He could not go back to Dominus, after his suicide attempt he no longer believed, he knew God had stopped believing in him.

"…Gabriella..." He finally said after a long silence: "…I am very sorry that your son, I guess, my half brother, had to die here this way..."

She started crying again, there was no consolation for this woman's pain.

"…I promise you that before the end of this week all the responsible parties will be dealt with, I promise this on my honor and on the bones of my father and on the body of your son…"

She added: "…You will also perish, because this bloodshed will continue until there is nothing left of your father's legacy. Hate is lack a black hole, even those who have been barely touched by it will be sucked up in it and will perish. Run away my boy, before you finished like my son…"

"…Is too late for me. I am already dead, Gabriella! There is no hope, no salvation for me. I am already in the center of the black hole. I just have to fulfill my destiny and hope for the best…"

"…I understand that you feel pre-destined to fall in the abyss, but you have the free will to ask the Lord's forgiveness, He will not ignore your prayers…"

"…My dear Gabriella, as far as I am concern, God abandoned me when he left me with the three sodomites from the Bravos Gang for three days. I don't understand how the "Supreme Being" did not lift a finger to save me from such torture and humiliation. I have been to Hell, believe me, and back…"

"…*Niño Sampayo!* You should not talk like that! You will condemn yourself and all around you. Your father worked endlessly to liberate you. Your perception was that of been left behind, however at the end he destroyed all your torturers and liberated you…!"

"…It is too late for my redemption, Gabriella, this baby its too late, I am already condemned. I don't bend anymore to the will of God, now I only have one master. Soon all the people of the Earth will recognize only one master, and I will be sitting, with his begotten son in his throne and we will rule this planet with an iron fist forever…"

"…You scare me, Mr. Sampayo, you have forged yourself a path and a future that I can not fallow. You fulfill your destiny with your cursed new owner, and that you may see the light before is really too late for you…"

"…The dice all rolling, soon we will read the numbers and there is no going back. If you can not work for me get out of here..."
She did.

Chapter 13
[[Somewhere in the Atlantic, Hercules Plane: 30,000 feet]]

Ana Sampayo was sleeping placidly on the plane when she had a dream. In her dream the plane was flying to Lisbon, rather than London. Her father had joined them in the passenger section of this cargo plane. He was playing with the boys while Ana was contemplating the whole picture with much serenity and peace of mind.

"…Daddy, I am so happy to see you again. It makes me very happy the kids will have a grandpa to share and play with. We both know you were never a saint, but you always tried to do what is right and honorable. Your son is possessed by Evil and has no honor…"

He looked at her with great love: "…Listen to me, dear. You don't have too much time. You are going to be traded. The DEA wants information about terrorism and drug routes. You and your kids are going to be sold to the Russian Mafia as sex slaves and your husband is too far away to protect you from them. You are on your own. You have to use everything you learned from me, and your husband to survive. You can only trust the Church, my good friend, Theodoro Nascimento, and the Israelis who owe me a bunch of favors dating back to the war in 1967…"

"…How do I get rid of the whore, take my kids to safety and make myself disappear…?"
"…Dear you are going to have to improvise. The world belongs to those who have learned to take every opportunity that their environment provides. The world belongs to those that can make hearts out of guts (*"hacer de tripas corazones"*)…"'

He kissed her in her forehead and she waked up. She did not see her captor in her chair. First she taught she had gone to the bathroom. Fallowing the scent of Charlie that the captain had she fallowed her to cockpit. On the way there she noticed on the walls parachutes and grabbed three.

Approaching the cockpit she heard the captain's voice:
"…It is a simple plan, boys. We sell her and the boys to the Ruskies, we get the intelligence and you boys get three days of R&R with me at the Hotel Eduardo VII in Lisbon where I will fulfill your wildest fantasies. And you know that what happens in Lisbon, stays in Lisbon…"

"…Don't take me wrong captain, as much as the offer is tempting, and it is tempting, I can not have in my conscience those two boys, I have two of my own. You will have to take responsibility for this one, you will fly solo on this one…"

The door was open slightly so that Ana could see part of the controls and both pilots. To her horror the Captain took out her gun and shot the pilot dead, point blank on the heart. Ana got a crank from the tool closet and bolted the door, which at this point became locked, from the outside.

The co-pilot realized his situation was precarious. A power mad woman had killed his best friend and lover. Killed, for his principles, in cold blood. His wife and kids would be so proud on how he stood on principle even while facing death. Too bad they will never know. The lights that gave the status of the cabin showed the door was closed shot. The smell of acetylene burning suggested the responsible party was welding the door shot.

He could not contain a smirk .He opened the parachute door and waited. To close the door they would have to close it in the parachute area. He hoped that whoever was out there would neutralize the plane and force a crash landing. He had very little to live for now that his soul mate was dead. What a senseless death.

"…Why are you smiling, I thought you two were inseparable…?"

"…I am smiling because you and I are as dead as this man…"

"…What do you mean, you dumb ass faggot? I can fly this plane so don't tempt me. Your life or death has no consequence to me, so behave…"

"…My life or death, has no consequence for me neither, but you should know that we are trapped in this cockpit and there is no way out, except death…"

She tried to kick open the door, but to no avail. There was no way out.

Outside Ana was looking for the fuse box to short out the locks and open several doors, including the one for large parachuted Hummer they had on board. At the distance she could here the cursing, kicks and shots coming from the cabin. She walked up the children put the in the Hummer and prayed. She was able to short open the bomb door for the car. Before leaving she shorted out the air conditioning and the motors. The airplane was, essentially gliding towards the coast of Portugal. Slowly just relying on its momentum, the plane reached the coast. She pressed the release for the Hummer and down they went, parachute opening automatically after going down 600 feet.

In the cabin the captain was considering her options. She has pistol whipped the co-pilot and realized she was gliding not crash landing. There was still hope. She had forty-five and some ammo. She could break the glass in the windshield and escape. She smiled, as she will save the last two bullets for the co-pilot and the bitch. She will still sell the kids to the Russians. She did not care if they used them as sex slaves or if they eat them alive. It was not her concern.

The Hummer seemed to float in mid air. It looked like a sub-realistic jellyfish, with no worries. She made an inventory. There were several M-16, ammunition, flairs and a heat gun. She was not much of a shooter. She hoped that she had an AK-47. That weapon is designed for people with little training or aim. A burst of fire and you get some bodies! She could not see where they were landing.

Ana could see the plane at a distance. To her horror the plane was not crashing, but floating, gliding down rather slowly. In the cockpit the co-pilot waked up. The captain was occupied in her thoughts. He pulled the pin of the grenade that hanged from his uniform.

Then he swallowed the pin. She heard the noise and reacted by pointing the gun at him, but not seen any treat she did not fire. He smiled a cordial smile.
Perhaps too cordial for her taste, she taught.

"…Something is wrong here, but I can not pinpoint exactly what…"she said in laud voice. Then it came to her seconds before the explosion. The grenade, which was hanging from the uniform, was no longer there. She looked desperately around for the grenade. He was not very cooperative with her quest to find the grenade. Finally she gave up and pointed her gun at the temple of the man:
"…Where is the grenade? Why are you risking your career and your life to save the honor of these people, that don't know the definition of honor…?"
"…And you, of course are the most honorable of all us! Bullshit! If someone should be sold to the Russians as a sex slave would be you! (He continued to raise his voice) You are a whore without honor! Only a whore trade innocent for money, terrorism or no terrorism…!"
"…Beautiful, empty words that have no real meaning…!" She retorted.
"…I am sitting on the grenade, you shoot me you die. If you

keep me alive you may crash land. You will not survive. Even if the landing does not kill you, there is no way to exit this cabin, windshield is made of bulletproof glass…"

"…There is always a escape to every situation, there should be a escape…"

"…There is no escape, this is a leased civilian cargo plain, after 911 all this planes were upgraded and there is no way out except the door, which in our case is welded shot…"

"…Why are you destroying your future…?"

"…You killed my future in cold blood. We had for years "an arrangement" with his wife. Beside all my male and female relatives sexually abused me since the age of three and I swore on my brother's grave that I would never be an accomplice to anybody's misery. There you are…!" He stood up the grenade rolled from the chair and he disarmed the captain. He smiled for the last time.

At a distance Ms. Sampayo saw the plane burst in flames in the cockpit.

This was fallowed by a series of explosions that caused the plane to crash. There was no way anybody could have survived, not even that daughter of a Jackal. After a couple of minutes more she felt the car doing touchdown. There was water splash. They have landed in the ocean she braced for the worst. However they had landed in a riverbed.

She found the keys in the ignition. The car turned on. All the lights were on. To her horror she was going into the ocean. She skidded around and went back away from the ocean, up the Riviera and up the bank until she was out in the fields. There was wheat, and barely and miles of vines. She lowered the window to take in the aroma of the fields.

"... Boys, do you realize that the smell of freshly rained earth actually come from a Bacteria, which make the aromatic phenol that smells like that..."

They looked definitively bored. Without thinking it twice, like this have been rehearsed in her mind for many years, she went off-road, making patterns while going in circles that strongly resembled crop circles. She had destroyed some wheat, but the farmers would get postcards and royalties out of this adventure.

The kids applauded, this night has been the greatest adventure of their lives. She mocked a reverence, kiss the air an accepted an imaginary rose from the imaginary audience.

Now if she could only find the road to Lisbon they would be on great shape. "Her New Hummer" was equipped with a GPS computer. One of the kids entered Lisbon and the pathway appeared in the screen.

"... Mamma is idiot proof, even Dad or Grandpa could find the city this way...!" Said her oldest.

"...Or maybe not...!" Added the youngest and Anna in unison. After that all went silly and laughed in unison, remembering the two men that had made the practice of getting lost an art form, especially if they were together.

They continued driving towards Lisbon, or virtual Lisbon. They drove for two hours due south until the reached the viaduct that would normally take them back. They drove toward the greatest accumulation of light. Ana had told her boys about the beauty of the city, about the cobblestone roads and about the beautiful tiles, which serve to give directions to pilgrims (Ah! An old GPS system decried the youngest boy). They kept driving towards the light

Much to her dismay, there was a massive fire in the middle of the viaduct. A major accident was in the middle of the road, carnage of many cars, hundred of people dead. There was blood, limbs and guts everywhere.

She drove towards the nearest policeman, a young officer born in Angola half African, half Portuguese. He was raised in the slums of Lisbon.

He had worked his way in the ranks of the military .He looked at her car with suspicion. She asked in perfect Portuguese: "…What happened, what seems to be the problem…?" He answered with a familiarity tone, with one single phrase: 'Al Qauida'. His heart had been bewitched ! He was a hopeless romantic. This woman was not a terrorist, she was a bombshell! She was an exotic American beauty. She was ripe but still promising. He was not just her admirer, from now te let her pass, even though she was driving an American Military Car, without a uniform:

He made a mental note about her plate: "USA-GI69".

Ana in the car was very grateful for having a Brazilian nanny after the death of her mother, after the birth of her infernal brother. It was an omen. She remembered the dream about her. She was convinced it was a real apparition. The ghost was real. As a child she had seen the ghost of the pirate Cofresí. The Sampayos were related, only God knew by how many degrees of separation to the Cofresí. Corsecan pirates, cutthroats,highway robbers. Her father had kept the family's traditional values!

"…Luis, could you please check the data computer for a man called Theodoro Nascimento…?" His son jumped into it. Her oldest son was quite a computer aficionado. He had hacked the CIA, FBI and MOSSAD systems by the time he was nine.

"…Mom who is this man…?" Angel, her other son inquired.
"…Friend of Grandpa, old business associate...I think…"

"...Mom, this man has a longer rap sheath than grandpa and dad together, if that is possible. He made his first millions selling weapons to the Biafrans during the Nigerian civil war. In association with the pilot and Engineer by the name of Mark Borg..."

"...The Mark Borg...!" Angel added. "...Grandpa talked about him all the time. Mr. Borg was an Swedish aeronautical engineer with a very Nigerian wife and dreams of building a factory of ultra-light planes to save the African Savannah, by preventing the construction of superhighways and stressing air travel and fuel savings..."

"...When the civil war erupted the good Mr. Borg, bought ten Spitfires planes and made it possible for them to shoot short distance rockets, he place them pointing downwards, rather than forwards, making it possible to improve accuracy and deadliness..." Angel added, imitating grandpa's old speech.

"...In one single night, they raided the Nigerian high command in Lagos, killing the five most important generals. Precipitating a backlash and ruthlessness from the Nigerian military the Biafrans were starved into submission. The Nigerian government executed Borg by hanging, with his Biafran wife and three children the youngest of which was only six. Of course they burned their bodies along with the surviving Spitfires. They were buried in a secret location thereafter know only to the President of the country...." Ana completed the train of thought.

"...What a great storyteller, I mean grandpa...!" Said Angel
"...Going back to Mr. Nascimento, Luis, do you have an address...?"
"...Yes, we do, is in the warehouse district, Independence Street #340..."
"...This may be dangerous, boys, so keep your eyes open and your mouth closed..."

"...Roger, momma, 'Eyes opened mouth closed'..." Luis added.

"...When we get there we do the direct approach. We go completely un-armed, I speak without a peep from you. We introduced ourselves as Papa's heirs and ask for help. Apparently the Nascimento owes grandpa quite a lot, the code of honor would force him to honor his commitment, even to an enemy..."

They drove to the address. As they got out of the car they noticed the stillness and silence was worst than expected. A silent warehouse is a very ominous sign. Hesitantly they entered through the main gate, which had a poor excuse for a lamp, like a concentration camp lamp. There acrid smell of blood filled the place. There was no powder smell, no shots have been fired, the place felt like death.

Out of nowhere came this man. He was short and bold, and thin. His eyeglasses resembled coke bottle bottoms "bottle ass" He had a transparent plastic apron under which he was dressed in business casual. Fresh blood dripped on his apron to the floor and to his shoes, his hands were gloved with disposable globes, also bloody.

He was startled when he saw the three in the middle of the entrance.

"...'Obbligato'! You scare the living daylights out of me. What can I do for you...?

Have I seen you before? Do I owe you a swine...?"

"...I am Ana Sampayo. I am looking for Señor Nascimento. These are my children Angel and Luis..."

"...I have been expecting you for the last six months. Your father's ghost appeared to me in a dream explaining you would be here this week and that you will need some serious help .Where is your truck? The Empire will start looking for it soon..."

"...He mentioned I would be coming in six month with a truck? That is remarkable. I have no money to pay for any of this..."

"...He also told me that you have the number for Swiss Bank account inked in the base of your breast. You will need to get back to the island a considerable amount of money. I will help you for free...actually your father promised to tell me the location of the Borg ashes in exchange for giving you full cooperation, which I will provide to you on my honor..."

"...'Multo obligato'; why are you so bloody? I don't want to be a witness to anything inappropriate..."

"...You will not, we are killing pigs for the holidays of the Saint Patronof Portugal. They are shipped to Fatima cooked and ready to eat. We are doing 500 here. Is big business..."

"...Did you herd about the Al Qauida attack? We passed the scene, it was horrible...!"

"...The pigs that perpetrated the deed have been taken care of persuasively and effectively..." He said, winking to Ana. We refused to sell the weapons, because we recognized them from our data file as Al Qauida. Two nights ago they broke into one of our warehouses and stole explosives. Six guards were killed, some of them were with us since the days of Borg. It was a terrible blow to us. We notified our contacts in the national police and Interpol. Ten of our best men were on the case and discovered them on their way to Lisbon, the National police and army was notified. They were intercepted in the viaduct. Their commander ordered detonation of the three vans they were going to park at the National Plaza where U-2 was giving a benefit concert (I guess we can not get rid of Bono one way or another).The leader van had no explosives, and very little weaponry so he was easily captured..."

"...Where is he now? How many people were expected to be at

the concert? How many were killed in the viaduct…?"

"…Ah, Ana…! Just like your father, you are into numbers. Well, that was the only way Sampayo could evaluate situations. Expected at the concert, 65K, give or take a few. In the viaduct one hundred soldiers and policemen, half of our men, close to 2000 civilians so far and the hospitals in Lisbon are full of the injured…" He looked at his bloody hand in a dramatic gesture, clapping ever so lightly, with minimal splashes of blood. He looked like a sculpture artist. Ana had goose bumps in her back. This man was very dangerous, not to be trusted, but since her father's ghost had recommended him highly, she will fallow along, but she will leave for the island ASAP..."

"…Mr. El Hazan is hanging out (literally), most talkative, with a little incentive he sang like a bird. As we speak the national army is arresting everybody in every cell in Portugal and Spain. Its amazing how much real information those USB ports can handle, two Gigabytes is two Gigabytes…!"
"…You mean that Ben Laden's war of "reconquista" is over. Spain will never be Moorish again…!"
"…Nor would Portugal! He added with pride. "…We found close to 8,000 names in the list. The government will be busy for the rest of the year. All the borders have been close and the syndicate has joined the army and police in the dragnet, on both sides of the border…"
"…What an attack of good luck! It's amazing…!" Angel said, looking at Mr. Nascimento with true fear.
"…And you know the best…?" He asked rhetorically. "…The best of it is we know where Mr. Ben Laden is right now. The reward for his capture is $75 million. We can do it and after that we retire. I will rescue the remains of the Borgs from obscurity, and will give the a true Viking burial, and I will move to some Island in the pacific to wait for my death, surrounded by the best wines from my personal

vineyard, food from my personal chef and scantily clad oriental women..."

"...I am sorry to interrupt your fantasy, but remember there are children around here..."

"...I know dear, I know...!"

"...Do you think is prudent to risk you and your loved one lives, would it not better give the information to the agents of the Empire...? They will still give you the reward and you would not risk your lives in the mountains of Pakistan..."

"...He is not in Pakistan, he is in Barcelona...!"

"...Again, why don't you leave this misadventure for the professionals in the field..."

"...We are quite professional. I will personally capture him in Barcelona. In the meantime you and the boys will be my guest. Let me clean up the mess and we will drive your vehicle to my house where you will meet my family. This will be my last adventure prior to retirement. For Motherland and glory...!"

Chapter 14
[[Island Capital,Airport Hangar,Isla Grande Airport: Noon]]

In the capital, Jose was in the warehouse, guarding Zola's son. The plan had gone like planned. Out of a crew of 60 only the captain and the guard had "tragically perished" in the" tragic accident". The government of Israel had formally apologized to both the government of Iran and the local Island government. Zola's son was relieved not to be under the custody of the Iranians, who treated him well but that would not have hesitated to execute me under Al Qauida orders.

Zola father was on his way to pick up the son in exchange of some information that the Israelis wanted. There was still the problem of him coming here with his Al Qauida posse. The question was how to neutralize them without jeopardizing the Israeli plan or their lives. It was noon and Jose was starving. The three horse riders of the apocalypse were napping with their rifles. Only two well-armed and trained guards were left at the warehouse.

He will have to stay put for now.
One of the guards called Jose:
"…You know what, your plan was brilliant. A lot of unnecessary death was avoided. And you reminded us of our own history of abuse. There is no justification for what we were about to do…"
"…I am glad that you feel that way. There is still hope for your people when you stride the keep the moral high ground no matter how hard the other people hit you against the ropes…"
"…We can learn some from the gentiles, your people have provided shelter to all the Iranian sailors in spite the fact they belong to another, and very intransigent religion and that they do not speak the language. You Islander have a lot to teach us…."
"…Do you have anything to eat around here? I am starving…!"
"…Stereotypically, we have salmon, bagels with cream cheese

and lox..."

"...I would kill for beans and rice with two over-easy eggs..." José said.

"...Not on the menu, sorry...! Our food van is outside. You are welcome to anything there but push the fridge door tight, as it will not close properly unless you make it close properly by making everything fall in its place...."

"...Is that not the case with everything in life? There is no closure until everything is in its place. The tree is not truly appreciated until is seen in the perspective of the forest. Nothing in nature works well until al its pieces fall in their place, and then the effect of the total is more powerful and mysterious than its pieces. This rule applies to al natural phenomena from the fusion on the surface of the sun to the female climax on the surface of your bed..." said Jose with a wink, as both guards smiled in appreciation of the jest and in admiration to the five foot six inches 'giant among men'.

"...The "Butcher of Mindanao...?" The first guard asked.

"...The Butcher of Mindanao...!" Said the second, laughing at the absurdity of the whole concept.

Jose walked towards the food van, which was more like a RV with a kitchenette, sleeping quarters and several refrigerators plus a microwave. The floor was decorated in early American linoleum, the one imitating bamboo. It was quite tacky. You will not think anything in particular about the place except for two things. The kitchen table, that fitted four conformably, was place against a wall with a poster of a life size Jewish mother, in a dress circa 1945 , with Jerusalem in the background and an inscription that read: 'If you not pick up after your mess I will kill myself'. The other unusual thing about the RV, were posters of three former Miss Israel in string bikinis located at the entrance of each of the sleeping quarters.

He smiled at the human condition. How these beauties will eventually become these mothers!

Then he smelled her. Like a blast from the past. Charlie perfume emanated from the direction of the bathroom. It was funny, after all these years a smell like that could paralyze the resolve, albeit for a couple seconds, of a warrior like him. But a couple of seconds of distraction is all you need to loose a battle, even a war. He came out of his meditations when he heard the toilet flush. He exclaimed:

"…Mercy…!", in laud voice , "…God why have you forsaken me…?"

Out came this tropical beauty. She was about five foot eight inches. Her skin was darkened residual sugar cane syrup. Her features, were more oriental than Hispanic in nature. She had hazel-blue eyes. Her must obvious and powerful weapons were those incredible long muscular legs that were barely covered by a miniskirt, legs made to kill and for love.

"…Jose Lopez, the butcher of Mindanao…! In person and Technicolor…!"

"…Martha Molini-Mayol, the killer from the Bronx…!" He retorted.

"…I don't know weather to kill you or the make love to you on this table. It has been a while. I may have forgotten how to love a man…"

"…I sincerely doubt that! Unless you have been turning gay on us! And from my past experience I sincerely doubt it... God! What do you do to keep in such great shape…?"

"…I spent my days taking numbers and kicking but…!" said she with a malicious smile.

"…Are you the chief of "the macheteros" these days…?"

"…Yes, and thank you very much for the tip, I was flattered that you remember my number and sorry that you are still working with your sexual issues…" She said almost giggling.

"…That was the only password I can remember from my days with you…"

"…Sure! Anyways, thanks for the warning. Ever since your uncle died we have been waiting to avenge him. As a matter of fact we have planned a big surprise for today. We have planted a bomb at the concert hall where they have the" Concert For Peace" somebody is raising funds for the Peace School at the Catholic University to learn to negotiate with the Yanqui. What a joke! The only negotiation the FBI understand is" lead negotiation". Look at what happened at your uncle…"

"…It is very unfortunate what happened to my uncle, but killing innocent people in a Daddy Yanqui concert is not the solution to our problems, neither a proportional revenge…"

"…There are no innocent people. It's either your comrade or your enemy…"

"…Please spare me the Maoist/Marxist- Leninist rhetoric. Bombs, either falling from the ski or strapped to your chest, are tools of cowards. In addition most of the population actually sympathizes with your goals. Even the most rabid 'Petite Yanqui' found uncle's execution an abomination. It has been the unifying event in our history. You have a martyr, don't waste it, a martyr is a terrible thing to waste…"

"…What would be a proportional response, smart ass…?"

"…Are the FBI agents still in the island? Then hunt the ones responsible for uncle's death, and only the ones involved in uncle's death. Kill them one by one, without much publicity. I guarantee you that will put more fear in the heart of the culprits, than blood and guts in the concert hall. Armed resistance is recognized as morally correct, unarmed resistance is morally superior, but pragmatism dictates action, not inaction…"

"…Would you help us? With you Ninja knowledge it will make it possible.…"

"…I will help you under two conditions…"

"…And those are…?" She asked with a smile.

"…I have something very serious to attend to on Saturday. So any hunting has to be postponed for next week..."

"…That is reasonable…" She added: "…Do you need help…?"

"…I was counting on you. Second condition: No bomb in the concert hall…"

"…OK, we can detonate it at 3:00AM, when not even the janitors would be around…"

"…Third condition is that if we are still alive on Sunday, we get a hotel room at Rincon By The Sea and spent Sunday making love like rabbits…"

"… I thought you will never ask! I look forwards to "greasing the engines", it has been way too long since the last time…"

"…So, let's close this with a kiss…." They kissed passionately, for a long time.

Suddenly, the offer of the dining table sounded better. They were interrupted by one of the guards: " Mr. Lopez, our look out has send report. Zola is here, surrounded by 10-15 Al Qauida, they are armed to the teeth…"

"…Wake ups my friends we will need them. Which car is Mr. Zola in…?"

"…We are pretty sure is on the black Mercedes…"

"…Martha, do you have your bow and arrow…?"

"…Yes, I do. Also some C4…"

"…I am David, I want to be your sex slave…" Said the guard to Martha

"…Sorry that title belongs to Mr. Lopez, here…"

"…You can always dream…" He winked her with a smile.

"…Excuse me, can you get the weapons and you wake our friends…" David ran to the warehouse making such a racket that the snipers had to be awake.

He fallowed her to her car where she had, among other things bow and arrow, C4 and detonators. She, who was better trained in explosives than him prepared the projectile. They got on the roof of the RV and waited. Both cars approached at low speed.

Jose pulled back the string of the arrow with all his might and let it go. It penetrated the windshield and stuck there. The passengers attempted to escape but Martha had already push the trigger to the detonator and the car blew in pieces.

Eight men came out of the second car and started shooting at them, before Martha could reload, so they have to drop on the roof of the RV to avoid the bullets.
Suddenly the heard it, a shot like an explosion produce a deathly silence and a run for the car. But it was too late. A second of hesitation would cause their demise. One by one the snipers took the all.

Zola came out of his limousine, fallowed closely by the last Al Qauida operative, who had placed the gun to his head and was in the process of starting demands until Zola was able to disarm him and push him away. Three shots from the snipers to do their jobs, three shots to the head and he was out. The snipers dangled from the roof and met Martha and Jose.
"...Let me introduce me to Martha Molini-Mayol. She is my former wife and commander of the "macheteros"..."
"...With you there is never a dull moment around here. Eh...?" We did not even know that he was married, and to such a beauty...!" Said Moreno
"...As beautiful as a black widow..." Added Jose
"...And as deadly..." Added Garcia
"...Do you arrest her or get her phone number...?" Added Jerry who was the last to arrive, and was not aware of the previously transpired conversation.

"...Well Mr. Zola, my name is Frank Moreno, I am in charge for the time being, until Silverman and the boys are back. I was told to start negotiations with you..."

"…There would be no negotiations…" Said Zola pointing at his limo wit his hands in his abdomen…" "…Furthermore I demand my son back…!"

The two IDF soldiers made a trot towards the warehouse, distracting whoever was in the car to permit Jose to slip behind the trailer. He took the bow and armed the C4 The front door was open and he could see two men, one armed with a sniper gun, pointing at Zola's head the other with a grenade launcher.

José took a deep breath and penetrated the gunman's heart with the first arrow, fallowed by reloading and passing the arrow fro ear to ear through the base of the skull. As he collapse he triggered the grenade launcher. The grenade bounced a round until it finally blew, raising the limousine two feet above the ground.

"…Any more surprises, Mr. Zola…?" Frank asked.

"…No more surprises, except that I want to hire your team as chief of security…"

"…How if you join us for the weekend, in Rincon, train with us for a tournament we have on Friday…"

"…I have a little hotel were you can stay…" Zola said

"…We may take your offer, for now we have to pack up here, arrest Mrs. Lopez and get rid of the bodies..."

"…You can not arrest Ms. Molini. She needs to go defuse some C4 before a bunch of innocent people die…"

"…Well we need to get rid of the bodies…"

"…We will do that…" The two young guards said

"…We need to file a report..."

"…Almost finished Captain, Silverman lent me his computer program from MOSSAD, he let me burn a copy...'

"…I guess is up to Rincón..."

"…I will fly to Aguada in my jet, you are invited. Don't worry you killed all my Arab friends, I am a free man again…!"

"…OK boys and girls, let's pack, we are in our way to Aguadilla, since the airport is there…"

"…You are right, let me give you a copy of the information the Israelis wanted..." He took a USB port from his pocket and passed it to Frank. He tossed it to David, who smiled. They disbanded.

"…You have some interesting friends, Jose…" said Martha.

"…Just wait until you meet abuela, she broke the mold. Please be there tomorrow at noon, we need you to be there to practice…"

José looked at her get in the car. During their first year at the State University they had fallen in love. During the strike of 2000, they had become very political. They had seen the students brutalized by the police and several had died, albeit not for lack of medical care, but because the nature of their contusion.

They had decided then and there about joining the "Macheteros" because his uncle, who was a foundling member, had escaped the Federal Prison in Florida and gone underground. His uncle was very well know for his bank heists in the late 1980's. However he singled handled have placed the pipe bombs in the F14's at the Air National Guard depot at the capital to prevent these plains to be used against "Our Sandinista Brothers" during the Contra Wars. The rumors that permeated the capital were that the National Guard was going to be used to topple the Sandinistas.

His uncle volunteered to be the pipe bomber. He was bare 35 at that point, with very little military training. He placed the bombs in the motors with devastating results. All 20 of the F-14 had to be replaced. The Guard commander, made up his mind that this was a very well coordinated commando attack, with at least 5 men involved, maybe even more It took years to convince the Pentagon to replace the darn things.

After 5 missions, he had become the "master executioner" he had enough! He quitted, much to the surprise of everybody, especially Martha and his uncle. Martha proposed that he will kill him after their next intimate session. His uncle, a truly noble man refused to give that order, and advise Jose of the offer.

Jose went underground for a year, until she was one of the ten most wanted, at which point she escaped to New York where she became a model and the regional commander of the "Macheteros" or Army For The National Liberation. In spite the fact she was a cover model and was actively catcalling, she was never recognized. She even posed for Playboy, and her cover was never blown!

As Jose saw her drive away in a stolen sport car, he had very mixed feelings. He new she would not hesitate to kill him, especially if it involved the vendetta against the killer of his uncle. She hated police, and he was fully cooperating with them in spite all his moral issues.

He was very deep in his thought when Moreno approached him.
"…What a catch you have there, how come you are not with her…"
…Difference of opinions: she thought that I was a traitor to the cause and that I deserved execution and I thought she was nuts…"
"…You mean she literally wanted to kill you, the butcher of Midanao…?"
"…Yes, and she was going to do it during sex…"
"…Then you would have come and go at the same time…!"
"…Very funny…"
"…Pick up your stuff, Zola is not a patient mind, we need to go…"
"…We will be able to take a nap in the plane…"
"…That sounds good, God knows I am overdo again…"

A tear fell down Jose's cheeks. He was melancholic, after all these years he still loved hopelessly , but could not make himself kill such a remarkable and beautiful woman, even to preserve his own life.

"...Frank, let's go, we need to practice for the next couple of days...."The group entered the Navigators and left for the private strip in capital. It will take only the traffic to stop them. Real training started today

Chapter 15
[[Añasco Compound, Sampayo's House]]

"…It has not been a good week for Mr. Sampayo…" The Supreme leader of the New Babylonians said. He was referring to himself in third person, with supreme irony. "…My dear sister, who I deposed as the heir apparent to the West Coast Cartel, escaped her execution by minutes. Her bastard husband, whom I pay good money to get rid off, is at large, with millions of *my* dollars. The police, who had the audacity of liberating my sister, also had the audacity to advert an all way out civil war between the two main gang lords…." That would make him the supreme commandant of all the drug distribution industry in the island. He could have bought his way to the governor's office and before you know it, the kingdom of Satan would expand again all over the Americas, and subsequently the world. So has been His promise.

He had left the house for two purposes. De Mello, the Devil's consort on her nine month of pregnancy, had become insufferable and whiney and refused to let him anywhere close to her, never mention sex. He was looking forward to the birth of the Son of Satan and her ascension in the flesh to Hell, where she will be Lucifer's favorite. He also had a cession with his spiritual mentor in Moca.

He drove his Jaguar through the windy road that took him from his fortress in Anasco to the main West Road, number 2. The streets were in perennial construction because the governments over the years had play the bankruptcy gave with all the construction companies. Moneys from the Metropolis will come and between kickbacks and delays, the money will be wasted between lawyers and politicians and nothing tangible will be done, except close to tight elections in which the miracle of last minute construction will produce in six months what eight years could not accomplish. A devilish plot, produce by very "devout" Christians.

He drove into the road for Moca. *La hermana Alicia* was a frail 110-year nun. But she was not the usual nun, with the usual story. She had been a prostitute since age eleven. The bastard child of a prostitute from Zaragoza's Bordello in Ponce and the mayor of the city, at that point a man by the name of Francisco Sabater.

She became a legend when her virginity was sold to her own father for a record of 15,000 pesetas (about $20,000). She had learned from her mother the trait very well, and he had been well compensated for his investment.

Her father had never learned to love a woman and when he realized this may be his daughter he proceeded to give her a beating, "what she deserved" for causing his eternal damnation. He also got sure that he would be the last client by slashing both her face and her clitoris. Her mother got the old fool drunk, castrated and strangled him, for which she paid with her life at the hangman's noose. Her last words were: "…I would do it again, *el muy Maricón se lo merecia* (the faggot deserved it)…" Surprisingly, Alicia survived. She was ruined merchandise. No man would touch *la cortada (*the one with the cut).

Well, almost nobody. Alicia worked in the kitchen, did beds and cleaned sheaths. She had very little education, and with the loss of her mother, nobody in this world. She will never fill the 'rapture of womanhood'. Her father had made sure of that. She had conformed herself to a life of serfdom when he met Andres Chardon.

Mr. Chardon was a Corsican migrated to the Island via Canary Islands. He was a man with heightened sensibilities, an artist. His wife and children had died during one of the Corsican revolts. This one against France. The French, after been beaten, decide to slaughter everybody in his town.

He was spared because he was restoring the altar at the cathedral in the capital. When he learned about the fate of his family, he swore on his wife's grave that he would avenge their death.

The French were eventually victorious. The prepared a big celebration. They brought from Marseilles three hundred caskets of wine. The country had been subjugated and pacified, nobody will dare to mess with the "conquering heroes".

Being a painter gave Chardon more than a rudimentary knowledge of chemistry. Several of the colors required significant amounts of cyanide and arsenic. He carried enough to kill more than a battalion. Painstakingly, with the help of his brother, a monk assigned to the church of *Les Miracles,* they made a tunnel to connect to the warehouse were the wine was stored for the great celebration, adjacent to the church. By candlelight he placed enough of both poisons to kill on contact.

The French, in their usual arrogance, bloodthirsty manner had schedule public executions of the three leaders of the revolt. Luckily they refused any French wine and drank the local brew, in a last act of defiance prior to their execution. The commander of the garrison was so moved by the gesture of bravado, that as the hanged squirmed their last breaths, he proposed a toast to their bravado. Five thousand cups when up, five thousand gulps of wine, five thousand glasses broken, five thousand dead French (the words to a popular nursery song). That was the last time France sent soldiers to mess with the Corsicans, after that everything was done through Swiss diplomats.

After the little stunt, Chardon feared for his life. Eventually he migrated to the Island where he would have been a rich man, concentrating on restoring altars. However he had developed a passion for alcohol and loose women that could have been his demise.

His salvation came in the form of Alicia. He felt deeply in love with her. At first he found him repugnant. Specially the leg ulcer. However, she learned, by accident, that when she packed them with the green stuff that grows in oranges when they are spoiled, his ulcers would heal. He eventually bought her from virtual slavery and married her. By that point, gonorrhea had made him infertile so they never had a family. He thought her everything he knew: art, restoring. She learned organ and piano playing, and to read and write, in addition to theology. Specially the forbidden Gnostic Gospels. These were more metaphysic, resembling a mixture of Christianity, Hinduism and Buddhism. She was an avid pupil. When he died five years later, she was as excellent at all the arts as he ever was.

She continued his work for another 10 years. The First World War started, at that point, and she made a fortune selling *guano to* German imperial army.

However, an angel appeared to her in a dream, ordering her to join the Church. She bought a farm in Moca where she made a church in an old abandoned mine. That was church and monastery. With her money, she bought a charter in Rome and continued for the rest of her life to instruct her novices, many of them former prostitutes like herself, the path to Salvation, in the Gnostic tradition. Because she continued to support every Pope, monetary and spiritually, she was left alone. She published several very erudite books on the Gnostic Gospels, under a pseudonym. However the local bishops invited her regularly to discuss them, knowing wholeheartedly that she most be the author. She had met Sampayo at an early age, and after his fall from grace and visit to Hell, she realized that he was the one to fulfill the prophecies in the Gospel of Andrew.

Like John, Andrew had a prophetic book, which was never finished because he was skinned alive. His disciples, because of the unorthodox and scary nature of the revelations, never published the book. When they saw what the Church was doing to the other Gospels, and their followers, they opted to copy a limited number of copies and pass generation after generation, leaving copies in banks, castles walls and universities.

Chardon had found one in the wall of the cathedral when he made the tunnel to punish the French. He had brought it back to the island with him. They spend a year restoring it and she had mimeograph copies done and distributed among her disciples and several liberal and influential families that had supported her through the years.

The gospel of Andrew predicted the coming of the Son of Satan, who will be 'begotten', not created from the seeds of Lucifer brought from Hell by his servant the Son of Payo. In her wildest dreams she ever thought that this would be fulfilled in her own backyard. The prophecy also predicted that in order to eliminate the Son of Evil, three knights, one of which would be the disciple of Jesus' Brother, the two others disciples of Peter . They would corvine the spear of destiny, the blood of Christ and the tears of his Brother to defeat the Evil one. Interestingly the Gospel did not mention the anti-Christ or the great tribulation. She always thought the two events were independent, like a dress rehearsal to Armageddon. She was very exited. She had sent a copy of the restored Gospel to the both John Paul and Ratzinger.

She knew the German would send investigators. He actually sent two. Each was independent, to make the proceedings more "objective" and impartial. By now, they most are working together. The Brazilian, a hunk of a man had one of those Inquisitor letters that made her exited and fearful at the same time.

He had knowledge of the Gospel of Andrew, perhaps as extensive as hers. They both speculated about the meaning of the "Brother of Christ"

There were hints in the Gospel about Asian ancestry for this character. It mentions "tears from his Brother of the East" will help defeat the Son of the Devil. They all agreed that in order to fulfill the prophecy, Sampayo had to be left alive until the incarnation and birth of De Mello's child

It was twelve when he drove his car to the doors of the monastery. She opened the doors herself. She did not trust the novices with Mr. Sampayo. She could feel the aura of erotic energy and shear evil that emanated from him. This was completely unknown to her. Most of the pupil she had mentored had been substituted by total desperation and emptiness.

"…Holly mother, I came to confess…" He ventured.

"…Father Macario won't be here until Friday…"

"…Only a saint like you will understand my confession…"

"…I am not a saint; you are confusing my age and patience with sainthood…"

"…Holly mother, please hear me out, you will advise me, not confess me…"

"…Agreed then, speak your heart out…"

"…I am the biggest sinner mother, I deserve and I am sure I will obtain eternal damnation…"

"…No sin is unforgivable; our Lord's tender mercies are endless. You can refuse Satan and embrace Christ, is not too late…"

"…But the prophecies have to be fulfilled for the future to be bright…"

"…You still can give your back to the Devil and continue to do God's work…"

"…It is too late for me, the prophecies will be fulfilled! The holy text is clear, the Son of the Devil most be born, the fight for supremacy will start! It is my future; my preprogrammed way, I am the Son of Payo…"

"…Even the 'Son of Payo' has free will…"

"…When you must fulfill His will, you loose your will, just ask Judas…!"

"…Son, what was the first rule you learn when you came here for catechism, when you were *an" enfant terrible*"…?"

He remembered when he first saw Sister Alicia. In spite of her suffering, and her age she kept herself so beautiful for the Lord! The good woman cleaned her hair with a shampoo she made from the *azahar* (the orange blossom)   She was his first crush. Now she had nothing for admiration for the Saint. He smiled because he remembered the purity; he had at that time and the magic of her presence.

"…*Madre,* you domesticated me, I was a wild one, and made me human…"

"…I civilized you, God made you human, and God does not make mistakes, son…."

"…Is it too late for me, I was in the presence of the Devil and his army of demons, after that you are never the same…"

"…Who do you think brought you back…?"

"…Dr. Mendel-Worth. He died several days after of shear fatigue; he administered CPR for 30 minutes and brought me back…"

"…The good doctor was an assiduous character, he was also a priest. He anointed you, with Holy Water and exorcized you while doing CPR. Those demons you mentioned had surrounded your soul; they were getting totally incorporated into you, he had to command them out. The CPR lasted 20 minutes, the exorcism 3 more days. The good father was never the same. He was affected and only wanted to rest for all times. Some fellow priests claim he died of sadness after seen the emptiness of your soul…"

"…The only tenant in my soul is *Odium* (extreme hate). The only thing that keeps me animated is hate. Hate defines me and in the dictionary there is a foot note for hate that says "see

Sampayo"…"

"…So the good doctor's sacrifice was in vain, he saved you the external demons, but could not save you from your own…"

"…My internal demons have kept alive; I don't want to get rid of them…"

"…So go out and fulfill your destiny, condemn yourself to the fires of Hell…"

He left, never to come back.

As she heard the motor of his Jaguar speed up in the distance, Alicia's heart was full of sadness. She had lost for good her favorite prodigal son.

She had not felt so sad and empty since the death of her husband more than 80 years ago. What she would not have given for another kiss in the forehead, for another hug. Just to feel his skin against mine. If anybody was a saint, that was her husband. In spite of her best efforts he died as a consequence not of his diabetes, but of disseminated Kaposi's sarcoma. He suffered terrible pain; she could feel his pain, just by looking at his eyes, or kissing his tears. He never complained ounce.

As she placed the last lock on the door, she felt her name being called. At first she thought it was the wind, she realized that there was a force that had entered the convent. A force for Good. She could feel the wind carrying her name around , getting closer and closer until *IT* reached the kitchen where she had gone to prepare her tea for the mid -afternoon prayers. She stood erect waiting for the force to communicate.

"…ALICIA, do not fear me. I am here to cover you, as with a blanket, with Eternal Joy. We understand your sadness after you lost your favorite disciple. I am here to help you cope with the loss of your best pupil…"

She felt a might push, fallowed by a pain in the chest. She recognized it as the entry site of a knife. She kneeled in the floor in agony. The pain was as severe as the one she suffered at the hands of her father more than 90 years ago.

"…ALICIA, I am the Holly Ghost! Now you are intact again! Rejoice! Your body will bear fruit after all these years of prayer and intense meditation, you will be rewarded for your staunch service, my true daughter…"

Alicia who now felt all her female organs rejuvenating in the inside and outside, was completely flabbergasted: "…Lord why me and why now…?"

"…It was God's time! Don't you dare to question the Almighty…!"

"…I am a complete woman, again, am I dead? Is this heaven…?"

"…No, dear, you are not yet in heaven, but you are witnessing the power of God! You have been a faithful servant and your name will be glorified at the throne of Bema forever…!"

Her head was forced to the floor with great power but she did no hurt her forehead. She began to pray. A fire so intense that she felt she was going to pass out, invaded her pelvis. It was a fire that burned her flesh, but did not consume it. The pain intensified to the point it was shear agony, she had a generalized seizure, levitated 4 feet above the ground, to the great amazement of the other nuns who had come to see the source of the commotion. Then it happened: she was transfixed into pleasure while her face change into Christ's face and blood came from the feet and wrists. This was fallowed by the disappearance of all the changes and the persistance of her rejuvenation.

"…Alicia, nobody will ever doubt that the child you carry is Holly or that you are a Saint. You have levitated, rejuvenated, transfigured, and stigmatized. Your followers are your witnesses. He will be called Gabriel, and he will baptize in mass again, to prepare humanity for the coming of the Messiah, which will be in your lifetime.

Are you ready for this…?"

"…May your will be carried and may the Lord's kingdom be built on earth…"

"…AMEN…" The other nuns replied which was fallowed by a powerful illumination of the room, which brought great joy to all present. Then there was TOTAL PEACE.

CHAPTER 16
[[MOSSAD Headquarters, Tel Aviv]]

Eli had been at the command center for three days in a row. He was simply exhausted. Coordinating all these movements of people and material had been quite an adventure. His replacement has been "sick". That could mean anything: from dead to actually killing people in the field. He had never killed anybody personally, but had ordered the death of many.

Since Hammas had won the elections the bureau had been on high alert. Sharom had taken a hell of a time to have his stroke. And this was the "big one" The old Warrior was passing the baton, but there was nobody to pick it up. There was a leadership vacuum sucking the country down, bureaucrats and technocrats ran the government with very little imagination. There was nobody left with a good pair of *cojones,* and the Palestinians under Hammas had figured the government was powerless, the emperor had no cloths, the tiger had no teeth, and it was made of paper, toilet paper.

Across the room was the only remaining man in Israel with testicles, Uncle Middleman. He was tired of the Iranian Rhetoric. Iran with nukes was very bad news for Israel. The crazy new President had sworn to obliterate ISRAEL from the face of the earth. The only thing standing between total annihilation and prosperity were the ten hydrogen bombs Israel possessed. Middleman has his finger eternally in the trigger. Of course there was the Israeli Air Force, but that was **always part of the equation.**

Eli had a poster behind him of the valley of Armageddon. He could not imagine a sustainable confrontation. But again, the history of these sands was one of blood and gore. He read ounce that Canadians could extract oil from some of their sands. He was sure that he could extract blood. They have witnessed Violence beyond imagination; century after century. Given enough time and enough bullets the Arabs will eventually destroy every Jew and then celebrate in the streets of Jerusalem. The Nazis, in conjunction with the local Mufti, had plans to that effect. The whole Jewish population will be shipped for relocation to the death machines in Europe. Eventually dead ships would be built to accommodate the Zionists from the Americas and Asia, when the Reich dominated the world. All that will be left of these vermin would be their ashes in the Atlantic and Pacific oceans, with their carbon prints as the only memory of their presence in history.

The new Arab leadership was not far from their ancestors. Arafat would gladly drop the Zylon gas pellets to activate the gas chambers if he ever was in a position of power to do so. The bastard died before Israel could be subjugated. But Hammas was Fatah on steroids.

"…We had no friends, now is every man for himself and all against the Jew, even God…".At that point it was Garcia calling from Zola's airplane.
"…Hi Mr. Eli, I am e-mailing all the records Mr. Zola has about his former abductors. There are a halfway houses in Egypt, the occupied territories, Europe and Asia. There is also Hammas warehouses in Israel proper and also bomb producing factories. Looking forward to meet you some day. Over…'
"…Thank you very much, any intelligence you find in the future, send to me. Over and out…!"
Well, Israel had some friends, not very powerful, but after all information was power. He smiled, picked up his things as to go home. Middleman stopped him on the hallway:
"…Go get some resting, you are going to South Africa tomorrow to coordinate the attack on the nuclear infrastructure of Iran…"
"…So is a Go, commander…?"
"…Yes, next Sabbath, go and sleep, you will not sleep again un-

til this is over..."

"... I have heard some information provided by Mr. Zola and Mr. Garcia..."

"...The Island Police? Can you trust them? Can you trust Zola...?"

"...The Plutonium we have we owe in part to the Islanders. Mr. Silverman, which is a pain in the but, was highly impressed. He e-mailed me from South Africa. I think that their intentions toward us are noble..."

"...The road to Auswitch, is full of good and noble intentions..."

"...So far we should not complaint about this people, it has been real..."

"...How about Zola...?"

"...One fourth Jewish, the islanders liberated his son and destroyed his Arab "escort". He offered the policemen work as security officers for him. He is much obliged, and is cooperating with us..."

"...So far they have been, I must admit. But, why are they spending so much of their time helping us...?"

"...They like us, they are very friendly and they consider us (for a change) the "good guys". As a matter of fact the have a Messianic religious ritual this coming Sabbath, I was looking forward to go..."

"...The future of Israel will be in your hands, I want you, the most efficient operative in charge of the very delicate operation. I am counting on you..."

"...I'll rather listen to Matisyahu in the Island beaches sipping a "sex on the beach", but sine I have no discernable choice I accept the commission. Here is the list that Zola send us, happy hunting. There are about 360 addresses and about one thousand operatives. Again, Happy hunting...."

"...Go to sleep Eli, and give me the list, I will take care of this tonight. Sleep tight..."

Eli left. Middleman, who had serious political ambitions, reviewed the list. He meditated for a while, understood that Israel was more important than his petite political ambitions. He picked up the phone and speed dialed the prime minister. His boss picked up the phone:

"...Number 1, this is number 2..."

"...Hello Middleman, at what do I owe the honor at this time of the nigh, and with such obscured reference to The Prisoner..."

"...Moshe, I am not going to beat around the bush, I have intelligence and planning that will bring you up to 100% approval rating. In exchange I want to be Prime Minister when you step down..."

"...Shoot my old friend, this better be excellent to ask to be my heir..."

"...You know the Iranian Option...?"

"...Yes Said Moshe...But this will be a last resort... we don't want to loose favor with the USA congress, and we don't want to be at war with China, Egypt, Jordan and Arabia...!"

"...We have plutonium with their signature, Moshe, **with their signature**, my friend...!"

"...We can fake a nuclear accident! Bravo Middleman, Bravo! When is the operation scheduled for...?"

"...This Sabbath! Our operatives are in South Africa, we have 6 bombs, one for each of the sites and stealth bombers. We can destroy their nuclear infrastructure in one night! They could not accuse us because it will be with their own plutonium...."

"...Approved. Anything else before I go back to sleep...?"

Middleman hesitated, but then went on: "...Moshe we have enough information to destroy Hammas in one night..."

"...Now we are talking early retirement for me and you running in the next election. Approved. Anything else...?"

"...Your son in law is in the list, you want him captured or executed...?"

"...Execute him. If he is an operative he deserves death as a traitor, but that would destroy my daughter. Make it swift, and make it look like an accident....'

"…Sorry Moshe, truly I am…"
"…I know, my friend. Go out there and give them hell…"
"…It will be done…."

Middleman hanged the phone. He called the Operational Command. The chief of the section answered. After faxing the list, he smiled at the silence that came from the other side as David Mayer reviewed the list. Finally he asked the next question: "…Boss, when you want this done? It is 12:30 AM…"

"…Tonight, I want all the vermin in Israel destroyed. Outside of Israel by next Sabbath…"

"…It is doable, if we coordinate with the air force and the army, we do not have enough "exterminators " in OC to accomplish this in one night…"

"…Son, do what you need to do. But be swift about it. And bachelor number 42 is a friend of the prime minister, so make it look like an accident…."

"…Consider it done, commander! Anything else…?"

"…Yes son, if we can accomplish this we can push this bastards into the Mediterranean Sea and they would have no choice but to really negotiate, as they will face the might of God's Wrath. Please don't screw it…" He hanged.

David looked at the list. He could not believe their luck. He had arrested some of the people on the list, before. Now the boss and the Prime Minister wanted everybody in the list dead. They will be police, judge, jury and executioners. This made him feel uneasy. But Hammas has hammered that suicide bombing was a moral and legitimate form of defense and that they were justified, no matter how many woman and children had to be sacrificed in their altar of hate. It was not revenge, it was poetic justice.

He picked up the phone and called the IDF commander, the air force commander and the police commander. He had about 4 hrs before the attack and they were in a tight schedule. The ball was rolling, hopefully no rebound will hit the in the own balls. There were rumors that something big was on the pipeline from Hammas, ever since they won parliamentary elections.

David took pride in his work. He considered the prime minister's son-in-law a priority. He had to be eliminated first. His dozier did not mention any military or paramilitary service. In addition he was a converted Jew from Yemen. There was a large Jewish colony in Yemen and over all they were respected and left alone. There was no mention of this man before 1985 in any criminal database or in the MOSSAD database. He was a doctor. So he will use a bait. A sick Palestinian girl with seizures and while she is evaluated he will cut his car brakes. The good doctor would die as he lived, he will remain a hero, not just for his people, but also for the people of Israel. His father -in- law will continue guiding the nation during this difficult time, and hi loyalties will never be questioned. David was fluent in Arabic, Hebrew, English and Spanish.

As planed, he picked up the good doctor at his home. They had a Palestinian family that had been a plant for years. Their house was on the top of a hill. They entered the house with most respect, leaving the two cars outside. The doctor examined the girl, which actually suffered from seizures and was post-ictal. David excused himself and went outside to the latrine. It took half a minute to sabotage the car's brake.
He entered the house. The girl had another seizure. The doctor decided to take her to the hospital in his own car. David, who was passing as the uncle, convinced him to call the hospital in advance and to let him drive the girl to the hospital, with the mother and then he would catch up with them at the hospital.

By the time the good doctor reached the bottom of the hill, he had no brakes and plenty of momentum. He finished encrusted as part of the wall, close to the Arab gate. This was fallowed by an explosion and instantaneous death. He will be remembered as a hero. All around the city, explosions and gunshots echoed in the night. Operation God's Mighty Breath was in progress.

CHAPTER 17
Road to El Estoril, Lisbon: Portugal

Nascimento's driving was tenebrous at best, the Vaelga-Sampayo family was petrified. There was a pregnant silence in that car. Ana would have scorned her husband violently if he practiced such driving. No one dared to criticize this dangerous man, after seen him playing with the blood of the man he had tortured for information. That had left quite an impression on all of them.

His driving was so erratic and haphazard that he was living marks of the Hummer through every corner of Lisbon proper, they were taking the scenic route on their way to El Estoril, where Mr. Nascimento had changed a casino into his living headquarters. They drove around the city. He assumed that they were being fallowed.

"…Years ago I took the M6 driving course. I passed it with honors. Best scores in 20 years. I am preventing people from fallowing us. Furthermore, I don't want to explain your presence or this car to anyone, I have enough problems as it is…"

"…Mr. Nascimento…?" The oldest boy asked: "…Can you stop somewhere, I am about to puke…"

"…We are almost there, ounce we get home will eat some food prepared by my wife, will make you feel better. Personally, I am starving. I hope you like sea food, and here it is so fresh and available all year long…"

"…What are your plans with Ben Laden…?"

"…Capture and provide execution services, as soon as possible, not before forcing him to squeal on all the members of the Al Qauida High Command. We will send these bastards back to Saudi Arabia where they belong. We will clean Europe of this filth, this cancer that threatens our western civilization. Al Qauida will be a foot note in the pages of history…"

"…Like Mussolini…?" asked the youngest son.
"…No, more like the "Dream Team", or the "A team", or "Mr. "T", perhaps…"

After much erratic driving; they finally reached Mr. Nascimento's compound. Four armed guards greeted them after apparently materializing from thin air.
"…Dominguez, I want this car painted black with enough gas to get to Granada, get pictures of everybody as we need Passports tonight…"
"…Consider it done, Boss…"

They entered the formal entrance to the casino. There were tile frescos on the wall and on the ceiling. They imitated life in ancient Rome.
"…Are these imitations of Roman frescos…?"
"…Pompeian, they belonged to a famous bordello in Pompeii . The owner, whose partner had died in some vendetta, had a dream in which his partner told him to abandon the city because a cataclysm of epic proportions would happen. The man took it seriously, sold the business and took the beautiful tiles with him. In Rome he was rich but not happy, he missed one of his girls, the only one he loved. Even though he knew the exact day of the cataclysm, he decided to venture property, life itself to rescue his love. He bet everything for his woman. Thanks to his efforts all the girls in the bordello survived, however he had a massive heart attack and died…"

"…How romantic…!" exclaimed Ana. You know your father would have rescue me too…"
"…Yes mother, but he always needs a little help from everyone…."
"…But he trays! He is dependable, a warrior. You should be proud of him, not make fun of him. I hope you grow to be half the man your father ever was…"

"...I am already half the man he is...!" japed her oldest son.

"...He is Papa Bear, he is not really fat...!" jested the youngest son.

Unknown to them, Nascimento's wife came to greet her husband under the chandelier , as she had done for the last 30 years. These people understood each other and lived their live to make each other happy.

Even in her sixties Helga Nascimento was a woman of outstanding beauty. She was tall, blond and quite pale. She did not look Portuguese and in spite of years in Portugal, could still not speak the language. This was an issue of choice. She did not particularly hated the Portuguese, but she did not had a love affair for them. Originally from Sweeden, she had moved to Holland, where she had been part of the "live sex acts" in the red zone. She was on drugs at that time and she owed a significant amount of money to the Amsterdam under lords. Her brother, an idealist at heart, spent more time and energy to liberate the people of Biafra, than his own sister. He single handled supplied them with fresh weapons and ammunition in addition to providing them with their air force. Of course he could not rescue his only sister. She made it to Lisbon, with the idea of hiding in the underworld, having a good time and when things cooled down in Amsterdam, she would return home.

But there is no way to escape the Amsterdam Mafia. They finally caught up with her and after beating and torturing her for a week, she was left with an overdose in the gutters of Lisbon to die. The universe conspired to put Nascimento on her path to destruction. Dominguez, his right hand, and Mr. Borg passed next 3 months healing her. Nascimento would be her nurse, physical therapist and drug rehab technician, all in one. Nascimento also bought her liberty from the Amsterdam Clan so that they would never bother her again. Over those months her brother gave her more love than in the first 28 years of her life. Eventually, however he had to leave for Biafra.

The day she was going back to Sweden to stay with her parents, they got news of the fall of Biafra. This was fallowed closely by the capture and execution of her brother, his wife and kids. That literally killed her parents.

She had nobody in the world, except Nascimento. He was fifteen years older than her, but she knew this was a good very man. That night she showed up to his bedroom, wearing nothing except her smile, and for the first time ever she made love to somebody she actually loved. After hours of passion, pleasure and extreme emotional pain, they lay on their sides, facing each other in the darkness, with only the sound of their respirations to distract them. He looked at her, with the eyes of a man in love, he said the words that would define their relationship for the rest of their lives: "…Welcome home, my love…" She was home, and wherever this man was, that was home for her.

"…Welcome home, my love…! Dinner is served, have your guests freshen up so we can have our dinner in their company…" She kissed him in the forehead and later in his lips. He smiled and fallowed her to the kitchen. Dominguez guided the others to the guest room.

"…Is that for real, Mr. Dominguez…?" asked the youngest son, faking disgust.
"…Very real, I fear. I don't want Done Nascimento or Donna Helga to suffer. The day one of them dies, the other will die of a broken heart…"
…That is the plot of a romantic tragedy, too stereotypical, cannot be real, no love can be that strong, or that intense…" said the oldest one.
"…It does not any real than that, I am afraid. I am his bodyguard, Perez is hers. I would take a bullet before it hit the boss, any

day of the week without thinking it twice…"

"…Do you know he is seriously considering going to Granada to hunt for Ben Laden? It seems to be his "retirement plan"…"

"…Actually is the whole household retirement plan. We have been practicing, you know! With seventy five million, we will all retire in Tahiti. I have been practicing my French you know. I will get myself a nice Tahitian girls, without too many tattoos and we will start producing little Dominguez clones…"

"…Some dreams can be nightmares…!" joked the oldest son.

"…Be as it may, he has made his mind, his wife supports him, and who am I to get in the way of his Tahitian dreams…'

"…The little I know about your boss, I like. My father chose him among all his acquaintances, to help us in our time of need…."

"…Who was your father…?"

"…Gregorio Sampayo…"

"…Gregorio Sampayo! How is he doing…?"

"…He is dead, but now he appears to me in dreams. My brother killed him…"

Dominguez laughed with all his heart and belly. "…Old son of a gun, he was able to con his way to heaven…"

"…Did you know grandpa…?" asked the boys in unison.

"…I almost married your grandmother, he beat me to it…"

"…Oh, you are that Dominguez…!" exclaimed Ana. Mother talked about you with great fondness. You save her life and my father's too…"

"…Yes that Dominguez! Here to serve you and God. I guess you could have been my daughter and these kids, my grandchildren. Is funny how the decision you made in a split second continue to reverberate in the forms of consequences for the rest of your life, each time you get into a fork on the road, the decision you make not only affect your future, but maybe the future of millions of people…"

What if the Apostles missed Jesus when he walked around the

fishing boats? What if Hitler had been accepted to the Berlin Polytechnic as an Architecture or Art student? What if Mussolini had become an opera singer? What if Lenin, or Stalin for that matter, had become college professors at Oxford? Mankind has an incredible capacity for evil or good, even apparently banal decision have consequences that are never intended.

 But I digress. Welcome to your home. We will try to make your presence here pleasant and short. God willing, you will be back on the Island before too long…"

 "…Mr. Dominguez, I have a very bad feeling about this whole patriotic vendetta that Nascimento is embarking into. Ben Ladin is battle tested, has defeated or kept at bay the two most efficient armies ever assembled. As compared to you, the have unlimited resources…"

 "…Dona Sampayo! That is the beauty of it all! A man has to live by faith and die by faith. Life by itself, on a vacuum has very little meaning. God gives life meaning. Both warriors always think that God is on their side. This is true in particular with religious wars, but applies to all wars. We all agree that there is only one God, so it's impossible by the nature of his Devine Justice that he can be on both sides. The logical consequence is, then, that he had to take a wining side; there can be no Neutral Deity that would be an Amoral Deity. The Devils is the Amoral Deity. God is not the Devil. The difference is that God took sides at the beginning of time, as he knows all the consequences, that is why he sometimes seem to choose the" wrong side" is because on the long run permitting the "bad guys" to win a battle is the path to the overall least destruction and suffering, even at the time is happening it seem that nothing could be worse than what is happening…!"

 "…So God has no free will? Is he a slave of the consequences…?" asked the oldest Vaelga-Sampayo.

 "…No. He is a Slave of His love to us. When He created us he committed Himself to die for us, because on the long run the consequence of not understanding in His Own Flesh our humanity would have condemn us to life without Salvation, life without meaning. Endless, pointless trek through the centuries ended for humanity when he experienced our nature and decided that we could not do it on our own, that nothing that we did would win us Salvation, it had to be His Present to us…'

"…Be at it may, my dear Dominguez, I fear for Mr. Nascimento. He is no match for Ben Laden…"

"…What is written is written in the mind of God. The boss feels strongly that this is what he has to do, and he will die if necessary. This is his destiny, and if he has to die, fulfilling it, be it…."

"… But that is stupid ! Let me give you an example. If God always picked up the consequence which produce the least suffering, how do explain the Holocaust…?' asked Ana in desperation.

Mr. Dominguez demeanor changed dramatically. For two seconds she could swear that a tear rolled down his cheek. He looked at her with a mixture of love and pity. He rolled his long sleeve shirt up, and there it was, for the rest of his life a set of numbers written not only in his skin but also in his soul forever.

"…I am very sorry, I had no idea, please forgive me…" said Ana, more ashamed than she ever been in her life.

"…My dear, you did not place this in my arm, you did not send me to Mengele's lab. You did not permit my family to be exterminated, including my twin brother, you did not injected phenol in my penis week after week with the justification that this would make me a Stud for the future pornographic industry that would poison further the minds of the German nation…" said Dominguez looking at the floor deeply embarrassed.

"…Still you were there. How can you justify your stand, when you lived that Hell…?'

"…When I was liberated I had no relatives alive. I was destined to die. I was in the section of those waiting to die because they were "beyond hope". I was terribly emaciated, and my edematous member was the size of a maraca…"

"…I felt life slowly abandoning me, I could not keep my eyes open. Then I saw him. He was riding a donkey. He would approach the dying children and chant the Jewish prayer for the death, give them a piece of chocolate to eat, moist their lips with water and kiss the on the forehead. By that time, most of them were dead. However they have died with an act of kindness from a stranger and a smile in their face. He repeated his protocol until he reached me. For the first time he smiled: "…Son, I finally found you. The Angel of the Lord appeared to me in my sleep and revealed what I thought was Hell to me. Later I realized it was an actual place on this planet the entrance had a sign in German that said: "Liberty through work"…"

Between the dying and the suffering the Angel pointed toward me. He told the old man: "…I will carry him back to Portugal, he will bear witness to what happened here. He will guide you and you will guide him. He will teach you the true nature of God…!"

The funny thing is that I saw the Angel, he carried me from Poland to Portugal. Nobody ever questioned the good Father Dominguez carrying a dying Jewish child that eventually recovered through several countries in Europe. Nobody question the good padre having a son. I was never molested, Dominguez adopted me. He thought me everything I know. He thought me philosophy, mathematics, physics, Greco-roman wrestling and poetry. In return, by pure accident I showed him the true nature of God. While braking a wall to make space for a library we found some ancient writings in Greek. Father Dominguez was a Greek scholar.

"…What I found was a translation of the Book of Andrew. All that we have discussed here about the nature of God was there revealed to us. We made copies and send one to the Vatican. Lucky for us it fell in hands of the future Pope who will open the church, more than ever. He incorporated much of the writing to his encyclicals. However, the apocalyptic second part was ignored on purpose. It was hard to understand the book of John. This was the Apocalypse on steroids..."

"...Although this explains the origin of your philosophy clearly, you have not made a clear case for the Holocaust as God's "less of two evils scenario". It does not fit the theory. What could be worse than what happened to your people...?"

"...I am a student of history. My mentor was a poor Portuguese priest that was full of the Holly Spirit. The answered to your question was revealed to me when I visited the National Archives in Washington. It was 1955, I had a scholarship to study the period, and I was 19 years old. I have studied Andrew's Gospel for ten years. I even had a bound copy in Portuguese with me. I felt asleep reading some documents. It was an inventory found in the central office for the SS in Berlin. There was one factory producing Zylon gas in Germany. They could produce enough per month to assassinate one million people. By the end of the war they have stockpiles to eliminate 200 million people. They had plans to eliminate at least the total population of Russia and maybe any "undesirables" They could have done it, if their hatred for the Jews was not so virulent. By concentrating on mobilizing, concentrating and eliminating them first, while trying to conduct a war in two fronts they wasted precious resources that they could have used to destroy the Soviet Union, then to turn to England.

By the end of the war, they had V3 rockets that could reach New York from England or North Africa. A bacteriological or nuclear attack would have destroyed and demoralize the Americans. After consolidating their power, they would have eliminated all the "enemies of the Reich', race by race, every country. Hundreds of millions, like cattle, would have perish, ashes in the oceans of the world, which would be a big "living space" for Germany. Eventually billions may have perished over decades. Our sacrifice saved humanity, is sad that so many people hate us now. If it was not for us, they would be selling tattooed lampshades in the internet, many colors to choose…"

   At this point Nascimento interrupted them. He escorted his guests, towards the dining room. The host was the only one talking. Everybody else was meditating upon the words of Mr. Dominguez. Eventually, with the help of a wonderful meal prepared by Helga and the three chefs, their tongues loosened.

   "…My dear Ana, I know you fear for my safety. Neither Helga nor I fear death. Dominguez has already being dead before, and thus, does not fear it either. I will get Ben Laden or die in the process. I am sure my old friend has explained to you the theology of the Gospel of Andrew. If we die, which is a possibility, I want you to go with your father to Nigeria and rescue the ashes of Borg and his family. We have made a monument to the people of Biafra in a park in Lisbon, please bury their ashes there. Tomorrow we go to the Swiss bank so you can get the monies needed to finance your return to the Island and for us to get Ben Laden. My budget is ten million in dollars, the rest of the sixty million is for you to keep. That is a nice nest egg, a good education for your kids…"

   "…Consider it done, Boss…." they all said laughing, as they retired for the rest of the evening. Tomorrow was going to be a long day.

CHAPTER 18
[[Aguadilla Airport, Monday: 3:00PM]]

The trip to Aguadilla was short. The Gulf Stream jet landed without difficulty in the old military airport turned civilian tourist hub. The homeland security office was there, mostly to remind the natives that their loyalty in the war on terror , not only was it assumed, but without any questions, enforceable.

Zola was a happy man. Former Foreign Legionary, he felt more comfortable among soldiers and mercenaries than among lawyers and accountants. There were no mercenaries, and thank goodness no lawyers, but all of them were soldiers, at heart.

As they landed Zola reflected to the fact that they were all free men and that his son was still alive. He was convinced that Al Qauida would have order their execution without thinking twice. But they were completely neutralized. That had seemed effortless. Four men had taken over the situation. Men like that were essential to have as friends and avoid as enemies.

They were in his Mercedes limo when he broke the ice: "…Gentlemen, first let me thank you for saving my life and that of my son. You will be amply rewarded. In addition I like to offer you to be my security detail. You can ask any price, as you know I am the richest man in Europe. I would be honored if you accept this offer…"

Garcia stood up, with faked formality, bowed to Mr. Zola and spoke:
"…I think that *speak for all of us when I say to you that the offer is quite tempting. However, we have a date with destiny on Saturday that we cannot postpone. I we are still alive Sunday morning, we will quit our jobs and Moreno and I will join you…"*

"...*What is so darn important that you will postpone a life of luxury and security. Surrounded* by gorgeous women and unprecedented wealth...?"

"...We have a date with the Whore of Babylon and her earthly husband, Mr. Angel Sampayo, the Pope of Babylonians..." interjected Jose.

"...You have to be pulling my leg! The time of the Whore of Babylon is upon us? How did I miss the signs? Such a shit-head! Where is this going to happen...? Ah, of course, in the "island at the end of the world"...!"

"...What are you talking about...? Jerry asked. "...Do you know something we don't know...?"

"....When I was in the Legion, we guarded one of the monasteries in the Sinai Dessert. I befriended the Abbot, an American with training in the Greek Orthodox religion and mysticism. He explained that years before he had found a document on the wall that separate the wine cellars from some cells in the basement. He translated it to English and realized that this was the long lost book of Andrew, possibly the most controversial of the Gnostic Gospels and the one that most clearly explained the divine nature of Jesus, the Trinity and the end of this world, the emergence of the Son of the Devil and the eventual reign of the incarnation of the Devil himself, the true and only Anti-Christ..."

"...Do you have a complete copy of the book we can read...?" said Jose.

"...Yes indeed, all the 20 chapters are in the process of publication, with references and comparisons to the "four official Gospels" and the Apocalypse when appropriate. Is ready for publication, but I can give you a hard copy. All is translated from the original Greek with the help of a famous Greek scholar at the University of Wisconsin…"

"…OK, Mr. Zola, I am all ears. We are supposed to fight the Son of the Devil and his "legions of acolytes" next Saturday. We need to know the rules of the game, so we have a chance to win, without getting ourselves killed…!" added Moreno.

"…I will put my fortune and maybe my life at your disposal. That may even the odds…" proclaimed Mr. Zola.

"…Odds are calculated to be about 1000 -2000 to one…" added Jose

"…Ok, let's concentrate on the text for now, later we can ponder about the odds…" said Maurice Zola. I will join a cause, especially at the side of the men who rescued me and alongside my father, but let's improve the odds as much as we can. Can we gentleman…?"

Mr. Zola smiled at his son with much pride. He wished his dead mother and his assassinated mentor could see him now, they would be filled with pride. He cleared his throat after downloading the text, and began:

"…Not all the sacred text survive, some pages are missing, some paragraphs have been inferred, this is the Greek translation, I don't have access to the Aramaic originals, that was hidden in a church in Corsica during the rebellion against the French, last century. Lucky for us, the passages referring to the battle for the destruction of the Son of the Devil and the future birth of the anti-Christ are, for the most part, intact…"

"…For the MOST PART…?" said Garcia. "… I hope we don't die because we are missing an important verb or conjugation somewhere …"

"…I don't think that would that make a difference, perhaps we can procure, for your peace of mind, the Vatican version. There are two Inquisitors visiting the Island. I am sure that they are in Rincon mustering the troops…" Said Maurice

"…Can we trust the Inquisitors…?" asked Jose

"…We truly have no choice, they are here, personally ordered by Ratzinger…" said Mr. Zola. "…We may even get the Pope here, as my spies have discovered , there is too much at stake, not to send their best two agents to cooperate with the locals. Let me proceed with the readings of the Gospel of Andrew…:

"… In those days, the Martyr Andrew was with the rest of the disciples in the house of Joseph of Arimathea, the former Pharisees, who lent us use his tomb for the Master. After the Resurrection, and ascension of our Lord we had a supper to discuss strategy of how to spread the Good News and how dangerous it would be. A great wind entered the house and much to our surprise the Angel of the Lord, Sylvac, landed among us. He took a deep breath and blew on us. Immediately all the disciples received the Holly Ghost: the capacity to face the future without fear. There was great joy and the brothers of Jesus spoke in all the languages of the world, Babel had been cancelled. The Angel Sylvac, took the humble servant and martyr aside and spoke to him in the greatest terms of endearment:
"…Andrew, tonight in your sleep I will put a vision of the future. I want you to write everything you see, no matter how mundane the detail, so that Holly Warriors of the future can defend themselves against the Son of Lucifer…."
"…And who are you, my Lord…?"
"…I am Sylvac, the Angel who the Holly Spirit has chosen to fulfill his wishes. His wish is that everyone finds the Divinity inside him or her. I am Christ's brother and I am in He, and Him within me.

I was cast from Heaven to Earth, even thought there was no question regarding my loyalties toward the Father or Christ my brother or my main support and love, the Holly Ghost. I humbly accepted my punishment and through many centuries I procured to get closer and closer to God..."

"...Lucifer, the wisest and most beautiful of all the angels, opted to challenge God and to plot against him. Since he cannot destroy God, he opted to make his Son suffer along with all humanity, after being cast from Paradise, never to be accepted back in the Kingdom. Me, I never left His side…"

"…When the living God needed me, I came back to infuse the Holly spirit back in the body of His most preferred Son. So lay still, listen and learn. The fate of humanity is in your hands…"

"…I went home but could not fall sleep, so much about the actual nature of God had already been revealed to me with the infusion of the Holly Spirit and the presence of His Angel. My head felt like it was going to explode. I will have to get willow bark in the morning. I decided to go for a stroll along the walls of the old city. As I approached the main cistern I realized I was entering a very lush garden. There were plants so green, they had to belong to an oasis. Two guards approached me. I felt that they might use me for their entertainment by humiliating worst or me. As I approached them I realized that they were not in Roman armor, although they had chest plates that could deflect all kind of projectiles: these were concealed under a habit. They carried an arched piece of wood and metal they use to propel small spears through great distances at greater speeds. They also carried spears in a sack that hanged from the back. Instead of their ranks visible in their chest the carried crosses with likeness of our Lord hanging in agony from the nefarious instruments of torture. They approached me and I settle between the two of them .The one that actually looked and sounded Roman spoke fist:

"…Listen and lay still, Andrew, remember our words to come: The Son of the Devil(i.e. Lucifer) will be born in the Island at The

End of the World from the Whore of Babylon. His mission would be to facilitate the escape of the Father from Hell and the coming of the Anti-Christ..."

"...The Son of the Devil can only be defeated by lacing with the blood of Christ and the tears of His Brother on the Spear of Destiny. Three warriors have to insert the spear in ITS heart. An unequal battle will ensue, and if you keep the faith and have an open your eyes and listen, you will be victorious...!"

"... Remember the Psalm: "BE CALM AND LISTEN" If you defeat the Son of the Devil, the coming of the hideous anti-Christ will be delayed and the birth of the prophet of the Lord will be possible, he will baptize the nations and prepare the righteous for the Rapture of the Lord...."

"...I waked up with a fever and I was on the presence of both Gabriel and Slavek. They cleaned my feet like the Lord had done on the night he was arrested. A Roman soldier approached me and proceeded to skin me and eat the skin of my feet. This was extremely painful..."

"...You will protect the prophet of the Lord! You will protect the prophet of the Lord...! The cannibalistic Roman repeated, like a bad mantra, while he continued eating my foot... "

"...Wasn't Andrew skinned alive...?" asked Jose. "...So this is truly a prophetic dream ad we should study it thoroughly..."

"...Yes my friend, any reference to numbers or order, have to be taken very seriously..." said Zola.

"...We need to check the other versions of the book. It happens that in Moca there is the world renowned Sister Alicia, the expert in Gnostic Gospel. She may have a more complete copy of the Gospel laying around the monastery. We should investigate that possibility. We also need to figure out who is the "prophet of the Lord" to see if we can protect him…" said Moreno, talking mostly to himself.

Zola smiled. He knew he was in good hands.

CHAPTER 19
[[The Green House, Rincón 6:00 PM]]

His entourage, known affectionately as the "three stooges", had left him at the care of his father at the Rincon Green House. The monks received them with great joy. The Llama made the other "children of the light"

"…Promise to come back to learn to do Zen Archery. The needed as many able hands as possible, as the task was colossal.

Jose was deep in a dream when his long dead Accu-ninja mentors appeared. They were in the Rincon Plaza, making sketches in the floor with chalk. Trying to phantom the logistics of the defense against the Son of the Devil and his prophet. While the floor was getting messed up and the three men were getting full of chalk powder, a child approached them with a big contagious smile:

"…Can I join you…?" asked the eager child. "…I have seen you labor restlessly, getting nowhere in a hurry. You do not need special coordination. What you need is not differential calculus (or integral either). You need is to develop the rhythm of the situation, to learn to dance with your partner. You need to do the Tango…!"

"…What is your name, dear…?" asked José

"…Carlitos. My last name is Gardel…"

"…Oh!, Like the singer…?"

"..Not like the singer, but the singer…"

Music came out of the town square sound system. La Comparsita blasted pretty loudly, in the gazebo a troupe of monks played the accordion, guitar, flute and drums keeping the 2X 4 rhythm, without missing a note.

"…But how do I adapt this to Zen Archery…?"

"…Do I have to explain everything? Simple…" answered one of his former masters.

"…Shut up and let the Tango master guide you. Listen to the music, incorporate the beat to your basic archery attack, the Zen part of it will fallow the two basic gyration variations in step 2 and 6..."

Gardel, now looking about seventeen, pick up a bow and arrow from the floor. He smiled at Jose and started as fallow:
"…You keep the arrows on the anterior left aspect of your body, pick up an arrow in(beat #1), at the same time your right foot moves backwards, the left to that side (beat #2), while attempting to insert the arrow in the bow string and moving the right foot ahead of the left (beat#3), while initiating , the pulling back of the string . Move the L foot forward while pulling further the string (beat #4). Join R foot with left as you aim (beat #5), move L foot forward and shoot (#6), move R foot to the right looking for the next target and trying to avoid the incoming arrows(#7)and L foot finishes side by side (beat 8) ready to start again. For the actual Zen Archery passes you do either on 2 or 6 the gyration and let the arrow fly in #7 movement the recipient will receive in #8 , variation in step two passes the arrow to the Left , variation in six to the right. Repeat as necessary and good luck…!"

By **this time he already was in his late thirties, the Gardel he remembered from all those movies from so long ago. "…Be sure you mention this dream to the Llama…' said Gardel before getting into a plane,** a propeller plane that will lead him to his death, again, parked in the middle of the plaza.

He walked up in a sweat. He went to the kitchen where he met the Llama, late meditating with his closest advisors. They smiled, he smiled back. With some hesitation, Jose shared his dream its entirety.

After a long, pregnant pause, the Llama added: "…Yes, Tango may actually be an useful short cut, given limited time available to the group members…"
"…The rhythm, the passion, the talent, what a concept! Have you mentioned this to anybody other than us…?' added abuela who

was in the meditation circle by this time.

"...No, I was afraid to be burned in the stake, or something like that. I am glad that you find it amusing. Of course I already took note of all the movements associated with the steps. On the other hand, finding a Buddhist monk that plays the accordion makes the whole point mute, don't you think...?"

"...Not quite, brother Sanchez IS ORIGINALLY from Argentina, and he is a musician by training, a dance instructor, who plays a very good accordion..."

"...Lets not forget Mr. Manuel, the Scottish toreador, he used to play the Conga in Edinburgh in his youth..." added Mr. Goya who entered the kitchen looking for a glass of soymilk.("You know, nothing better for the lactose intolerant") "...I can teach you to dance, including the Tango..."

"...Much to my regret, ladies and gentleman, I am a much better archer, than perhaps a Conga player. I do know how to Tango..." said Manuel who had moved to the Green House to coordinate the deliveries of weaponry, including ten thousand arrows and fifty eighty pounds competition bows. "...The local high school has a classical quartet and they do play a mean Piazzola..."

Emma entered the room. As usual, her voluptuous sensuality turned heads. Even in fleece and robes the woman was sexy. Even the three monks were inebriate by her presence. She walked towards Jose, stopping one inch short of his face.

"...Tell me that you took care of Mr. Zola, that he would no longer be an issue and that he got the death he deserved..."

"...Well, not exactly..."

"...Did he suffered the fate that he deserved...?"

"...Not exactly..."

"...I hope that he suffered a painful death...!"

"…Not exactly, Ms. Emma, if we survive Saturdays "get together", Mr. Garcia, Mr. Vaelga, Captain Moreno and me are all going to be working for him as personal body guards, he is joining us for training tomorrow, I personally think is an excuse so that he can get close to you, so that he can get some…"

"…Most likely..." said Father Ignacious, as he entered the room with Father Pereira.
"…Most definitively..." added Pereira with a great Brazilian smile, almost Pelé-like in nature.
"…God I am glad this kitchen is so big, we bring freshly baked French bread and cheap cheddar cheese. In addition we bought the cheapest Mortadella this side of the Atlantic, for the non-vegans among us added Pereira.

José accepted an impromptu sub. He thought: "…I guess this is all I am going to eat during the rest of this adventure, I am getting tired of eating bread and cheese, I hope the menu improves when we start working for Zola…" He added:
"…Gentlemen, as much as I would love to stay and harass Ms.Goldman, is three in the morning, today is Tuesday and tomorrow we have dress rehearsal all day and we need to become proficient in Tango dancing…"

Pereira and Ignacious, dropped everything they were doing. Ignacious assumed the female stance while Pereira assumed the female one. Manuel, the Llama a abuela hummed the harmony to Cambalache and the former enemies danced flawlessly. Goldman took out a very tired and reluctant Jose. She was a great dancer, and within thirty minutes she thought everything she knew to Jose. Before too long everybody was dancing at the harmony produced by the three impromptu musicians. Before too long everybody had learned to Tango. Abuela smiled, there was a possibility that they may actually pull this off.

José bowed to all the present. It was five Am Tuesday. He looked at his watch. Mr. Zola was due to arrive with the three friends at nine thirty. He needed some sleep.

Everybody bowed back and they all left the kitchen with Jose. All except Manuel and Ms Emma. They have been lover's ounce; the music was still in their heads. They slowly disrobed and made love on top of the kitchen table for about 30 minutes

"…Emma, why are you doing this, I thought you and Zola were an item…"

"…You were my first and only love. Zola was just another sexual assignment, I was his distraction. I will never forget you, I will always remember you. In my deathbed your name is the one I will mention in a whisper with my last breath, along with the other secret names of Yahweh. Our love was beautiful, it had to be of divine inspiration…"

And with that she picked all her clothing from the floor, and kissed him in the forehead. "…I will love you forever, think of me when you are lonely, think of me when you make love to your next wife, be careful that you don't start finding similarities between your daughter and the memories of me. Think of me with every great sorrow or great joy. I will be here (she pointed towards his head and towards his heart), forever…"

"…I am a widower, the Islamic bastards kill my wife and kids, stay with me and help me re-start my life. Please stay with me forever…"

"…I wish I could stay, however I am of Israel and Israel is of me. I am Israel's daughter and mother and goddess and whore. I will go to bed with whom the great state of Israel deems essential…"

He looked at her naked body and his heart was filled with nothing but love and compassion. He approached her lovingly and embraced her. He put his hand above her left breast and hers above his. For a period of time, they only felt each other's heartbeats. They realized that their heartbeats were running at the same beat, something neither of them had ever experienced.

He looked at her with his blue eyes into her beautiful green ones, then, he said: "…You are so used to your chains that you don't even realized you are a prisoner. All along the keys to your chains have been right here…" he said, pointing to hers and his heart. "…The secret is to learn to unlock those locks, love is the key to your freedom. Please do not go back to Zola…"

She cried for several minutes like she had never before. She felt like two tons have been lifted from her shoulder. She looked at him, grabbed his arm and guided the love of her life to her room. The door closed and silence reigned, two hearts as one, close to each other in perfect harmony.
In the middle of the silence in the kitchen abuela was cleaning out the last vestiges of their lovemaking from the table. She was a romantic at heart. Being a ghost she had the course of witnessing these kind of sessions ad lividum(no pun intended) . She never mentioned it to anybody, as not to scare people from lovemaking. This world was so sad, the only joy in life is love and inhibiting love was inhibiting life itself. She was remembering her own wedding night and how much she had loved her groom when she heard the music.

It was the melancholic sounds of the accordion, crying out for the rediscovered love between two old lovers. She looked up and so Mr. Gardel, in full dancing gear extending his hand for the dance. He looked about Abuela's age, the way he would have looked if his rendezvous with his destiny had not cut his life short. He was a very elegant and dashing gentleman, with his classic hat, small feather and leather rim. Fire in his eyes, passion, calculated in every movement.

His hair, was white as snow, he had charming smile and eyes.

    Suddenly, they were both eighteen again, all their body parts toned and ready. They joined their hands and danced the sensual steps, all variations, all fancy steps, a cadence of sensual energy whose energetic rhythms fueled its own passion, a perpetual sensuality machine, the Kama Sutra of ballroom dancing.
    They collapsed, exhausted, even at their tender age. They laughed with abandon and cried without hope.
    "…Madam, that was the closest to sex I had in eighty years …"
    "…My dear man that was the closest thing to sex I had ever had, even when I was alive and married…!"
    They looked at each other, lovingly and smiled merrily. Gardel bowed and disappeared, and her heart was full of joy, there was hope for her even if she had to stay as a ghost forever, at least he could take Tango lessons with Gardel himself…!"

CHAPTER 20
[[Lisbon: At the Bank Swiss, Tuesday Afternoon]]

Ana, as long as she could remember carried the key to the Swiss Bank account deposit box at Lisbon. It was a good luck token. Father carried one with him. She, as heir apparent had the 10-digit combination tattooed at the base of her breast, five numbers in each bosom, had to be seen in a mirror to use correctly...

The old bank manager, an old aristocrat, whose great-grandfather had fought Napoleon as a Swiss mercenary and was advisor to Wellington, thought he had seen everything until he ask Ana for her combination and she exposed her ample bosom to retrieve the combination. The old chap almost had a heart attack.

He had a light arrhythmia, however, when he saw the withdrawal of sixty million dollars.

This money was sin money, but who cared if it will help Nascimento capture Osama and her to liberate her family back home on the Island. It was a necessary evil. She will be sure her part will serve her family well, open a legitimate business and educate her children and keep her husband at her side, avoiding high risk jobs that almost had cause him to loose his life.

Interestingly enough, she also found about one hundred million dollar in Microsoft, AT&T and Sun Microsystems, original opening day prices, worth about one billion dollars present prices.

She did not trusted Nascimento, so he will settle her debt to him and without ever mentioning the stock. She could build an empire, legal and otherwise, with that money. She joined the kids in the Hummer. Nascimento and two armed guards, all in bulletproof vests were also there. She handed him the duffle bag with sixty six million and six hundred thousand dollars.

"...I see that you have been a woman of your word, Ms. Sampayo, I will be a man of mine. This Old Portuguese was a man with no honor. You have brought honor back to him. Actually, Osama, by bringing the war to Lisbon, brought the best in all of us. Now, according to the government, we are heroes of the motherland. They will be rich "heroes of the motherland". We could leave for Fiji tonight, if we so desire..."

"...What is stopping you, why put yourselves in jeopardy when three governments with billions of dollars in resources are on the hunt...?"

"...It is a matter of Honor, we guys are descendants of proud fisherman that fed this peninsula for millennia, learned to co-exist with the Atlantic. This great ocean is like a whore, you may enjoy the ride, you better be ready to pay the price, or you will finish with a stiletto knife in your heart, or worst..."

"...So what is your next move? Where do we go from here, my friend...?"

"...You get a refund, so you can get back to the Island. According to your father's ghost, we will both be involved in epic battles. One of us will not make it alive, the other will. He will help us both as long as is possible, as long as there is life in all us, he will not abandon either..."

"...But, you still have time to abort this mission, please do, I will give you all the money, as long as you send us back to the Island..."

"...I am afraid that fallowing your suggestions would be against your father's wishes, his specific instructions..."

"...Think about those as guidelines, my father liked to give liberty and flexibility to his workers..."

"...Be as it may, you will receive all the money that is due to you, and we both will go to our rendezvous with history..."

"...Ok, take me to the airport as we need to get back to the Island…"

"…First things first…" He handed her two backpacks, one with sixteen million dollars, the other with
 Brazilian passports. The money is in a certified check, plus one million dollars in cash, for bribing and surviving. Transport has been arranged for private plane, will cost you a cool two hundred thousand, but you will land in Aguadilla tomorrow night…"

"…Thank you, my friend…"

"…The pilot is my brother in law, quite a cool guy. You can contact him if you have any need in the future to go to Biafra-Nigeria. That trip, he may escort you around. He was Borg's co-pilot. He knows the place as he has done commercial flights there and move weapons for the government after the civil war. Money and politics make strange bed fellows…"

"…But only love makes the real strange, bedfellows…"

He looked at her and smiled. He loved this woman like a daughter. They embrace and both cried:

"…Your husband is a very lucky man…"

"…You have no idea…!" they both laughed.

The car approached a private hangar. There a gulf stream was waiting for them. Two officers of the USA army were there. There was an apprehension in all present, but Nascimento calmed them down. He parked along the other Hummer there. He took four hundred thousand dollars out of the bag, got out of the car and ordered everybody out. He signaled his men to enter the other Hummer and the family to the Gulf Stream.

"…General Perkins…?"

"…Mr. Nascimento…? I have your order here, enough ammunition to storm a palace, all bells and whistles. The delivery includes some stealth technology. The price for Osama is now 200 million…"

"…Of course you will get a percent…"

'…Of course, that is my retiring fund…"

"...In that plane is Mrs. Sampayo-Vaerga, wife of Jerry Vaerga. I can promise you he will find you and kill you if you try anything funny with them..."

...The Jerry Vaerga, most commemorated soldier of the Second Iraq War...?"

"...The one and only. So, no hanky-panky. No messing with my brother in law's flight plan, they have to be back home tomorrow night. Comprende...?"

"...OK, boys you can come out..." Out of nowhere 20 marines appeared, as of thin air. "...At ease, change of plans. This people are OK. Get the civilian Hummer to the base with you, we are letting these people to go..."

The marines did as instructed, the only thing that could be heard was echoes of "...Jerry Vaerga..." among them, a mix of fear and admiration. Ana and the kids were at the top of the stairs, Nascimento wave them away and they entered the plane. The door was closed and they were shown to their sits.

"...Mother, dad must be something else, when these soldiers acted the way they did..."

"...Your father is a man without fear, honorable man, when a man like that fights, time stands still for the rest of them. More than five thousand soldiers owe there live to your father. That is a debt they will pay one way or another..." she said while playing with both kids foreheads and hair.

Nascimento's brother in law, Frank Guice , approached them. He collected his money and welcomed them.

'"...We will be departing soon, I have made plans to go to Nigeria, I am afraid it will be with you. If your husband is in the Island, your chances are better..."

'"…They also have Jose - the "butcher of Mindanao" …" Said the younger son. Of course they will be fighting the Devil himself.

Before he could answer, a voice came out of the cockpit. It was oddly familiar and engaging.
"…You mean, the son of the Devil.…" This large rotund man walked surprisingly rapidly for his age.
He had a thick German accent, but spoke in perfect Brazilian style Portuguese.
"…Let me introduce myself, I am Mr. Ratzinger, most people know me as the Pope , but you can call me Helmut, that is my "war name". I am trying to pass "incognito"… "

He sat close to them. This was going to be a long trip. The plane took off without incident. The children were engaged with the Pope. He had an I-pod autographed by Bono with all the U-2 songs, the good , the bad and the very mediocre. Some Beatles, some Vivaldi, some Bob Marley.

"…You know I am the first I-pod Pope…' He said smiling.
"…Let's hope that you are not the last, pray be God…"
"…The Pope smiled at Ana, she went to sleep. Eventually all fell to sleep, including Mr. Helmut.
His last thought was: "...Praised God…!"

In the cabin, Mr. Guice opened a compartment. There was competition style martial arts gear, in addition a bow and an arrow set, also competition style. The sacred dozen was complete. He thought: "…I wish I could help Nascimento not to get killed, but this is a date with God's Will. I carry precious cargo, the future of humanity is in my hands…'

Chapter 21

[[Moca Monastery]]

Alicia, the one hundred and ten year old nun, international gospel expert, puked one more time in the toilet and flushed. Her newly rejuvenated body, pregnant with the prophet of the Lord was having a bad case of morning sickness. She was a saint.

She will be the saint patron of woman with morning sickness, she smiled: "…Saint Alicia of Añasco, our official patron of the pregnant pucker…"

Her heart was heavy and was also her butt. In 48 hrs her breast had engorged to three time her baseline, and so was her butt, she had gained eight pounds in thirty-six eight hours.

She has never been this alive; but at the same time what kind of sick joke was this? She was looking at her nude body in the bathroom mirror and suddenly realized that, without any question whatsoever, her body has never been this sexy. She exuded sensuality. She felt ashamed, and at the very time, extremely excited. This was her third rebirth, and she was going to do the best: she had decided to be happy and full of joy. If only her late husband could see her now, he would be very proud!

"…Mother Alicia…!" she heard the voices from outside the door. "…We have visitors. Please come down here. This people are from Rome, they have news from the Pope…"

She kneeled on the floor with much difficulty and prayed to God with all her might to give her patience. Slowly she dressed up with her habit, which concealed her voluptuous young body. She walked down the stairs, again with some difficulty. She walked towards the main entrance not realizing her visitors were already in the formal dining room. She heard the voices and entered the dining room. Her assistants were serving tropical juices and freshly baked bread with butter.

Mother Alicia sat down on the table. All men raised in unison, as a sign of respect…

She thought: "…These are military men, strong, coordinated and proud. I wonder who send them and what is the purpose…"

The leader of the bunch kneel before her, and kiss her feet: "…I am Captain Ives Pastore of the Swiss army, Vatican division and Knight of the Holy Spirit Guard. I come here to escort you to our headquarters in Geneva. We are here to protect the prophet of the Lord from the forces of Evil. The Pope sent us ahead. He is expecting tremendous danger to your future son if the New Babylonians and the Son of Satan have the upper hand. He is on his way to the Island to supervise the conflict. He is covering all the bases…"

"…Can I trust you, Mr. Pastore? How do I know that you are not one of the Babylonians…? How can I trust you personally…?"

"…Of course. Trusting us is a leap of faith. You will have to cross the abyss. Also I have a letter from the Pope…" he said smiling. "…And if everything is still in doubt…", he raised his arms and showed both forearms. "...the marks of the Shaolin Temple, the Sacred Dragon and Sacred Tiger..."

"…You are a Buddhist monk? You work for the Swiss and the Vatican…?"

"…You know that Jesus and the Enlighten One where brothers, so I don't see why I can not serve both…!"

"…You mean to say that their philosophy was similar in some respects, which I tend to agree. The Gnostic Gospels suggest direct contact but there is no proof. Cross influence, no question, shared basic philosophy perhaps. Goal: Nirvana…!"

Alicia opened the letter; indeed that was the Papal Seal.

He continued: "…In an old document carbon dated to twenty AD, there is a drawing of Jesus and Buddha wrists cut, exchanging blood… There is also a document explaining that Jesus visited

Buddha, and how he traveled to China where he stayed at the temple and where he used his extensive knowledge of language to communicate with the priests…"

"…Bravo…" clapped Mother Alicia, "…The only problem is that The Buddha expired 500 years before Christ…"

"…Jesus met a Buddha, not "The Buddha"(semantic aside) Both religions influenced each other. Muslims hate us because we are not "People of The Book". They are right, we do not fallow a book, but many books. Not one Buddha has inspired us, but many Buddhai. We are all and we are one…"

Alicia read the whole letter, compared the Papal seal to her memories of John Paul's letter and thought that it was authentic. "…I agree with going with you on one condition…"

"…Shoot, I rather take you voluntarily than forced…"

"…Kneel, you insolent fool, behold the power of The Spirit…"

The four men hit the floor with their faces, paralyzed….a force bigger than gravity pushing them down. Pastore started crying in severe agony. He was in terrible pain. The marks of Sacred Tiger and Dragon burned as if the were on fire, like the first time he had them burned in place.

"…So, I was saying before you rudely interrupted me, I will go on the condition I am never gagged or bonded, the bride of The Spirit deserves at least that respect…"

"…I know this is all hypnotism, you have no real power, you are using previous memories of pain to torture us, I have seen done before…"

"…Have you ever had a bad headache…? asked Alicia, apparently devoid of malice. "…I get them all the time…"

"…I never get them…" said Pastore. He holding his head in agony, crying like a girl, arms were on fire again, fallowed this. After five minutes this all subsided…"

"…OK, you can elicit pain even where there are no previous memories …"

"…My dear sir, look at your arms, tell me if you notice anything strange…"

Pastore looked at his arm in astonishment and owe. The tiger and the dragon had exchanged arms, their axis had inverted and a Christian Fish had appeared at the base of both figures.

"…But, still..."

"…I would not tempt The Spirit again, next time your penis may fall off..."

Pastore became pale. He was going to call her a witch, etc. However, he had an Italian girlfriend who liked her entertainment, so he could not venture the loss of his manhood…"

"…Mother Alicia, I give my word of honor that we will not force you into any situation, will not bond you in any way…"

"…Bravo, you are trainable! I have already packed, please send one of your men to pick it up with my novice and caretaker, Milagros. You have to forgive the child, she is just eighteen, impetuous and can make love like a kitten. Have been with us only a month, some vices are hard to forget. She could do a man in five minutes. Had a brain injury as a child, make her tragically hypersexual. While she is in this place and guided by the Holly spirit she can control it, if she wishes to. We have not taken the free will, we just have given great strength to be able to control it. The Spirit have returned to her the free will to do what is right n not what is natural with her. She has much to learn, and she will be my quarter maid in Switzerland. If one of you touches that child, all your penises will get the Christian fish symbol in quite a painful way. Comprende…?"

"…Yes Mother…" they all replied in unison. The youngest guard fallowed Milagros, whose habit barely covered the beauty of her forms. He was getting quite exited. They finally arrive at Mother Alicia's quarter. As he picked the luggage, Milagros bent over to pick up the second luggage, revealing all her glorious anatomy.

"…Are you well, you look pale…" she said, while they walk

down stairs.

"...I am very well indeed... it most be the tropical heat..." he said, as he thought to himself how difficult was going to be this assignment.

"...What is your name, brother...?"

"...Gustaff is my first name. My rank is First Lieutenant. I am 24, single and gay..."

"...However, you are exited with my body and the thought of making love to me, you are failing as a gay person, or maybe you think you are gay, but deep inside you want to emulate those priests that abuse you when you were fourteen. Four to one was never a fair fight, probably not even now..."

He remembered the incident as it was yesterday, the pain, the nausea. It was stopped after three days of torture, when the abbot, an openly gay man returned from his vacation, whipped the four men almost to death.

This was fallowed by branding of their L buttock with a 4-inch S (for sodomite) and literally kicked out of the monastery nude in the middle of the winter. None of them survive the exposure. The abbot nursed his wounds and hypnotized him to forget the whole incident. However he never abused him. He even got him his commission in the Swiss army, insisting that he would be assigned to the Vatican eventually. Instinctively he knew the only person that had loved him without taking advantage of him, to whom he planned to emulate in every respect.

"...Four to one would be a fair fight now, sister. I would kill them all. You may be right. I have not consummated with any of my boyfriends..."

"...Gustaff, I promise you that if I ever decide to love a man again you will be the man, pray that you are also touched by The Spirit..."

"...You mean make love to a man...?"

"…You need to listen, I know well how to make love, and I need to learn to love again…"

They arrived at the entrance of the monastery. She help him place the luggage in the trunk and assumed her place in the car, adjacent to the Mother Superior, no before giving Gustaff a tender kiss in the forehead and a brotherly hug. Alicia looked at her with infinite pity and love.

"…Mother he is the one, he is the chosen one. The Spirit has placed him in my way. I love him…"

"…Does he loves you back. Pastore claims that he is gay..."

"…He is not actively gay, except for a period of molestation when young, he has never known the flesh…"

"…Did he tell you all this in five minutes…?"

"…No, The Spirit reveal it to me the first night I was here, he said that he will cure me of the anatomical Nymphomania and will give me the choice of becoming a nun for the rest of my life and that he will make me the standard bearer of the Spirit or He would get me the best man for me…"

Alicia pointed at her womb and added: "…So this is plan B…?"

"…No Mother since five minutes ago that is plan A…!"

"…Milagros touched the Mother in her belly and the Mother felt the child move. She thought is too early for that it has been only 48 hours...

"…What was that…?" said Milagros, after thinking exactly the same.

"…I think it was The Spirit confirming this as plan A…" she said smiling.

Pastore closed the trunk of the Papal Limo, the two women, the four men and the Holy Spirit where all in the car. They sped away towards Aguadilla to the Papal plane and back to Zurich.

Gustaff looked at Milagros, through the rear mirror as he was driving. His heart swelled withed love. Pastore entered the car and looked at him.

"...I think you are bewitched, drive my friend, we are in the presence of real power. Drive to the airport. We will have plenty of time to sort this all out, down the line..."

"...There is nothing to sort, I will fallow the will of The Spirit. I am in love, like I never been before. I will be a tool of the Living God. You have to make up your mind and clear it up from all your doubts. These are the end of the days. You better take sides today...."said Gustaff.

"...I have already taken sides, Gustaff. My faith is not as strong, but I am here, I am not, anyway...?"

There was a pregnant pause in which the two nuns smiled at each other, very contented of their present state, one carried a prophet, the other the promise of true love and a life under the continual guidance of the Holy Spirit. The four military men were praying for prompt resolution of this mission. Gustaff had a second chance at happiness and he was not going to blow it!

"...Boss, we are five minutes from the airport and the pilot is heating up the motors, the tower has our flight plan, we are priority one , we will be out of here in twenty minutes top..." said the communications officer.

When they arrived everything was ready, the crew, the same that had served John Paul the last ten years, now Ratzinger. The pilot, an Italian full of the Holly spirit smiled widely at the nuns, ignoring the military. He embraced them with a brotherly bear hug, and disappeared into the cabin and off they went towards Zurich.

CHAPTER 22
[[Casa Verde: Ten minute before sunrise]]

It was five minutes before sunrise when the Ninja infiltrated the "Green House". The ancient warrior avoided the two very capable monks posted at the only entrance to the centuries old mansion...
Slowly, like a fly, progressing, hanging from the wall arriving at the first room. A sniff was all needed for the warrior to realize that his target was not there. I smelled like incense and sweat: probably the Llama. Continuing through every room he ascended to the second floor. First room at the right a couple was there. The smell of freshly cut bean sprouts, characteristic of human semen, was the prevailing aroma. "…Alas, a night of intensive love making, easy targets, tired man, satisfied woman, nobody in the mood for war…!"

The warrior continued towards the end of the second floor hallway. "…Ah, here we are…!" There was the smell of Aramis, characteristic of the enemy to be defeated. The Ninja could count on at least three bounties that could be claimed if the master was killed.

Slowly and silently the sword was taken out of its sleeve. The sword had an inscription in Japanese that read "Silent, Fearless Warrior". Simultaneously the door opened. The enemy was covered head to toes in sheaths, as it was cold. The Ninja pointed his sword toward the center of the bulk and stroke without hesitation. The room filled with feathers and foam. Out of nowhere a kick stroke the Ninja straight in the face. Jose who had been hanging between two cealing beams had let himself fall and kick the Ninja square in the face, now sucker punched and semiconscious, he struggle for balance.

Jose applied pressure to both temporal areas, paralyzing the Ninja. He position himself for the "coupe the grace" a Karate chop to the base of the skull. He stopped himself halfway down when a whiff from the past entered his brain.

"…God darn you Martha, son of a gun, I almost killed you, you crazy witch. My allergies are killing me, so I can't smell shit…!."

"…I was able to hear you when you passed the guards, all the pauses you did. You were quite interested in the first room at the top of the stairs, couple having sex? You were always a peeping Tom, Molini. I did not smell the darn Charlie perfume until I was aiming for your neck…!"

He was furious. To her it was always a joke, everything was a Joke. This one almost cost her life. For better or worst that crazy witch was his wife. Maybe she was attempting a first-degree divorce.

She was still paralyzed, barely breathing. He grabbed under the kimono both nipples and pressed hard. She jumped like a cat. The pressure spell was broken and she went with the sword for his neck. She stopped two centimeters from the jugular and laughed.

"…Thanks for not killing me, and for taking me out of the paralytic trance, I guess we can consider all this foreplay, nipple accupressure and all…" she said as she threw her sword against the wall, where it landed impaled. She disrobed completely, diving into the bed, making a mess of feather in the air. José relieved that his wife had not been killed, joined her, making another mess of feathers.

After taking off his underwear, she positioned herself on top of him.

She was ready for action, but then and there Hell broke loose. Goldman and Manuel entered the room, after braking the door, dressed only with their bows and arrows. The Llama and the three permanents priests entered the room armed with Samurai Swords. The two guards, also armed with bow and arrows, closely fallowed them.

"…I guess if you are not going to join us, do please leave the room…" said Martha

"…But we heard fighting…" said Goldman

"…We smelled blood…" said the Llama, quite embarrassed.

"…We heard everybody running this way, Mr. Zola is here, he brought breakfast, and your friends are also here. We should start training in one hour…"

Everybody left the room to start getting ready for training. Jose and Martha went on with their business.

The Llama spoke first outside the room, as they walked toward the stairs:

"…God makes them and the Devil joins them…!" he looked at Goldman and Manuel, who had mad the best to cover their nudity with their bows and arrow holders. "…How about you two, when this started…?"

"…Several years ago, this gentleman here let me win the European Archery Championship. He lost the championship but won my heart. At that point he was married, so we never consummated our love for each other. We did share hours of conversation and spiritual closeness. For the last couple of hours we have been picking up where we left…"

The Llama smiled and added: "…Its amazing how God has placed the desire for true, reciprocated love as one of the most powerful forces in the universe. Love is in the air. Hopefully it will serve us, rather than hinder us in the coming trials and tribulations. When love is real is a very powerful force, when it is only Porno, or carnal love, it is a very destructive force. I hope that in our case is the former, rather than the latter…."

"…I hope you can excuse us, we need to dress up a little more, give our regards to Mr. Zola and his friends, we will be joining them for breakfast, shortly…"

The Priests who had been doing mass in the little town cathedral, went up the stairs, after greeting Zola and his bodyguards. They had a glimpse of the naked bodies as they disappeared into their rooms.

"...What is going up here...?" asked Pereira, with a childish grin in his face. "...It seems that the Buddhist can not keep people from making love shamelessly...!"

"...I'll say...!" answered Ignacious, in a mocking tone.

"...I am sorry to say that what we can not control is people loving each other, I am not so sure whenever you really want to control such a creative force. Anyway get ready, we will have breakfast shortly and the Tango lessons will start..."

"... Do you know that great Tango dancers, male or female often dance with partners of the same sex, as they can learn how the opposite sex feels when they are dancing , so they can improve their dance...?" said Pereira

"...Well, dance with me, Mr. Pereira..." said the Llama as they went out for breakfast.

Out came the Llama and the Brazilian dancing the Tango, towards the courtyard where the Buddhist priests were preparing the tables for the breakfast. This took everybody by surprise, except for Zola who asked Garcia to dance as to get the feel of the dance. Soon all the people in the Green House were dancing in the courtyard. The Buddhist combo was playing at full swing, and after a while they have become very proficient. Everybody was getting into the rhythm of the music, which they hoped will help them defeat the Son of the Devil. The next two days were going to be something else. Moreno and Vaelga actively avoided dancing with each other, more out of incompatibility, than of homophobia.

All sat at the table. Ignacious gave the blessing. Martha and Jose finally made it down. They sat together in the only remaining empty chairs. Their long-term plans were conflicting in nature. Short-term plans are usually so much easier to fulfill, particularly if it involved sex between people that loved each other dearly and without preconditions. The short-term goals are usually and often satisfied, repeatedly.

Martha stood up after breakfast was finished and invited Moreno to dance. Both were consummated Tango dancer, Martha had work as an instructor in the Bronx with some success while she was in collage. Her timing was without fault, Moreno was a pretty good dancer. However the place shined when Jose took her out to dance, every cut , every eight , every sandfish fell in place , passion was in the air . Jose understood that clearly that this was the love of his life and hoped upon hope that she could become pregnant so that she could give the "macheteros" a vacation. She looked into his eyes and realized that she still loved him in spite of himself. She would love to pro-create with this man. If they survived Saturday she will stop taking her birth control pills and would get pregnant. They still had fifty years until the prophecy of the second coming will be fulfilled, they will see their children and grandchildren, provided that they defeated the Son of the Devil.

Zola approached Emma. He had no regrets, did not felt betrayed by her, as a matter of fact he was still alive because she was spying on him. He also understood by her proximity to Manuel that they were in love.

"…Emma, I want to thank you for your services to my organization and for been instrumental in the survival of both me and my son. I would be honored if you continue working for me. I understand you may want to have Mr. Manuel around, and that I will find a position for him. I carry no grudge against you…"
"…I appreciate your candor Mr. Zola. We might take your offer. We have not decided what we will do with our lives yet. Everything depended on Saturday's outcome. Let us sleep over it, Mr. Zola and thanks…"

"…It is easier to employ a former enemy than to destroy it; less blood and less paperwork…."said Zola.

"...Any warrior than can destroy an enemy is a grate warrior, any one than can defeat himself is an invincible one..." said the Llama

"...Choose your weapon, old man...!" said Zola. "...I will teach you who is a great warrior..."

"...Maybe you should be concentrating in becoming an invincible one, Mr. Zola. I choose the Bo..." said the Llama in a half aggressive tone. "...I built these two Bo from local bamboo. They were dried for six month, after a bat in polyurethane for two weeks. They are made from the golden bamboo; very sturdy and at the same time, light and ever lethal. The dark polish painted to make it difficult to see a night, and thin coat of fiberglass. This 'baby' is my pride and joy. I only manufactured fifty units, each have my signature, plus a little Buddhist prayer in Vietnamese, all for $99.99. But if you act now, we will include this pair of nunchaks, made by the same process with my instructional video, and a shuriken star with my autograph..."

"...You have to be kidding, ah...?" said Zola.

"...Of course I am kidding! You pompous ass! You are willing to compromise our mission here for your ego. You may jeopardize the mission if you don't conquer yourself! He passed a Bo to Zola. "...See what you can teach an old man...!"

They bowed to each other and the contest started. The Bo was moving so fast that if they have been of any other color, they would have been invisible. The quality of the instruments was superb. Each blow sounded solid neither of them had been able to hit anything but bamboo. It was quite a show of expertise. The old Buddhist monk was in a trance it seems that he was able to predict all Zola's moves and have been concentrated in blocking him. Zola was giving all his effort but could not touch the old man. The Llama smiled, he knew that Zola was at the verge of exhaustion after fifteen minutes of this. Then the most incredible thin happened. The Llama used his Bo as a vault to jump over Zola in a rotating motion with Bo in hand, behind

Zola, who was wide open for the kill. He hit the man in the three main accu-points, above each kidney and on the base of the neck. Zola collapsed on his knees in terrible pain, but without any major real damage. The Llama bowed and said: "…Not bad for an old man…? You realize that I could have killed you? Have the Bo as a souvenir Mr. Zola. No hard feelings…?'

"…No hard feelings, you need to teach me that, would you like working for me…?"

"…Only if you pay for the Green House…"

"…Consider it a deal…!" with some trepidation, Zola shook his hand and the Llama gave him a hug.

"…At this pace I going to have the whole town in my payroll…!" He looked at the Llama with great admiration. "…It is a deal, I am glad that I am not your enemy, I will buy the Green House and even will support the monks if you teach me to fight like that…!"

"…If we defeat the Enemy, we will teach you everything I know and more…"

"…It is a deal, then, and lets seal this with a toast…" said Ignacious, who had served as referee

"…May the gods be with us, may the Enlightened One, the Living God be with all of us…" said Zola.

At a distance Sampayo watched the scene, tonight would be the Black Mass and the birth of the Son of the Devil. For now they will have to hunt a female surfer from the beach in Rincon for the human sacrifice. The Son of the Devil will get his strength from her body and soul.

Chapter 23

[[Old abandoned army Base, Pretoria: South Africa]]

Omar waked up with a terrible headache. The bed was as uncomfortable as any hospital bed. His head was throbbing, every muscle ached. When he was conscious enough he began to analyze his surroundings....

He was the only patient in a huge open ward, probable capacity of 20 inmates. All the windows were barred. There were only two doors in that room, each door had an exit code lock. Two armed Black guards, on each door. He was not tied to the bed, there was an alarm to signal the two additional guards in the monitors (with IDF uniforms) which were communicating constantly with the outside world. He had three distinct surgical incisions. The circumcision, a wrist repair (busted in his capture and some kind of neurosurgery procedure)

One of the IDF men approached him. He extended his hand as a friendly gesture, Omar gave him a half effort handshake.

"..I don't blame you for being pissed. These people are not professional. You cannot beat the "Jew-ness" out of anybody. But you were less than cooperative..."

"...Well I was attacked by four ruffians who tried to infuse some drugs into my body..."

"...That is exactly my point. There are more elegant and inconspicuous ways of kidnapping a subject... I have written manuals on that precise subject, the problem with the MOSSAD these day is that we lack finesse. My father could abduct you in the middle of the Cairo Bazaar and nobody will know any foul play was involved! What a giant...!"

"...Can you tell me why am I here...?"

'...Of course, you are my apprentice. I get all the difficult cases. You are the most difficult ever..."

"...What makes my case so difficult? Pray I ask...?"

"...First is the issue of the traumatic memory loss while you were deeply undercover in a Palestinian camp, your real wife was abducted and almost killed by mistake…"

"…I see..."

"…Then is the issue of being Ben Laden's right hand for years, and becoming a devout Muslim for more than 10 years..."

"…OK..."

"…Then there is the issue of being kicked unconscious by your wife of many years, she can not forget that you kill her brother in a raid to Gaza in 1993…"

"…Oh, I guess is complicated... Can you explain the issue about the circumcision…?"

"…Oh…! That was not my idea. The MOSSAD's commander prerogative, he wanted to make you useless as a Arab spy, specially on your frame of mind, in which you don't know which way is north, who is your enemy and who is your friend…"

"…What is your name…?"

"…Eli, first name basis only. You can not escape .We implanted a G.P.S. location devise in your brain, also has a very concentrated explosive that can kill you and whoever you may be hugging instantly..."

"…You did what…?"

"…Again not my idea, notice I am keeping a distance here ..." Eli said half jokingly

"…You have to be kidding! Where am I…?"

"…Pretoria...'

"…Pretoria, South Africa…?"

"…The one and only… I have been here myself for two days only. I am concluding a little project that fell into my lap...laptop five days ago. This project will finalize in two days. We are in the waiting period, anxiously expecting the arrival of either the Messiah or orders from Tel Aviv, whatever comes first…"

'"…You think you are a comedian, eh…?"

"…That reminds me of an old joke. It goes like that: "What is German?". Answer?:

"Is Yiddish without a soul or humor", answered Omar without

thinking. He was amazed at what he has just said. He was also very scared, the persona he had carefully created and nurtured was starting to crumble. But where has he heard that before? It was in a very distant past, for all practical purposes in another galaxy.

Eli interrupted his thoughts. He brought out of his attache case a folder as big as the "family bible' that Christians keep around their formal dinning room, perhaps because of the aesthetic value of reproductions from Donatello, Raphael and Michelangelo, rather than any eternal truth they can distilled from the inspired words in those pages.

"...This is your dozier, my friend. It chronicles your life from the moment your parents met at Teblinka to the moment you open your eyes here this morning. It has all your training from Kindergarten to your graduation from Tel Aviv University where you met your wife Fatima, to the training at the MOSSAD, to your undercover tours, to your loss of memory, to your command of Arabic, to the moment you met Ben Laden in Saudi, to your joining of the Mujahadin, your escaping with Ben Laden of the American dragnet in Afghanistan, to the planning and execution of "The Amal" Project, Your capture in Granada, your torture and surgeries , everything in double space black and white , Helvetia© stile...."

"...My name is Yuri, my father was Adolph my Mother Sarah. They met at Teblinka. My aunt, mother's sister cut off the electricity in the barbed wire and was killed by her lover, the camp Commandant. My father liberated the weapons from the storage shack and fought a battle for 30 minutes in which all the SS men died and two thirds of the inmates. However all were scheduled to be machine gun down, including the Kapos. It was 1943. It was the only Camp to revolt, both my parents survive they were smuggled out of the occupied territories and eventually finished in Israel. My father became one of the founders of the MOSSAD..." said Omar crying.

"…So I see your memories have been jogged out of you, my friend…"

"…This was the story I have made as Ben Laden's deputy, in case I was captured, and it turns out that all of this was true, that I was recollecting my past…"

"…Regrettably for you, you are a valuable asset for the state of Israel. Your wife hates you. You are a walking bomb, with a known target. Your days are counted, my friend. Again, I was given the package, you can fulfill your mission or you can kill yourself. Personally, I would love to kill Ben Laden myself, but you are the best equipped for the Job…" said Eli

"…You mean to tell I have no escape from this destiny which I have no voice, and no options…?"

"…There is a escape, but only if your heart stops beating. If the detonator senses that there is no cardio-electric activity it will disarm itself..."

"…So my choices are death as a hero, death as a coward or death from natural causes, provided that neither MOSSAD or Al Qauida terminate me first…"

"…That basically summarize your options, you could say that you have been privileged to be the sword of Massada, and your choices are similar, in your case and for the rest of your life the battlefield will be mostly in the privacy of your own mind? Like a nano-Massada…"

"…The only difference is that those peoples have a choice to make, I have being held into the fray, with no consultation, no pinion requested, no opinion given…"

"…You and I are pawns in the game of history…"

"…Be as it may, you are a pawn with free will, the moment they implanted that devise in my head without my consent, you kill mine…"

"...On the contrary, the final decision is yours. Weather or not you die or live, weather you die without a clear purpose, or defending your homeland is ultimately yours, as you are your own handler..."

"...You mean I have the control to the detonator...?"

"...You and only you..."

"...Where...?"

"...The blue button in your watch..."

"...You have to be kidding...!"

"...If does have a security feature, if you decide to abort, you enter a four number code in the calculator, your date of birth in the Jewish calendar..."

"...What is the range of the control...?"

"...The range is about one quarter mile, ounce activated you have five minutes to detonation, but you have to be within the range..."

"...We are cutting it short, ah...?" "...How many detonators are there...?"

"...Three with your sequence. You have one, I have the second one, and the third one is in the security vault at the MOSSAD's headquarters..."

"...Are you going to be my handler for the rest of my life...?"

"...No, I will be your handler for the rest of mine! Any questions...?"

"...Why are we in South Africa? Obviously is something extremely important, as this looks like a very expensive operation..."

"...We are bombing Iran's known nuclear facilities with stealth bombers with nuclear devices with enriched plutonium that has the obtained with the same signature as the main reactor in Iran, a stealth delivered Chernobyl..."

"...But there will be an investigation, especially if you loose any of the pilots, or they get captured..."

"...They will destroy their plane rather than leave any evidence behind. All planes have self-destruct feature, there will be no evidence, not even a misplaced hair from a pilot's head…"

"…Lets assume that this hair brain scheme actually works, what is next…?"

"…For you, Ben Laden, for me Rincon, to help some friends of mine that will need us…"

"…Am I free to go, Mr. Eli…?"

"…Not yet, not quite yet…!"

"…What other good news you have for me, Mr. Eli…?"

"…According to your information here, your wife became pregnant the night of the raid: twins, fraternal, different fathers…!"

"…Different fathers…?" he said in laud voice, before he could control himself. "…How is that possible…?"

"…That can be an outcome, when you get into those tricky threesomes, my friend. Two horny dumb blots, one steamy female with a tendency toward twins, and before you know it you have prescription for disaster. Not to mention the emotional mine field of the whole situation, who does what to whom at what time, where are the boundaries and who pays for the room…?"

"…You seem to have studied the phenomena well, Mr. Eli…?"

Eli smiled and added: "…Most of my knowledge is strictly theoretical..."

"…Most, not all, ah…?"

"…Well, this spy business is a lonely profession , those holly days hit the divorced lesbos in the secretary pool quite hard; that is when good old Eli and his trusty side kick, Woody springs into action, bringing happiness to all womankind…"

"…Oh brother, are you taking medications…?"

"…No, my friend this is natural. Is not deliriums of greatness, everything I do, I do very, very well: "nobody does it better, Um! ,Um!, sometimes I wish someone could, Um! Um!, why I have to be so darn good,…?"

"…Earth to Eli, come back for landing…!"

"…I was thinking, maybe, those twins of yours may balance to the situation and make peace possible in the future, "Luke they will bring balance to the Force"

"...You don't go out often, do you...?"

"...No I spent most of my life at MOSSAD, lately I have been sleeping with my cousin, the daughter of the Commander Middleman..."

"...You dog, you are sleeping your way up the ladder, excellent. Why are you telling me all this...?"

"...Your wife hates your guts and would kill you if you have a chance. She is a high-ranking member of the Parliament. You were a marked man. The threesome was your idea. As a Palestinian warrior you made several successful raids to settlements and kibbutz. In one of these raids you kill her brother, sister in law and nephew. It was a terrible blow to her. The only reason you are still alive is that you are a time bomb..."

"...But we made love, just before she kicked me in the head..."

"...She just widowed for the fourth time, she was a needy woman that knows what she wants, perhaps it was a friendly farewell, only God knows what is in that woman's heart..."

"...So you are telling there is no future for us...?"

"...Bingo! There is no us, there is the future Prime Minister of Israel, whose son is the half brother of the director of Islamic Jihad, and whose first husband, albeit Jewish, was a famous Islamic warrior..."

"...So, I am politically expendable...?"

"...A dirty Pamper has more value than you...!" he passed an envelope across the table where they were sitting. There are three passports, one of them your original one. The other ones you use to get back to Spain to join Ben Laden, your satellite cell phone will now transmit all your calls to us. There is twenty thousand for expenses. There is a combination for a Swiss Bank account, in case you can accomplish your mission without dying. Good luck! Go! You are a free man…"

Yuri looked at the envelope and realized it was not empty. A Casio sport watch was at the bottom.
"…So everything is real, not a joke…"
"…No my friend, this is all very real, this is all your ex wife's, fault. She masterminded the whole operation. She wants to see you suffer. I think is a darn shame they way they are treating you. You are a hero of Israel, a true son. Generations of your family have given their blood and toil for Israel, and this the way they pay you all. Your father probably is spinning in his grave! Nobody as Machiavellian and vindictive should ever become prime minister. She will sell the whole country for thirty silver coins, if it suits her passions! She is very dangerous…!"
"…But what can we do…?"
"…A large faction in the Intelligence community actually wants her dead, as they consider her a security risk. I have seen the memoranda…"
"…I will be happy to help you, but my hands are tied, or better, my brain…"
"…I will take you to the airport and explain the potential ways to bypass and destroy the triggering mechanism. If you survive Ben Laden assassination, we will support your revenge with all the available resources including national intelligence and very rich capitalist, in addition to a group of very courageous gentiles, which I have befriended and who owe me some favors…"
"…Eli, I don't think you know the magnitude of your enemy…"

A door opened and Middleman entered.
"…Mr. Yuri, never underestimate this young man, he get the job done, and done right. We will support you to the very end with anything we can. I hate that witch…!"
"…This is Mr. Middleman, my boss…"
"…Delighted, if I survive I will delighted to go back to the com-

pany. I would love getting my revenge…"

"…You make it back to Israel and we will help you, financing probably will be provided by Eli's friend, the billionaire, as he also hates the witch. She is trying to enact an ultra nationalist agenda, defining who is and who is not a Jew for the purpose of the military and tax exemptions and voting rights. Like a "Reverse Nuremberg Law". That makes you, Mr. Yuri, the only pure Jew in Pretoria, with all tax exemptions and military privileges. The rest of Israel will be given "certificates of Jewish-ness" to be able to work and serve as military. Of course only the Prime Minister would review each case…"

"…How much money are we talking here…?"

"…For our friend, we estimated one hundred million dollars per year. He owns most of the software and defense companies in Israel. He is "only one fourth Jew", so he will have to sell the defense-related companies and loose the 25% tax exemption for the sale and for the profits…"

"…Does she know about your secret operation here…?"

"…Only you and I, the pilots and Eli know exactly what are the targets, and the time of the attack…"

"…Do you trust me enough to let me go, just like that…?"

"…Not really, but I have no choice. Mr. Eli, escort this man back to Europe, stay within triggering distance, that is an order, not a suggestion. Do not join your friends in the Island. Intelligence says that they have enough men to complete their mission without you. We need you to coordinate the attacks from Europe on the same day of their showdown. Shalom…!"

Chapter 24
[[Rincón: Somewhere on Route143]]

The gorgeous beauty stretched like a cat in her bed. She loved the mahogany California Queen bed that the local artisan had created for her. Having four solid posts and a solid headboard was essential for her kind of business. This was a museum piece....

She remembered clearly the morning that Manuel Contreras deliver and mounted her bed: "…The total weight of the bed, ma'am is a close to a quarter ton. It has sixteen drawers under it, so if you have to store any piece of clothing, other than dresses, they fit here. It is equipped with sixteen lights fixtures, some of them spot lights pointing towards the four posts and the fifth towards the headboard.. This is the only piece of furniture you will ever need in this room…"

Today, like then, she was amazed at the beauty of the bed. It was not a bed, it was a Pagan Altar and she was the goddess of that domain.

"…It has a drawer of audiovisual control, there is music, DVD recording capabilities and the canopy is a plasma TV where you can watch TV, old films or live entertainment provided by the ten discreet high resolution web-cams mounted around the base of the canopy…"

She was intrigued by the fact that the headboard was covered with a sheath. She was going to uncover the headboard when Manuel stopped her. "…This is the finishing touch, this makes this bed a piece of art…" he unveiled it, revealing a relief sculpture in her likeness , dressed with her desire, passion and a smile, she was stretching, like a cat in all four legs hyper-extending her back .All her merchandise was in full view.

"…I used a video clip from your first movie, you were nineteen and in total control of your beauty…"

It turned out Manuel was a long term admirer of her work and has seen all her twenty six movies
At thirty-six she had retired to the Island, had bought this Villa. She had invested all her money on this beautiful house, planted smack in the latitude where the Caribbean and the Atlantic unite, in a hill dominating the beach, and a surf shop and restaurant at the base of the ocean. Business was O.K., she still received some revenues from her old movies. However her lifestyle was kept the way it was by working for the New Babylonians. She was the symbolic sacrificial witch for all the Black Masses. She got one million dollars plus a twenty grand a month from Sampayo. In exchange she had three sixes branded with an iron to her left buttock and was ritually tied to an altar at the old lighthouse in Cabo Rojo. She was symbolically slain and her heart was offered to the son of the devil, the high priest dressed in a disguised with a mask with ram horns encrusted with pearls. Sampayo will eat a still beating calf heart, freshly slain for the occasion, while he mounted her. Lately he will be rough with her, "caressing" her with the ceremonial dagger.

She finally stopped stretching. It was around 8:00 AM, she had to go to the market. On Thursdays, most of the area supermarkets received their fresh produce. She somewhat roughly waked up the twin brother she picked up at the beach last nights. Great-grandsons one of the old petroleum barons, they spend their days surfing and their nights "drilling for oil" with the local beauties. She had to by the product for her restaurant, or they would loose all the local vegans, which supported most of her business.

"…Rise and shine, sleeping beauties…" she said in a semi-motherly fashion. She could see they were again ready for action but she had no time for that now. Business was business and pleasure was pleasure and is cool when you can mix them both, but there was no time for that now.

"...Boys, I do appreciate your very vigorous enthusiasm, but I am running late, tonight we can continue our little sessions, but for now why don't you hit the shower and go surfing or something..." She picked up her keys and left the pair to their own resource.

She drove thirty minutes to the "Sultana del Oeste". They had the closest thing to a farmer's market, in the Island. It was more of a "Farmer's Circus", they had as many street performers as vegetable vendors. Families came here on Thursday mornings to have a good time. She looked around until she found a parking spot. She knew exactly who to approach. In the Buddhist Farm Cooperative booth, like every Thursdays, the monks carried their hard style of bargaining. The Llama was among them, with his Lennon glasses and his hot tea. Today, in a sub-realistic vein, the monks were playing several classic tangos. They were actually getting very good at it.

She smiled with surprising shyness the booth. She treated with great respect any man that upon meeting her did not propose a monetary transaction for her body. After 17 years in the business, she has never been able to seduce any Buddhist monk.

There was something in their demeanor and general appearance that gave them the deceptive look of apparent weakness. In other words, no matter their age, they always gave the impression of children. She was one of the lucky ones, she has never been abused as a child, had a collage education, even an MBA. For all practical purposes she could quit tomorrow and live comfortably for the rest of her, but she was addicted to the rush of sex and she has never faked pleasure, in or out of her movies, ever.

"...Good morning my child, how are you doing today...?" asked the Llama in a very friendly way.
"...What's up with the tango...?"

"...They are practicing for Saturday AM, we are giving a concert in The Rincon Plaza, around 8:00 AM, it will probably last a couple of hours, you are more than welcome if you want to come..."

"...It always surprises me how you guys treat me, you make me feel warm and special, like a member of humanity..."

"...My child, you are a child of God, your Christ and I suspect also The Enlighten One was widely known to keep company with woman of your "state and abilities", perhaps they enjoyed your warmth and spontaneity, perhaps they enjoyed your beauty for beauty's sake, like a work of art..."

"...Whores and tax men, one and the same...?"

"...Specially in this Island..." he said smiling and added : "...When we meet someone, fallowing the teaching of the sages of the ages, we tend to interact in the present, there is no past, there is no future, only the present has any meaning because only the present can bring change and redemption. When Christ said "go and sin no more" he was keenly aware of our weak nature and that only the present, which is the only action time, is where our week nature have to be nurtured and strengthened..."

"...What you are trying to tell me, is that its not worth dwelling in the past, as there is no possibility of changing the past, and the future does not exits, is a progression of the present..."

"...Exactly child, not bad for a Yale MBA..."

"...Tell that to my financial advisor..."

"...Stoke brokers and financial advisors are keenly aware of these facts, as they study present trends, hoping that they can guess the future, when they know well that they work in the present..."

"...Ah...! Zen Brooking! I like it...!"

"...There is plenty more where that one came from...!" he said, in a self-mocking way and the both laughed. Their laughter was children's laughter, they have introduced their inner children to each other and there was no coming back.

"...Maria Marconi...!

"…Yes Holy Father…?"

"…When are you going to quit working for the Babylonians, I fear for your life…!"

"…Don't you worry, everything is fake, with the possible exception of the sex, that is quite real, the only real thing…"

"…You know I fear for your life, I love you like the daughter I never had, I don't want you to get hurt by these evil men. Have you thought of the possibility that these are just dress rehearsals for the real thing…?"

"…You mean that the real Son of The Devil, will show up one day, eat my heart out while he mounts me with his disgusting and out of the common organ? Please…!"

"…My dear, laugh as you may, truth is truth, deception is deception and it takes very little to dig into the latter to find the former…"

"…You are serious…! OK, when is this going to happen…?"

"…Tomorrow at midnight, "the Son of the Devil will born out of the Whore of Babylon, and will be nourished by the Italian Wet Nurse". Do you realize that Ms. De Mello is of childbirth?'

"…The Whore of Babylon…? But...!"

"…You made a movie, which of course I have never seen, I Google you when we met, called…"

"…The Italian wet nurse…!"Quite a movie, we made fun of a lot of taboos..."

"…Stay with me dear, the point of the matter is that the prophecy will be fulfilled as we are "at the Island at the other side of the world", in the "lighthouse of the West"…" he finished up.

"…Why are you telling me all this…?"

"…I don't want you to die, if you persist in this way your soul may also be in jeopardy, resist so that your soul does not die with your body…?"

"…How about escaping now with both soul and body? Is that possible…?

"…As we speak, Sampayo is hunting down an innocent surfer

as a possible plan B…"

"…So I have to make the decision to die, so an innocent can live, but at the same time I have to fight so that I don't loose my soul…? This is not fair…!"

"…The present is in your hands, you can either fulfill your destiny or see a lot of good people suffer for a long time, and a young lady, who has not experience anything, suffer severe abuse and humiliation, it is your choice…"

"…I guess I will be nice I owe it to my adoring fans, how can I save my immortal soul…?"

"…I will give you the tools to resist damnation, but you can not enjoy sex with the beast, or you will be lost forever, understand dear…?"

"…So I have to become an-orgasmic! Talking about life little ironies…! I am ready, teach me...!"

Chapter 25
[[Granada: Spain]]

This was the scoop of his career. He was going to interview Simon Weisel, the famous Nazi hunter. After this he will probably be promoted to The Madrid Bureau. He had being working for Al Jazzier for five years now. He was the only Jew in the organization, a hard spot...

Ramón Bueso was in the Granada studios. The Moroccan girl who did the make up was getting him ready. She was a beautiful woman. Her allure and beauty probably was the only reason he had not quitted yet. Since the first time they met, when he interviewed her for the Job, her great and exotic beauty had smitten him. She needed a Job and a place to stay. He provided both. She needed papers to stay in Spain, and his lawyer provided them. The night she got her legal permission to stay, after a celebration with what seemed to be the whole Moroccan community in exile, she joined him in his bed for the first time. It was the most incredible night of his life.

The next day his parents visited them, they had a spare key. They found them asleep, sideways, holding both hands, completely nude and uncovered. They waked up with the walling sounds of his mother sobbing in the corner and his father's "…God at least he is not gay and if you ask me that girl is quite a beauty, he could have done much worst, specially that niece you wanted him to date, God what a cow…!"

His father, even without trying, has always being his co-conspirator. The old man knew that by bringing the niece into the fray, his wife will forget his son's unorthodox sexual preference and his enormous morning erection. His father, was personally shocked more by the latter. He had managed again to piss his wife more with the right button, than his son non-Kosher love live.

The Moroccan girl, his wife and mother of his child, planted a loving kiss in his hairline, where it would not affect the make up. She then held his face between her hands gave him a "breast hug", then looked directly into his green eyes and whispered: "...Go get them, tiger...!" Alicia was his best fan.

Waiting patiently in the studio, in front of the camera, was Simon Weisel himself, getting some final touches from Alicia's supervisor. He looked taller and somewhat younger than in the photos he had seen. However he was very thin and athletic, looking similar to his photos and younger than expected for his age.

"...Mr. Weisel, I want to thank you for the opportunity you have given me..." Three security men that obviously were not part of the TV station interrupted him.
"...I am Mr. Perez, chief of security for Mr. Weisel, these are my associates. We are here with two purposes: To protect Mr. Weisel from his many enemies present and future and to guarantee that he will be out of here in twenty minutes. MOSSAD can have agents here in 30 minutes, which is their response time. We want to be out of here in 20 minutes flat, commercial or no commercial brake, understood...?"

Bueso was dumbfounded; Weisel fearing the MOSSAD? That did as much sense as Churchill fearing an attack by the R.A.F.
Perez continued: "....Is 7:10, we are out of here by 7:30 , with or without you, so start now and make it smooth, Mr. Bueso..."
The security men disappeared behind the darkness of the studio. He looked scare, this felt like a migraine coming. He sat down and proceeded:
"...Welcome to our program, here is Mr. Simon Weisel, Nobel Peace Price winner and famous Nazi Hunter. How is the center in Vienna...?"

"…We abandoned the premises three days ago, after a raid from MOSSAD , they attempted arrest was foiled by my security guards and bodyguard…"

Bueso's jaw dropped, he looked in the direction of Alicia, who in sign language told him: "…Think about Madrid, keep your cool…!"

"…Those are quite serious accusations, Mr. Weisel..."

"…We have brought movies of the raid captured by our security cameras,   there is no question..."

Bueso swallowed hard before the next question: "…But why would the security apparatus of Israel be interested in destroying your life's work…?"

"…The Zionist madness has polluted the thought process of our government…!"

"…Say what…?" he was sorry it had escaped his mind before he could stop it.

'…Yes, I have been in secret negotiations with moderate Palestinian factions, who are working for peace in our lifetime, their delegation was abducted and massacred like cattle inside the state of Israel by the MOSSAD…"

"…Do you have any proof of this…?" asked Bueso, in full migraine swing.

"…We have both surviving witnessed. This was ordered by the head of the MOSSAD, Mr. Middleman himself…!"

Half around the world Middleman was watching Al Jazzier in his little compound in Pretoria adjusting final details with Eli by instant messaging. Yuri and him were at Barajas, waiting for the connection to Barcelona. He smiled, even at his relatively advanced age this man was as sharp as a knife. He instructed Eli to get a glimpse of the Arab News Network. Only the President, Prime Minister and members of the security committee knew about the name of the Commander at MOSSAD. There was absolutely no massacre; there were no secret peace talks. That is was a political ploy from a very dirty and ambitious female politician whose disdain for his organization was part of her platform. By mentioning his name, they have jeopardized his effectiveness, the organization's power and the lives of his wife, children and grandchildren. The bitch will pay with interest. He picked up the phone, called. the Prime Minister and offered his resignation on the spot. Much to his surprise the Prime Minister, in a fatherly tone , rejected his resignation, promised to send all his family to safety in Milwaukee and promised him that : "…The witch will pay for this, the cabinet will convene to decide her fate…", were the last words uttered by a very pissed- off man.

In Barcelona, Bueso tried to get some resemblance of control in his interview, focusing on Alicia and the assignment in Madrid, which he saw fading away, like water held in his hand; inexorably falling in the floor.

"…This is exactly what the left in Israel have been alleging since the death of Rabin, that we should continue giving the Palestinian concessions until we either ran out victims or the ran out of homicide bombers…"
Weisel looked somewhat perturbed about Bueso's interruption; but rapidly recovered:
"…Well you know that the fact that these arguments are coming from the left, doesn't make the less valid…"
'…Validity of an argument is highly dependant on its truthfulness…!" responded Bueso
"…Touché…."', responded Weisel.
"…Anyway, I am officially removing my support from the governing party and I an official supporter of Labor under Ms. Fatima Banger…"
"…But she is advocating returning all land taken in 1968 back to the Palestinian without any precondition, even an idealist like you can recognize the danger of the situation…"

"…We have treated these people like sub-humans, not unlike the Nazi's treated us, minus the gas chambers and the deportations…"

"…You have to be messing with me…"said Bueso, both of whose parents were concentration camp survivors, without thinking of the consequences. Alicia looked at him in desperation, understanding that Madrid was no longer in the plans; he will be summarily fired as soon as the interview was over, with luck. He could get a job for Israel TV, cleaning toilets

"…Of course the horrors of the Holocaust are real, but so is the plight of these good people…"

"…These good people…? Are you on drugs Mr. Weisel? These "good people" indiscriminately assassinate innocent people for political gain…"

"…You are losing your objectivity, my dear fellow…" said Weisel with a hint of sarcasm.

"…Objectivity? You have to be kidding! Who care about objectivity! The future of our country depends on our ability to negotiate with this people, not completely surrender to them…!"

He looked at the watch twenty minutes have gone by and he introduced a break ,for ads, to give a chance for this traitor to escape the TV station without intervention from MOSSAD. Weisel thanked him for the opportunity and rapidly exited the studio

Immediately his cell phone rang, it was his father, calling from Tel Aviv:

"…What are you trying to do…?"

"…What do you mean…?"

"…Mr. Weisel is dead, he was buried in the Heroes Cemetery three days ago..."

"…Who did I interviews seconds ago…?"

"…I do not know, but this will require some interesting explaining, I am very sorry about the promotion, you and Alicia are welcome to stay with me. With your mother gone I have plenty of space. It will give me an excuse to see my beautiful grandson, Sam…"

He sign-language to Alicia the invitation, she responded" we might as well", and started picking her equipment.

Mohamed El Salem walked towards Bueso. He was the programming director for Al-Jazzier-Spain. Much to his surprise he was not mad, neither has he cleared his cubicle.

"…My dear Francisco, that was shear genius! What a coup for us! You held your ground against one of the most intelligent man alive. The promotion is yours. You will have a 30 min program of interviews with international dignitaries. What a coup! Of course they're a bonus in this for you and also for Alicia…" after that he kissed Bueso in both cheeks and left.

"…Congratulations son, are you coming to visit…?"
"…The high command has approved the operative…"
"…You mean Alicia...?"
"…Roger, we are a go…!"

Alicia approached him with malicious eyes. "…We could celebrate all night, darling, Sam is staying over with the Rosenberg, my sister is also in town and you know how much she enjoys Sam's company…"

All the monitors went on in the station and Mohamed's ugly face appeared in a formal news flash: "…Today in our studios we have the honor of a visit of our Big Brother in the faith, the last defender of Islam. He demonstrated a sharp interest and his vast knowledge on Israeli politics and shine a light towards how to defeat Israel for good, from within using their own corrupt politicians…"

Fatima 10 feet away was signing frenetically: ..." What is he talking about, sounds like Osama…"

Then it clicked, Osama had been in he studio posed as a dead Jewish Scholar and had single-handed planted the seed of suspicion among all Israel.

Mohamed continued: "…The voice patterns have been compared with pervious recordings and there is no question that our brother, Osama Ben Laden has visited our studios today…!"

In Madrid, Nascimento had picked up the last of his luggage. His two associates and him had been granted hunting licenses for Al Qauida in Lisbon and Spain. The news flash did not hit them by surprise. The Interpol had rented car and chaffer to drive them to Granada. Their driver introduced himself and after the equipment was in the trunk they sped off towards the super highway, towards Granada. The old man was looking forward to having Osama at his mercy.

He will find none. He wanted information, by the time he finished with him, he would have distilled all the information out. He liked the cognac metaphor. Making torture akin to applying heat to Champaign made the horror more elegant. After all there is always pain in Champaign! He will sell the elixir of information to all the intelligence services at a fee that will make the fifty million rewards pale in comparison. After that Osama will be irrelevant and he will dispose of him as he fitted. He had not forgotten the fact that the Saudis, and particular, Osama's father, had siphoned hundred of millions to the Nigerian government during the Biafran War.

It was pay back time.

Nobody in the car noticed the blue sedan Honda Del Sol convertible that fallow them three cars behind. Yuri was driving and Eli was adjusting his long-range microphone receptor for the microphone and GPS tracer they have planted in Nascimento's car .

After spotting Nascimento in the luggage area Eli had decided to forgo the plans to connect to Granada directly. Instead, they rented a sport car and fallowed their escort, after implanting a GPS devise in the back bumper of their car.

Yuri, who was anxious to return to Osama, made the comment that it may have been more efficient to plant a bomb in the car, and get over it.

Eli made a mental note not to lower his guard. This man was a damaged goods, to be mistrusted at all time.

Chapter 26
[[Rincón: Thursday Afternoon]]

It was Thursday evening. All the archers present have been practicing both Zen Archery and the tango.

"…Do you think we will ever be ready…?" asked Mr. Manuel, more as an iced breaker, than anything else. Emma had been solemnly pissed all day; both at him and at the world. This could be something he said, something he forgot to say or something that she suffered twenty years ago. Life with Emma was like working clearing mine fields, which he had done in his stint with the foreign legion. You never knew which was alive, which was quite a dud. Because of that you treated every mine as it was the last one you were going to touch.

Emma smiled for the first time. "…It depends of what you want me to be ready and when, big boy! I am very worried about this whole affair. We should had have weeks, not days to practice. We are still looking for the last man. One of Jose's disciples broke his shoulder in a competition and will not be able to join us…"

"…Alas…! Have faith my dear! The Lord will provide. Just keep passing the arrows the way you are and at least we will have a chance to survive…" He was happy; she was worried, not pissed. He might even get some action tonight with the hottie. Life was good, at least for now. All the archer equipment had been delivered: we had four thousand arrows, more than enough. And yes, they were short an archer, but they still had more than 36 hrs to go. The living God will provide for sure.

Jerry was practicing both the Tango and Zen Archery with Zola. Moreno had refused to have direct physical contact with Jerry, so he had practiced with Garcia who had been getting despondent, partly because Moreno's incessant strive for perfection and because his wife had been unable to join him at Rincon because of the flu epidemic.

Today they had practiced more than six hours thanks to protective vests provided by the monks. Jerry was worrying about errors when they fought without them. He had grown accustomed to all these people, had developed certain affection for all, especially Jose and Garcia. He had accepted a job with Zola, his kids will have a future independent on crime. While he was musing, his cell phone rang with his wife's ring tone. She was a big girl and could defend herself, so he had not been worried about her.

He picked up the phone and opened it.
"…Jerry…?"
"…Yes dear, where are you…?"
"…Can you pick up us at Aguadilla, we are five, have a very important guest. Are you still short of manpower…?"
"…We could use a warm body that could do some archery..."
"…Would you like to meet the second ranked Olympic archer in Switzerland..."
"…If I had the choice I would go for number one, but I guess number two will do just fine..."
"…Please pick us as soon as possible, be discreet..."
"…How can I be discreet when I am picking you up in one Zola's limousines..."
"…Get your ass down here and don't argue with me..."
"…How did my old friend treat you…?"
"…First she wanted to sell me and the boys as sex slaves, then she changed her mind and wanted everybody dead, naturally the witch is dead..."
'…Naturally. How was Switzerland…?"
"…We never made into Swiss territory, we spend most of the time in Lisbon, getting money and planning to destroy Al Qauida…"
"…Wow…! We are getting international aren't we…?"

"...Stop the chit chat, the Pope is not going to continue to play Rummy with your kids until the second coming of Christ; he has a schedule to keep. The pilot needs to practice with you all..."

"...Does he know the Tango? Humor me and asked him..." said Jerry, in a tone she knew well and meant business. A couple of seconds passed and the pilot picked up the phone.

"...I am a little rusty, but I am sure that if I practice I can keep up..."

"... You need to integrate the Tango to Zen Archery, we got the instructions from Mr. Gardel's ghost...!"

"...Mr. Vaerga, are you on crack-cocaine...? What utter nonsense is this Boloney...?"

"...We will be picking you all in 30 minutes; ask my wife to give you classes, she Tangos well. Can the Pope Tango...? a couple of minutes passed in silence and the Pope came on the phone.

"...Jerry, my son, you have a wonderful family. I do know how to Tango, if it is important to the success of your mission, I personally will teach the pilot and anybody that needs it how to Tango, in exchange I want to eat some local fare when we get to Rincon..."

"...I will bring an order for everybody there from the best restaurant in town, El Rincon Tropical..."

"...Hurry up, I am starving..."

"...On my way, your Holiness..."

"...God speed my son..." The phone went silent.

"...Mr. Zola, I need your limousine. I need to pick up family and the Pope at the airport..."

"...We will join you..." said Ignacious and Pereira, without hesitating a second.

"...Ratzinger is here, what a sense of timing..." said the Llama, smiling.

"...Why don't we all go pick up Ratzinger, then we go to the restaurant together, my treat..."

"...His holiness will be disappointed..." said Jerry

"…No he won't as my monks had prepared traditional Vietnamese vegetarian appetizers that can bring a dead man out of his grave and bring ardor to a lover's heart…"

"…I want two orders to go..."said Mr. Manuel

"…Ditto…", echoed Jose.

"…We need to bring weapons, I have a gut feeling that the Babylonians will try something tonight, maybe a preventive strike, maybe even a bomb or an assassin sweep…" said Moreno

Garcia, who had grown accustomed to the accuracy of his boss's hunches did not hesitated for a second. He opened the trunk of the car and took a gym bag out, opened it up and offered the contents to all: "…We have mostly 45's and ammunition, sniper rifles, a couple of Berettas and one Uzi with only two clips, I will take the Uzi as I have more experience..."

"…I beg to differ…' said Emma with a smile "…I took classes from Mr. Uzi himself and used it in combat on several different occasions, the MOSSAD..."

"…Okay, Ducky…" said Garcia, highly disappointed that he will not be in charge of the firepower and handling the Uzi and the clips to her…"

"…We will rather use the bow and arrow…" said Jose and his wife in unison..." We need practice anyway, I have my bag of tricks with me and my wife is very proficient in the use of all of them…"

Moreno made a mental note of that statement, ounce a terrorist, always a terrorist. This was a truce, not the end of the war.

The group got in the limousine, armed to their teeth, went to the restaurant. Garcia and Moreno were dropped to check out the place the rest drove to Aguadilla to pick up the group at the airport.

"…I don't like it…" said Moreno, adding: "… too difficult to defend, many angles of attack, surrounding buildings are taller, albeit not by much, this is Baghdad all over again…"

"…The problem with you is that can't forget Baghdad...."

"...Of all people, my dear Garcia, you are the one that should not forget Baghdad, as you barely left the place alive! Or do you have amnesia...?"

Garcia looked at the floor deeply embarrassed. He was alive because Moreno had dragged his sorry butt out of harm's way after that IED blew the tank he was riding. Everybody else inside and in the perimeter died either of the explosion or because of the fallow up sniper fire.

"...Lets talk to the owner, get the activities room, and secure the perimeter as well as possible and lets start praying..."

"...Pray for what? Success? Peace...?."

"...Rain, lots of it, it would force them to come to us, rather than pinning us down like roaches, from a distance, the rain will make snipers less effective. Rain is our friend...."

They entered the restaurant. Moreno went directly to the kitchen. Nobody was alarmed as they knew him, and knew his business, they also that he was off duty and went to visit the cook and owner.

"...Hey Ramon, what's up Carnal...?' he shouted as he entered the room.

The ugliest Chicano you ever seen came out of the steam in the kitchen, cutting knife in hand, ready for action until he saw him, Pancho Villa moustache, his face made a map of the moon by very aggressive and untreated acne. He smiled widely showing all golden frontal teeth.

"...Frankus Maximus...! Hey Maria...! Look who was pushed here by the rain...!"Outside it was starting to drizzle. Maria looked like a model, a very strong woman, very athletic, had an artificial leg courtesy of the US army, as she had also served in Baghdad. She looked like a mixture between Sofia Loren and Angelina Jolie. She jumped on Frank and gave him a wet kiss in the mouth.

Ramon feigned disgust and anger and grabbed his wife with his muscular arms into his arms and gave her a long French kiss

"…Get a room…" added Garcia as he entered the kitchen. "…Maria I still can't see what you see in this ugly son of a female dog…"

"…In Baghdad, my soul was lost and my body in disrepair. And this hunk of a man, never abandoned me, or left my side until we arrived in the field hospital. After that he gave me a good reason to live, three beautiful children and a good, clean life…"

"…Not to mention the fact that I am hung like a horse…!"

"…Did I ever mention that he is hung like a Burro…!"

"…Horse..."

"…Burro..." said she with dose fiery eyes looking directly into his.

"…OK, Burro…" he surrendered, smiling. "…You get the point…"

They all laugh , except Garcia, who over the years carried the stigma of not been able to do anything for Maria that night as he was also being hit, her artificial leg present there as a reminder of his failures in life.

"…Garcia come here and give us a hug, we still love you in spite of yourself…"

He timidly went to her and hugged her, this was fallowed by a bear hug from Ramon.

"…I know you have the hot for my wife, If you come on to her like this again, I will cut your balls..." said Ramon jokingly.

"…Too late for that my friend, I have been .married for three years now, there are no balls left to cut…" he said with a smile .

Maria smiled and kissed him in the forehead. "…I know you have always loved me and that you feel personally responsible for my lost of limb. No need to torture yourself. Life has been very good to me and I am very happy, so be happy tonight for my sake, OK…?"

"…OK, for you I will be happy, just because you ask me to be…"

"…Your wife called, still tied up at the hospital because of the flu epidemic, will try to join you tomorrow…"

"…What bring you here tonight, to our humble establishment…?"

"…Ramon are you Catholic…" asked Moreno.

"…Born and raised, married in the Church and all the kids are also baptized in the Church…"

"…Well you are up for a treat! Carnal, in less than an hour Pope Benedictus (a.k.a. Ratzinger) will be eating in your restaurant..!"

"…We are making the reservation, securing the perimeter, checking for bombs and securing the place from attacks, Zola picks up the tab.…"

"…The Zola…! Politics make strange bedfellows, ah? I hope he is not expecting too much..."

"…He is a cool guy. We will start working for him next week. We are looking forward..."

Ramon joined the two looking for bombs, calculating which part of the building offered the best chance at security for the Pope and anybody else. No bombs anywhere. Taller buildings surrounded them: The Rincon Lumber Yard, The Transmissions Palace, two empty lots, growing the local version of the guinea pig grass, bad places to hide because of the rats and above all the rabid mongoose.

The Spaniards, who colonized it and pillaged it for almost 4oo years, imported them to The Island. After that the Empire had colonized and pillaged for another 1oo more. These animals were brought to kill the local snakes, they in turn would occasionally bit the sugar cane workers. The only problem is that their sleeping patterns were different, so they seldom met. The mongoose than ever bit more sugar cane workers by the snakes. Ah! The ironies of life!

After choosing guarding posts, the three old friends walk inside where Maria had served Garcia and Moreno. They had to eat ahead of the bunch and secure the area. They ate in a hurry, almost without tasting, almost impossibility with Maria's fines local cooking. Moreno explained his theory that a woman's cooking reflected her lovemaking. If that was the case, Ramon was a very lucky man indeed! His nights were filled with variety and spice! A smile escaped Moreno's face and was picked by Maria, who slapped him with the wood serving spoon across the face adding:

"…You don't know the half of it, and can not imagine more than ten percent…!"

"…Is she a mind reader now…?" asked Moreno

"…She is spooky, I thought it was just me, you know, we have been married so long, but no, she can read most men's mind, added Ramon…"

"…My dear, men's minds are very short books, and ninety percent is filled with desire…" retorted back Maria.

"…Touché… added Garcia in between chewing and swallowing.

'…Yes I know, we are one-dimensional, concrete and stupid…" added Moreno.

"…And most of the time we think with the wrong head…' added Ramon, smiling with his big Chicano smile, looking like Charles Bronson, on steroids.

"…And without women, men go back to a primitive form, where there is no love or mercy, in which the silver backs dominate and the others are use as currency among the dominant ones. That is why there is no God in jail, in order to have His presence, women have to be present...or something like that…", added Garcia in a self mocking way, having devour his plate, being able now to utter more than one word at a time.

"…Carnal, you have been married for too long…you have adopted the forbidden language of womanhood…and the battle cry of the Chicano Feminists: "Hembra y Diosa..." You are lost, you have officially lost your place around the camp fire…"

"…Perhaps you would like to join these two around the campfire…", retorted Maria ,with one hand in the apron and another one with the big wooden spoon ready for the kill, less than two feet from her husband, who jumped over the kitchen counter, putting a respectable distance between him and his beautiful bride.

"…Gentlemen this is called a strategic retreat. A safe distance is about five feet. I recommend one while you can…"said Ramon.

"…You have always been a coward. You never confront me, you avoid any argument, you prefer to be with these two asses around the campfire…" added Maria getting impatient and annoyed at her husband agility and physical power.

"…You know well that I prefer to be with you around any campfire, especially in the early morning hours when is cold and you like to ride the Burro…"

Garcia and Moreno abandoned the kitchen, Maria change into all the shades of pink and red, looking more like the Grand Canyon at sundown than her usual light tan. Her wooden spoon flew, like a circus knife, hitting her husband smack in the middle of his eyes.

"…You are lucky I am in a good mood. Go screw yourself …." she said turning around to attend to the stove where she was preparing the food for Zola's group.

"…Man she loves you. That could have been a knife…"said Garcia.

"…If that was a knife, there would have been a dead Burro by now…'said a voice from the kitchen.

"…She doesn't mince words, Ah! Carnales! if you knew this woman as I know her…!"

"…Crazy Bato, go help these Maricones to secure the perimeter, if you behave and stop embarrassing me, you may still get some today…" said Maria from the kitchen.

"…Hey man, I would be silent as a monk…" said Garcia.

"…On the contrary, the more annoyed I get her now, the hornier she acts latter, however when you get her to change colors like that, she is in for a vengeance …an all nighter…!"

"…I heard that…"said Maria from the kitchen

"…We better leave now…' said Moreno, tired of his friends strange form of foreplay. As he headed towards the outside, it was raining steadily, making sharp-shooting difficult if not impossible. "…One point for us…" he thought. As they arrived at the entrance of the restaurant he commanded Garcia to guard the back, close to the back entrance and the large trash container. The green containers had Zola© written in the side, to remind everybody that this man's tentacles were everywhere.

He gave Ramón the two loaded Berettas; and sent him to the Parking Booth and instructed him to turn off the light inside the booth or unscrew the bulb. He wanted to be in the shadows, not on the display case. Then he ran towards a group of Mango trees, climbing the tallest one with some difficulty because of the tree trunk been slippery with the rain, halfway up. He could see the buildings from here clearly, Garcia and Ramon had both control of the two empty lots. The three of them were crack shots, could hit 100% of the time at 400 yards, either the head or the heart, then efficiency went down to about 25% at 1000 yards. Now it was a matter of waiting, he picked up the phone and informed Vaelga that they were ready and in position, he informed him that they were ten minutes from delivery. They would not have to wait long.

Then he saw it. Actually he felt it. In Baghdad he had developed this sixth sense. No, he could not see dead people. Instead, he could judge dumb ones well. No he was able to perceive the presence of people in the area without seen them, general location kind of deal. Nothing, by any means precise. You never knew if they were friends or foe, of course. On a couple of occasions he almost shot Garcia dead, as he tried to play practical jokes when o guard duty, he almost died on several occasions.
He sensed a group of people in the roof of the transmission building, several "entities" in the roof of transmission repair place.

He sensed some more in the two fields. He could not see his friends now. He prayed that the mongoose would be awake to bother them enough that they would betray their positions.

He slipped down the tree without hurting himself too bad. He jogged in the rain hoping not to slip, toward the back of the building. There was no fire stairs or ladder around this area. They must had rope their way up. He looked around in the worsening rain without being able to se much. He closed his eyes, which were as worthless as in a sand storm and felt his way around. After he spent a couple of minutes in this task, one hand on the wall and one ahead of him, the rope hit him in the head. He opened his eyes and saw it there. The men upstairs were not professional, as they miscalculated the length of the rope by six feet. Usually you wanted more than enough, especially if you intended to rappel down for a fast escape, as a short rope will slow you down.

Moreno started climbing, placing the rope between his legs, and using only his upper torso and his feet against the wall for support. "…This is where the four hundred push up a day pay off…" he murmured in low voice to himself. He slipped a couple of times. He had no gloves and was using the sleeves of his trench coat as gloves to prevent rope burn with mixed results. He arrived at the roof and slipped in, with his back to the wall.

There was a promontory about fifteen feet away. Six men were getting ready a mortar for firing. He heard them speak in Arabic and Farsi. Iranians and Iraqi! First he thought they were there to get their revenge against Zola. However he realized that they mentioned the Pope by his German name on several occasions.

So, Al Qauida was involved with the New Babylonians and they were here doing their dirty work. They were about to start shooting when the darkness was made clear by a shot coming from the opposite side of the roof, hitting the man with the projectiles through his left eye , falling dead on the floor. The mortar shell started rotating towards him. He aimed and fired, causing the shell to explode and detonate all other mortar shell. The explosions that fallowed kill the rest of the assassins.

At that point, like if a signal had been given, men came firing out of each of the empty lots.

Ramon and Garcia, both hidden in the darkness and protected by concrete started shooting at the source of the fire. One by one they started falling, with great cries of help in Arabic spiced with an occasional curse. Within two minutes there was silence. No more shooting no more cries.

Zola's limousine arrived and Garcia and Ramon ran to open the doors and whisk everybody away to safety, into the banquet room. They left Vaelga and José in charge of security and climbed to the second floor to survey the area. A balcony with two spotlights surrounded the second floor, each one pointing towards an empty lot. García turned on the lights and there were fifteen bodies laying motionless on each lot.

"…Should we check them out…?" asked Ramon, more like an intended joke.

"…No, they are probably booby-trapped. We will wait until they go into rigor and then the traps will explode…""

"…Sounds like a plan to me, but we still need to check the unexploded ones…."

"…There is nothing more anti-climatic that a suicide bomber that only kills himself…"

'…Amen! Carnal. Amen…!" said Ramon, smiling…."

On the roof Moreno had rolled away from his previous position and taken refuge behind the air conditioning unit. Whoever killed the first terrorist was still armed and potentially an enemy. He took his fighting dagger out of his pocket. He carried it as a lucky charm.

Then he saw the person, gun in hand advancing toward his previous position. He crawled behind him and went for the attack, gun in hand. He stopped when he recognized the smell of her perfume, Charlie.

"...Jesus Martha, if is not your husband, is going to be me who will kill you..."

Martha turned around, gun in hand and pointed to Moreno's head, pulling an imaginary trigger and placing the gun back in her holster.

"...You are dead Mr. Moreno, I had the great Moreno at my mercy! The Macheteros will never forget me. I am a legend..." said Martha.

"...You are a sick woman, Martha..." said Moreno greatly relieved he was still alive.

"...Are you exited, Mr. Frank Moreno, as I am very exited. How about a quicky up here..."

"...Are you nuts, have you no shame...?"

"..I am nuts for your nuts, come to me Papa-Bear...!"

"...I would rather die..." he said running towards the age of the building, grabbing the rope and repelling rapidly down the wall, leaving the crazy half dressed witch behind. He rapidly ran towards the main entrance of the restaurant, greeting his friends in the second floor and entering the restaurant to greet everybody inside.

He met José in the hallway and explained what had happened .

..We left her behind, she knows the terrain, her father owns the transmission building, I hope she helped you..."

"...I almost killed the nymphomaniac..."

"...Saved again by her perfume, eh...? Was she all exited...?"

"...You better believe it...!"

"...I have nothing to look forward tonight, other than an all nighter with this horny witch..."

"...My most sincere apologies for exiting your wife into a sexual frenzy..."

"…It is a dirty job, but somebody needs to do it…" said Jose.

"…Amen! Have you eaten yet? This place is incredible. You should try the fish stew, it will brig a dead man from the grave, great for hangovers too…"

"…I will take your great suggestion. May need the strength for later…"

Ramon and Garcia made a last sweep of the empty lots with the spotlights, confirming the body count and descended to the first floor to share the rest of the meal with their friends. The Pope and the Llama were jointly giving the blessings, the food was served.

Martha joined them, as they had left an empty space at the table. She graciously acknowledged the presence of the Pope, thank Mr. Zola for hosting the event. and Maria for preparing it and sat down beside Jose, looking at Moreno and told him straight:

"…You owe me one, moron…"

"…Oh…! Thank you very much, I guess…"

"…You are very welcome…" she said with a wink, as she buttoned the last button on her shirt.

Then addressing Ramon and Garcia added: "…Has the perimeter been secured…?"

"…Thirty casualties, no motion through two confirmatory scans, we should start hearing explosions if they are booby-trapped in about half an hour' they have learned those tricks in the Sunni Triangle. Let them bleed and get stiff, before you go to check for documents. You have all the time in the world, they don't. Let them blow themselves, then you get the large pieces buried, and the Iraqi dogs and crows will eat the rest, quite efficiently.

"…Keep alive, don't drink any alcohol now, we need to be alert, they may have reinforcements…"

The dinner continued uneventful, dessert was served. Then the first explosion from the fields
was heard. This was fallowed by twenty-nine more. All the assassins have been booby-trapped.

Both Ramón, Garcia and Moreno kept the explosion count. All confirmed thirty.

"…Lets rap up this dinner and go to the Green House, the police will be here soon…" They herd the sirens, three patrol cars and a SWAT team. They inspected the empty fields, and witnessed the carnage. They could not believe it. They then drove to the restaurant where Zola had just paid for the meal and was ready to split. The commander car stopped, an imposing muscular blond man, with a M16 and bulletproof vest ascended out of the car, fallowed by all the masked member of the SWAT team.

Moreno and Garcia walked to greet them. They have served with Gavin Vicens in Iraq, did not particularly consider him a friend, but on the other hand he was not an enemy either.

"…Carajo…! I should have known that you too were involved with this crap! You two are bad news alone and when together, Jesus saves us! said Gavin in an unfriendly, exasperated tone. Thirty men…!

"…Top of the hour to you too, old friend…. said Garcia

"…You are no friend of mine…I am taking you two with me, at least…!"

A voice came from the table. The Pope stood up and with a very calm voice said:

"…You are not doing such a thing, this men are part of the Swiss Army Guard, so are all these men, woman and children, I have the paper work here somewhere in my attache case to prove it, so they are foreign diplomats with immunity ,so back off…!"

"…You are pulling my hair? Arrest everybody hear, including

this old man…!"

"…I have no interest in pulling my hair or intentions of staying at your prison one minute, I am Ratzinger, most recent and perhaps the last Pope, obey or you will face the wrath of God, remember there is no place to hide from the Father of Creation…!"

Captain Vicens finally recognized who he was talking to and ordered his men back in the car. All obeyed, except for one, who had no intention of leaving. He raised his M16 in the direction of the Pope, adding: "…You will die today, for the glory of the soon to be born Son of the Devil…"

Time stood still as everybody froze in terror. A butcher knife flew from the kitchen at high speed incrusting the man in his forehead, a second later another hit him in the heart, not giving him time to aim or shoot. Everybody hit the floor. A third knife hit him in the gun hand. He collapsed, dead before reaching the floor.

"…Nice shooting dear, you have not lost your touch, angel…" said Ramon.

"…Don't mention it darling, come here to help me load the dishwasher, while they pick up the trash…" Everybody understood she was talking about the masked dead man and laughed. Ramon gave his wife a big hug and a kiss in the forehead adding: "…that is my girl…"

Moreno grabbed Vicens by the elbow and exclaimed: "…We need to talk, this is nothing, Saturday we are expecting thousand to attack the town plaza and church…"

"…We do need to talk…" answered Giovanni, putting his gun in the holster again, in shock.

Chapter 27
[[Road to Granada: Spain]]

The road to Granada was full of curves, dry and boring, like most sister in laws. Yuri was still traumatized by the abusive behavior he received from the intelligence apparatus, orchestrated by his estranged wife, now a powerful member of the Knesset and possibly future Prime Minister of Israel. He did not trust Eli, even though he had been descent towards him, a good handler who treated him with respect and who had suggested ways of avoiding using the explosive in his head and to continue spying for Israel, to help to dismantle the Al Qauida organization. The Israeli secret service had extensive experience infiltrating Palestinian and Arabs organizations, usually in enemy territory. However they never had a GPS in anybody's head. They drove until the reached Granada. Nascimento drove to the Hotel Casa Morisca in Victoria Street.

"…Amazing coincidence..." commented Yuri. "…We have stayed in this hotel in the past, heavily disguised. Some of the employees are Al Qauida sympathizers and helped us navigate through the city and to obtain munitions and weapons when we where planning the Madrid Train Bombings. It was easier to get C4 in Granada than a good chocolate truffle…"

"…Is there a chance he may use the same hotel…?"

"…Possibly, as Weisel. They're lots of sympathizers in the staff. I imagine that the defunct Weisel is the most appreciated Jew in the Arab world. Who ever made up Osama is not keeping up with current events…."

"…The traditional press, which are arrogant and drunk with power failed to remember that he died three days ago! The bloggersphere must be full of reports, with picture of Mr. Wiesel's funeral. The New York Times will issue a correction in page 13, section D, just before the Obituaries. They would not acknowledge some mistake. The press is the fourth power, one hundred percent arrogance (full of themselves) and no accountability..."

They got out of the car, and fallowed Nascimento to the reception where they registered with another agent. Eli obtained his room's location. Yuri, been recognized by the Al Qauida's operative, was informed that Mr. Weisel will be arriving to the hotel shortly. Eli requested a room for three days. He was given the last room in the hotel. They went in to freshen. Eli left a microphone in Nascimento's room, fallowing the bellboy, leaving a bottle of wine with the microphone in the cork. This way they could monitor the competition and act if needed. Nobody, but nobody, ever opened those complementary wine bottles because the quality of the wine is at best questionable, except in the very expensive resorts.

Eli had been in the business since he was fourteen. Even though everybody called Middleman "uncle" he was truly related to him and was the only one in the agency with that right. Middleman was accustomed to hear from his agents at least ounce a day, especially since the inception of e-mail. He personally checked his e-mails every four hours. There was no spam in that domain, just encrypted messages that were the bloodline of MOSSAD.

Eli opened his Blueberry and sent the fallowing message:
"...Uncle, arrived at Granada, we are at the Moorish city, no question about it, my brother had a good flight and is in good spirits, our cousins found a good room and we are in constant communication. We think that they want to compete for the graces of Uncle Samuel, please advice..."

About ten minutes passed before the response came through:
"...Dear nephew, don't let your cousins intimidate you, Uncle Samuel's attentions are rightfully yours, arrange for your brother to stay with him for a season, be sure you meet your uncle in person, ask for a truce between us, we still have insurance over your brother, we need some leverage so that we can control Aunt Fatima. If "the

tribes" choose her, I will not quit as elder of our clan, they will need to eliminate me, I don't think she has enough clout yet to force a resignation or send me to fish in Galilee. Hope to hear from you…"

Eli showed the e-mail to Yuri who was astonished:
"…Uncle wants a truce with Osama…? He must be getting old…" said Yuri.
"…Actually is not a bad idea…" said Eli. "…The conservatives can defeat Rita, if the level of rocket attacks and the suicide bombers go down and they run on a "though security" platform. This appears to be a clever plan more than a desperate attempt. A vote of no confidence is unlikely before the election. The Prime Minister has a weak coalition, but a functional one. And they are still riding on Sharon's memory as a "warrior of peace". I have been living all my life among such warriors, Israeli and Arab, there is no peace in them, but they have a plenty of war and hate..."

Eli was really sorry he had not met this man before. He had several hours to share, he will have to suck information like a sponge. Very few people understood Osama like this man who had been his war and bodyguard and secretary for several years. Since the Afghan-Russian wars until present they have shared shelter and tactics, blood and sweat, triumphs and defeats.

It was a real shame that in order to pacify Fatima Newman (her third and late husband) this man was essentially forced to go back to a life they despised him for. If we had a couple of weeks we will get enough information about this organization to effectivelly neutralize it, and eventually destroy it.

Yuri eventually broke the silence:
"…How did my wife become so powerful…? How did she manage to influence military intelligence so much…? How come she gained enough influence to be a serious candidate for prime minis-

ter...?"

"...I will answer that if you tell me why Osama has not died of kidney failure. Is that a deal...?

Yuri looked at his watch and was pensive, like thinking weather or not to tell Eli but he went ahead: "...Its time for the prayers, do you mind...?" He had accepted his fate, that he will require to go back and that he would continue to be a devout Muslim, at least to act like one, in order to survive among the cutthroats, who will behead him without thinking it twice, if they had any suspicion he was a spy, they would not trust him in spite of decades of loyal service to Osama.

"...He is still alive because..." he took his shirt off to show a large posterior scar in the right side, "...I was the donor for his kidney transplant..."

Eli was stunned. He recovered himself, and smiled. He continued to smiled and added: "...Perfect match...?"

"...I am Osama's Kidney, immune system and heart, ready at the order, long live my commander...!"

"...Amazing my friend, did he pay you...?"

"...Twenty million dollars, hiding in my Abu Dabbi bank account..."

Eli checked the microphone receiver in his computer, there was absolute silence. Nascimento must be wining and dining his staff, he thought to himself

"...Well that is a hard act to fallow, my friend, but I will try. Rita was heavily damaged in that raid. That night she got pregnant, eventually gave birth to twins, one yours the other belonging to your Palestinian contact, we checked by DNA. She raised both and developed this Messianic complex, fed by her first husband, the Jerusalem Gazette editor, Mr. Selzsman, she established deep contact with the Jewish Marxist Leninists in New York, who would sacrifice Israel in the altar of internationalism. She was their Czarina, and they contributed to her cause, along with the prominent Hollywood Jewish Mafia, who would sell the greater Israel to pacify their crazy extreme left liberals..."

"...So what happened to her first husband...?" asked Yuri.

"...Heart attack during sex, apparently ritual strangulation, the man came and went at the same time..."

Yuri smiled, she was quite wild and quite deviant. He never went for any of that, he was very happy he never did, or it could have been him to die also.

"...The second husband was Moshe Perez. The Bill Gates of Israel, multi billionaire, weapons manufacturer. Had rights to reproduce any Israeli weapons patents from the Uzi to the Tiger tank, to the Massada intercontinental missile and everything in between.

He gave her legitimacy among the defense- industrial complex and bankrolled a second term for her in parliament. He died of a heart attack during sex, electrocuted, a flaming ass..."

"...Ouch...! How is Mr. Newman's health...?"

"...Mr. Newman controls semiconductors, programming, computers...is impotent, so he hires butlers to please Mrs. Kinkiness. So far three had died. They call her the Praying Mantis, every male she has, and she bites their head off..."

"...MOSSAD does not respect this woman at all, I assume..."

"...You assume right, we have contingency plans to assassinate her, if she becomes Prime Minister. I am not kidding, she is not to be trusted, especially with the messianic complex, and she is very dangerous..."

"...I will volunteer for the job; it would be my pleasure to see the witch suffer..."

Yuri then went for the nitti gritty: Name, addresses, contacts in Europe, the United States, The Philippines, Indonesia and Africa, sleeper cells in United States, Canada and Mexico; also safe houses in Italy and the Northern Europe. Explosive depot in Syria. Hidden WMD in the desert, transferred there by the Chetchen soldiers two weeks before the fall of before the fall of Baghdad, in Russian vehicles and uniforms, with the help of French Legionaries, massacred in the Bhaka Valley by the Syrian security forces. He recorded everything he said for two hours, until Yuri was exhausted and he realized that Nascimento was back. He transferred the recording to his laptop, compressed all the audio and e-mailed to Middleman. Months of intelligence gathering would not have produced this wealth of information. Middleman acknowledged receiving the recording and wished good luck with the "family reunion".

Eli started monitoring Nascimento's room . He added absentminded: "…If you are alive, you will have first shot at the witch, you have my word of honor…"
"…Appreciate it…" responded Yuri.
The microphone went to life:
"…Rodriquez, when is Osama due to arrive…? Is he still dressed as Mr. Weisel…? How big is his escort…? Did you tell the busboy that we were from the press…?"
"…He is arriving between seven and eight PM, dressed as Weisel. Have seven bodyguards. All veterans of the Afghan-Russian War…"
"…Those are tough cookies! I don't like the set up, a little bit. The odds are stacked against us…'
"…Boss…" confirmed Gonzalez. "…The odds have always been stacked against us…!"
"…Why don't we get locals from the syndicate to even things up. I am sure that they will be willing to come and help, even if they don't get part of the booty…" added Rodriquez.
Nascimento picked up his cell, and attempted to call on several occasions, but it was in vain, as the wine bottle was also a digital signal scrambler. Eli signaled Yuri to fallow him. They went down the stairs toward the telephone operator room. There an Al Qauida sympathizer managed the phone bank. Yuri caught up with Eli, was easily recognized by the man.

"…We need to intercept a call from room 203, we are trying to avoid a great bloodshed in this place, if you play with us, everybody will be secured and alive…" said Yuri

"…I am game, my name is Raul, what is yours…?"

"…I am Omar, but my best friends call me Yuri…"

"…OK, we need a second line that you can transfer us, so the intended targets never get the calls…"

"…There is an old telephone booth, is petty much sound proof. Is in the lobby I will transfer you there. The rest is yours..."

"…Thank you…" said Eli and sprinted to the lobby about 30 yards away. He got into the old, London-type cabin and after taking off the "NO TRABAJA" sign from the door, he entered the cabin and closed it behind him. The upper light came to life.

"…Just what I need, I am in public display, I might as well have a spotlight, I might as well have a neon sign over my head with the words MOSSAD flashing…" he said in the hope that the cabin really was sound-proof. He waited a couple of minutes and the phone rang. It was Raul.

"…I will connect you now, you are supposed to be Jose Salamanca, the local crime syndicate lord. You run truckers. I hope your Spanish is good…"

"…It is better than my Russian, much worst than my German. But it will have to do…" said Eli remembering the year he spent learning Spanish at the Toledo University, where MOSSAD had sent him when he was a lowly intern. The best Spanish he learned was with Ramona Leal, the assistant professor he enjoyed during most of that year. What a Spitfire! He caught himself saying in laud voice.

The phone rang.

"…Jose Salamanca, to serve God and You, not necessarily in that order…!" his accent was Andalucian, his diction crisp and clean ,so far so good he thought to himself. In the back of his mind he could see Raul and Yuri, laughing to death on the floor.

"…Mr. Salamanca, this is Mr. Nascimento. I am here in serious need of manpower, I am hunting a rat and will need 10-15 of your best men, preferably armed to their teeth...."

"...Mr. Nascimento, you must take me for a dope, do you think I was born yesterday, you sound like a cop...!" Eli smiled at himself, as he started used regional idioms he picked from Ms. Leal.

"...Mr. Salamanca, I assure you that I am not taking for a fool, and that indeed I am no cop, I deal with weapons from Lisbon..."

"...Oh...! That Nascimento. My boys had delivered to your some Czechoslovakian automatics in the past..." he said, realizing he was already getting away from generalities to specifics.

"...God, you have an excellent memory, that was more than three years ago...!"

Eli sighted, he had not screwed it yet: "...Lets talk business, my friend. For 10-15 son-a-bitches of mine, armed to "the teeth" I want ten percent of the action plus fifty per man, one hundred for the dead ones, will provide the weapons and munitions, you provide the target..."

"...Targets, all Al Qauida, including Osama himself..."

"...Well, well, my friend that is no simple target, and there is bound to be more casualties. How about if we double everything..."

"...How about if we pay you what you originally requested and in cash, prior to the job..."

"...My friend, "a paid musician always leave you short" you know the saying..." said Eli to spice the conversation. This might work after all, it's going smoothly, and he has taking bait, hook, line and reel.

"...I will take my chances, do we have a deal...?"

"...Yes, we do..." said Eli. "...Where do we want my guys, and at what time...?"

"...Casa Morisca, in three hours..." said Nascimento and hanged the phone, Eli joined the other two.

"...Good going, Jew boy..." said Raul. "...Now what...?"

"...As far as I am concerned, you know too much and have to be eliminated..." said Eli.

Both Yuri and Raul opened eyes widely and froze. They were waiting for a gunshot, but Eli gave them a middle finger instead and started laughing. He hated been called a Jew boy, except when Ramona Leal uttered the words, which usually suggested she wanted loving. Her usual complete phrase was: "...Recess is over Jew Boy, is time to earn your keep..." "...Definitively a Spitfire, indeed..."

The other two men were relieved, and moderately amused. Raul broke the silence.

"...Mr. MOSSAD, it is hard to hide your ethnicity, you the poster child for IDF recruitment..."

"...You would be indeed surprised, as I was, when I was assigned to return this running dog back to his master. All the cards will be on the table, and I think I will b able to negotiate with the Commander. We do know how to negotiate, and we know how to fight when cornered; that is why we have survived as an Idea for five thousand years and why, with Jehovah's blessing will last another five thousand..."

"...But in order to negotiate with the Commander, you must have things to offer him, little presents..."

"...I have many aces up my sleeve, I think he will be willing to consider my offers..." said Eli.

"...So what do we do with Nascimento and his henchmen...?" asked Yuri.

"...We take the direct approach: we negotiate. If it does not work, we neutralize..." said Eli. He paused for a moment, taking a camera from his side pack. He looked at Raul, who automatically smiled, mostly out of reflex. Instead of shooting at him he pointed toward the picture of the king behind him. He shot the first picture and a dart sped out of the camera, hitting the picture. This was fallowed by a dull explosion, which destroyed the frame and glass. There was no more Juan Carlos in the background.

Yuri understood at that point that Eli was a man that was better to have as a friend than an enemy. Cool, calmed, cerebral, collected and a faithful servant of the state of Israel.

Eli motioned Yuri to fallow him up the stairs. He obeyed his request and up they went. They knocked at the door. Rodriquez, armed with only a smile, opened the door.
"…May I help you…?"
"…We are here to speak with Mr. Nascimento…"
"…Are you from the syndicate…?"
"..No, I am from MOSSAD, he knew my father and I am here to pay my respects and to see if we can convince him to back off from what you are trying to do…"
Nascimento approached the door, he signaled him to come in. Both were frisked for weapons, none were found .
"…I am Ed Goldman's son, my sister is Perla Goldman..."
An automatic smile came out of his lips, Perla's first case, ten years ago and the man still smiled at the mention of her name.
"…How is my sweet petunia…?" asked Nascimento, signaling his men to let the men be.
Emma had a tattoo of a petunia on the base of her butt, at the beginning of her back, six colors, six cm long, six petals. Father was furious with her when she showed up with the tattoo and with him for finding it "sexy".
"…Your sweet petunia has grown up, now he only sleeps with multi-billionaires…"
"…They do have better pension plans and severance packages, after all…" said Yuri.
"…I knew that child would go far, I hope she is in good health…"
"…Nothing that a little bit of penicillin, a couple doses of Quinilones, plus a pinch of AZT can not help…"
All in the room laughed, Eli just smiled, calculating who should he eliminate first.

"…We know at the agency why you are here, and we implore of you to let us manage this, we will leave any rewards for you, but we want to do this our way…" said Eli in a convincing enough tone.

"…You should see what this animals did in the freeway in Lisbon, they claimed it was not even their intended target…" said Nascimento full of self-righteousness.

"…You should see what they do every week in Israel, and we are their intended target. Revenge is a poison, let justice prevail in the long run, the Sword of Gideon will prevail…"

"…How much of a long run we are taking about here…?" asked Rodriquez.

"…Months, maybe years. We want the whole Organization, not just Osama and a handful of his acolytes…" said Eli

"…If you kill a roach, you kill ten thousand more..." said Nascimento.

"…You are thirty years late for that one, said Eli. He added: "…at his point is not just one roach about to egg, is ten thousand roaches. We need to wait until the time has come to kill them all, now is the time to be patient and not to let you be guided solely by your emotions…"

"…If we are expected to back off, you need to give us something more specific, concrete..."

"…Regretfully, I can not give you anything more concrete than that. You have to take this on faith, like an eleventh command, "…You shall trust Eli…", he said

"…I am sorry , events are out of my control now, soon this place will be swarming with syndicate men, thirsty for blood…" said Rodriquez.

"…What if my men can neutralize them before they get here…?"

"… I am afraid that it is too late for your plan, we are sticking with ours…"

"…One last thing, can I take a picture of you and my friend here, I will like to e-mail it to Emma, she still speaks fondly of you, after all you were her first one. Then Yuri will take one with me on it. Put chairs for Rodriquez and Nascimento in the front and your other bodyguards will stand by you with his right hand on your shoulder, then Yuri here with the left hand in Rodriquez shoulder. When my turn comes, Yuri and I will simply exchange places, OK…?"

"…Sounds like a plan…" said Yuri, assuming his place, which gave piece of mind to the others, which got to their assigned spaces. Eli placed himself four feet from them using the table to steady his elbows.

"…Give me a big smile. Say Osama…!" Three camera clicks in seconds, three darts on their right eyes lodging in the posterior aspect of the brain. Yuri docked for the floor. The three men complaint of the flash being to bright, fallowed by the "worst headache of their lives", fallowed by three dull explosions, a small trickle of blood hanged from their right eyes, they were dying. Eli approached Nascimento and with a calm voice added: "…Sodomizing a fourteen year old girl does not make you a great lover, you pedophile piece of shit…" The last thing Nascimento saw was the sole of Eli's boot coming towards his face, the last thing he heard was his neck cracking, broken by the impact of the kick.

"…We seem to have multiple agendas here, my friend…" said Yuri standing from the floor.

"…You better come through, or I swear to God, you will die before I do…"

"…Mr. Eli, you need to lay off the coffee, a little bit. We are on the same side, remember…?"

"…Lay off me, this is not the time or place for this crap, Yuri…"

The heard running steps going towards them in the corridor:

"…Señor Eli, Sr. Yuri the commander is here…" he stopped at the site of the three bodies.

"…You are fast and efficient, Jew Boy, a worthy adversary, I am going to miss you…" said Raul.

"…I assure you, my friend, I have no intentions to die here. I am here to deliver a message, I have no intention of having the messenger killed…"

"…Sr. Weisel is here and he would like to see you both now…" said Raul

They walked down the corridor. There were at least ten guards securing the corridor to the meeting room…non-Arabic, looked like mercenaries. Some of them oriental, perhaps Koreans, some looked big, like Samoans.

For the first time Eli noticed the intricate Moorish mosaics that adorned the hallway to the conference room. Interestingly enough, all the walls depicted pivotal battles lost by the Moors in Europe and the Middle East. In order were the first and second crusade, Papal blessing, major battles, the fall of Constantinople, the division of the Church.

The second was the surrender of Granada, the lonely Caliph and his mother whipping him with the ultimate reproach: "…. Do not cry like a woman, what you could not defend as a man…" It was written in Arabic, Latin, Hebrew, German and French. It was dated 1570.

The third was the battle of Lepanto, were the Mediterranean Sea, at least the upper Mediterranean, was freed from the control of the early Islamists who had sworn to re-conquest all their kingdoms. Their Navy was destroyed. Cervantes lost his arm. Shakespeare got his "first blood".

The fourth and last one was a depiction of treachery as a last resort, how one man's sacrifice can change history. Was the depiction of the surrender of what was left of the Serbian Army to the Moors, the fake conversion of the Serbian King and the assassination of the Great Caliph, the Serbian popular counter offensive and the destruction of the Moorish Army?

"…Osama calls this the "wall of shame", it was painted by the great painter Bart Mayol, a monk which later moved to Mallorca, where he founded an order where the great Junipero Serra and Bartolomé de Las Casas learned their theologies and moral imperatives. As soon as he re-conquests Spain, he will destroy this hotel and attempt to change history, re-writing the past to fit his present agenda..." said Yuri.

"...Not unlike American Liberals..." said Eli

"...Not unlike Americans, period...." retorted Yuri

"...Touché..." said Raul, as he opened the door and introduced the two men to Mr. Weisel.

"..I see, Jew, you have brought my loyal servant and friend back to me..."

"...Most of him, anyways..." "...I just want in exchange him for my life and for you to hear a proposal for a truce..." said Eli.

"...There is no need for a truce, my friend. We are winning in all fronts. We will overcome in Afghanistan, Iraq, Syria, Jordan, Saudi Arabia, Egypt and Palestine..."

Eli, who had been looking at his watch, responded: "...By all possible objective accounts, you are losing this war. Thinking otherwise is not visionary, is delusional and you know it...!"

"...You have little faith, Jew...!"

"...This is an issue with reality, in spite of what the liberal media may suggest, you can not sustain a war with suicide bombers. The Americans have very good intelligence, for the most part. You have been ten yards ahead of the game, but the distance is getting shorter and shorter and you can feel the sleeping monster breathing on your neck, about to devour you. They know where the Chetchen drivers deposited the three eighteen wheeler full of WMD. If they try to mobilize them, the Americans will blow them to the moon, the Palestinian factions cannot be kept at peace, so a civil war in the Palestinian territories is imminent. Don't give me that crap, only the New York Times will buy your bull crap like that..."

"…OK, I would not insult your intelligence with the propaganda, what do you have to offer in exchange for your life…?"

"…Information…Intelligence…Propaganda… perhaps a more effective way of waging the " war of the minds", than accusing the Americans of atrocities in Iraq and Guantánamo…"

"…The truce is not in Iraq, the truce is in Israel..."

"…I don't have any real control over what Hammas or any other..."

Eli interrupted him: "…You are insulting my intelligence again…! We know that you and the Iranians fund their enterprise. The Americans after 911 finally cut off the pipeline of funds coming from American sympathizers and Arab-Americans who buy the crap about education (Islamic fundamentalism of the Saudi-type) and healthcare…"

"…You want us to strangle the Palestinian, abandon my suffered brothers..."

"…Only for 3 months, so the ruling party can win the election, so that we can sit in secret talks with all the Palestinian factions, yes including Hammas, to see if we can truly find a solution other than this slaughter. There is too much blood on the sand already…"

"…But if the money stops, they will starve..."

"…No, they won't, we will open the pipeline of food going from relief agencies, stored in government facilities for months and held because of your politics of death. The food will be handled by the red crescent, who in addition to distribution will establish a network of "soup kitchens" in the territories...nobody will starve…"

"…But your distribution system is too slow, because security issues..."

"…We have designed a system in which a single operator and a platoon can clear thirty eighteen wheelers going each way per hour with one hundred percent efficiency of capture goods (contraband). Is ready for implementation and sustainable…"

"…Impressive, we have been working..."

"…We stole the design from your father's company and improved it to make security work..."

"...OK, you have grabbed my attention. What it is there for me...?"

"...This weekend there will be a major offensive that will destroy, or at least hamper for months the activity of your group in both Afghanistan and Iraq. Fifty thousand American troops will be imported from Europe and Korea. In addition twenty thousand well trained mercenaries from South Africa, Angola, Guatemala, Colombia, and El Salvador, armed to the teeth a ready to kill..."

"...So what are you offering me that I don't know ...? Or at least suspected...?

"...We can give you the time downs for the American Satellites, so that the whole army can slip through their dragnet and escape to Iran. The can re-enter later with more vigor on the next time down next month. We estimate that you have about twenty thousand active members in Iraq and probably another one hundred thousand sympathizers. You can avoid a big bloodshed and a Palestinian civil war..."

"...Do we have a deal, then..." asked Yuri. "...Three month of truce in exchange for a chance to redeploy and organize, for a new offensive in the future..."

"...Do you have a computer with you...?" asked Eli.
"...Yes we do, are you going to e-mail me the information...?"
"...You bet, I don't want to be anywhere near here when you get the information. My life will be not worth much..."

"...You don't trust me...?"
"...Not with my life..."

"...As you wish. Some day when you least expect it death will come, the angel of Allah will find you and destroy you! That is a promise..." He gave him one of his business cards with his e-mail in it. "...Of course is secure..."

He smiled at Yuri bowed out to Osama. He ran, after he left the building as fast as he could .They had left the rental Del Sol three blocks from the hotel , a couple of blocks to the entrance to the freeway, in case they have to make a fast exit. He had the metabolism of his Grandfather, who could eat six thousand calories a day and remain slim, like a crane. He ran as fast as he could until he reached the car. He sped until he had fifty miles between him and Osama. He was able to breath. He consulted the portable Magellan GPS and turned at the exit for Barcelona. Not until he was absolutely sure that nobody was fallowing him did he sent the info. He had promised that he will visit his grandfather in Barcelona prior to any escape from Spain.

His mother would be off his case and he could check the local Hebrew girls.
He was exhausted. He had to take a break. There was a safe house in the next town. There was a truck stop. He pulled over, bought some coffee and decided to take a nap. He immediately fell asleep, in spite of the coffee. He dream of him as a child, running through a port, fallowed by his dear sister Perla and his cousin,
Moshe. Grandpa was fallowing closely. They stopped at a sign saying Soyer: Monasteries De Las Casas 140 km (Casa Mayol). Grandpa smiled and said: "…Go now your sister needs you…".
The tapping rudely awakened him in his window. It was a Gipsy, begging for money. He took five pesetas and gave it to him. He sped up to Barcelona, was going to Mallorca to meet the Ghost of Bart Mayol at the Monastery of Las Casas. He made arrangement for a flight from Barcelona and asked his grandfather to meet him at the airport. His mother will be happy that he visited him. He e-mailed a report to Middleman…"

Chapter 28
[[Rincón: Casa Verde]]

It was Friday morning and the vivacious Apollo, doting the celestial vault with his chariot of fire, galloping the firmament for willing maidens, settling for his old lover, the faithful one, Earth... It was sunrise.

The kitchen in the Green House was alive. The monks, both Buddhist and Christian worked with more or less joy beside each other. Everyone was worried about last night. Mayhem and senseless violence takes its toll on the human soul, even when the violence is justified by all standards.

Real human beings get post-traumatic stress syndrome, animals continue to kill all their lives without an iota of regret. The old Buddhist monks that had spend all their lives attempting to conquer their worst enemies, those passions that darken a man's soul, wept while working in the kitchen. Violence against yourself, at least in a metaphysical sense was always justified. Violence against yourselves as a religious statement, self-immolation, could be forgiven. However, abetting violence against other beings, no matter how lowly, rapidly approached moral relativism. Even the prospect of keeping the Tango- time while others did the killing caused great concern to these gentle souls. The Llama himself has required this of them arguing that they will not engage in any killing themselves. "…Tango does not kill people, only people can kill people…" he told them at the end of their communal meditation, half jokingly, sensing great distress on the part of his friends.

Apollo found Ratzinger and the Llama walking through the rose garden, in vivid conversation. Both men were polyglots, and easily change from Vietnamese to German to Italian and French conversing in all, enjoying the idiosyncrasies and little ironies. An occasional laughter will roar from each other man when the other attempted this exercise on each other's native tongue. In the background the warriors and monks helped each other with their archery skills.

"...Ratzinger, I am feeling uneasy about your presence here. You know that we can not guarantee your safety here..."
"...Be at peace, my brother, only the Supreme Commander can make such an unsustainable promise during these circumstances..."
"...The police, I am afraid, are antagonistic at best. They seem to have great animosity towards certain members of our group, tensions were happening yesterday, which I hope does not jeopardize the success of this mission. Those guards outside the gate that the left behind, I don't trust them..."
"...AL Quaida has infiltrated the police here. That is not reassuring on several levels. I would be dead it was not for that remarkable woman. I have seen every circus in the world while working in the Vatican. I have given absolution to every tattooed man and woman from every continent in the world that worked for the circus. I have never seen somebody with such exquisite control of the knives, any knife..."

"...Did you realize that she has an artificial leg? She has learned to make advantages of what other people consider handicaps. And that husband of hers is a joke..."
"...Of course, after all is said and done is "The Mexican" who is left behind to pick up the trash..."
"...That was truly priceless..." said the Pope.
"...Even that pompous police chief had to laugh at that one. Not everybody can use black humor like that..."

They stopped their conversation. José and Moreno approached them. Both men had heard them approach as soon as they entered the backyard. Hours of meditation will make your other senses more refined. Your hearing acuity improves when your eyes are closed. You learn to listen, both to the people's mouth, and to their hearts. Great lovers close their eyes while kissing and lovemaking, not because they fantasize about people not present, because we are such visual animals that in order to enjoy other sensations we have to filter our eyesight out. Vision is needed for arousal, but then it impedes paced enjoyment.

"…I understand that you met Satan's wet nurse…" said Moreno.

"…Yes indeed…" replied the Llama. "…Beautiful soul, she has cooperated with us fully…"

"…Build like a Goddess…" said José.

"…It's amazing what they can do these days with plastics…" added the Pope in a mischievous tone.

"…Amen…" added Jose

"…You two have to visit the lady in question and get proper garments for the birthing of the Son of Satan, so you can pass incognito. That way we know, in advance, what we are facing. That may or may not help in our strategy. It's good to know well your enemy. Try not to get killed, as it will spoil our line of defense…" said the Pope.

"…How is the situation with the mayor, Mr. Moreno…? asked the Llama.

"…At first he was incredulous, but after inspecting the thirty craters left behind by our friends from last night, he has pledged full cooperation, particularly since took the liberty of threatening him with excommunication . Of course, that was done in your name…"

"…Of course…!" said the Pope, smiling and admiring the young detective.

"…They are evacuating most of the town to Aguadilla, so that no innocent by-standers is hurt in the defense of the town. In addition to our troop of archers we have Maria, the knife thrower and her husband, the SWAT team and the Mayor. We may get help from our Israeli friends in the capital, but would not bet on it…"

"…Most of them left for Israel, but the ones left behind had pledged their cooperation…"

'…Now is a matter of training until the end of the day, and may

God be with you…" said the Pope

They left the rose garden and separated. Jose and Moreno left in Garcia's Explorer and drove toward the porn star house near the surfing beach, through route 413. The Llama and the Pope retired to their quarters to meditate. A feeling of apprehension, like a fog pressing on everybody in the house, they were scared, they will face Ultimate Evil. They may not make it!

They arrived at the mansion in road 413.
As hey have never been there, they did not know what to expect. There were guards in uniform, with communication apparatus, semi-automatic weapons and samurai swords. They gave the guard at the gate a card with the seal of Babylon that has been provided by the Llama. The seal was a frame of olive branches with a pentagram with a mighty scary goat head in the center with the words inscribed in Latin "Deux Satanicus", or "Son of Satan". They were brought into an Internal Garden where Satan's Wet Nurse waited for them, She was surrounded by flowers, and tropical plants. She was sitting across a fountain of the god Baal consorting with his concubines. He was built like a horse, only the neck and face resembled a male human.

The woman, who was dressed in a fine linen robe with hood with very little left for their imagination, addressed them:
"…Welcome to my humble adobe. The Llama spoke highly of you. You are here with the pretext of been my new boys. You will be provided robes like the one I am using, which does not permit to conceal much. You will be armed with not much but your wits. Jose here probably can take care of himself. You, Inspector Moreno, on the other hand, make me worry about you. You are not the young stud I used to know.
"…You two know each other…?" asked Jose, genuinely surprised.

"...Let's say we have carnal knowledge of each other, albeit very brief..." said Moreno

"...He is too modest, he made Satan's Wet Nurse the movie classic it is today. I have met no other actor with so much depth, scope and endurance...!"

"...Let me guess, he played Satan..." said Jose.

"...You got it, karate boy, and let's say that he did not need any props for his "tail". He made "quite an impression" on all the actresses in that movie..."

"...Moreno, Mr. Stud himself...!" said Jose.

"...Please give it a rest. If truth needs to be said, you do some things that you later live to regret. I am not talking about selling my body for money. I was an adult at that time, way above eighteen. I knew exactly what I was doing..."

"...I needed the money because I had been mugged and all the money was gone. I regret having sex with woman that had no choice, they were practically slaves. They were hooked to a system in which their pimps kept them indentured by drugs or by physical abuse. It was a perverse foster care system in which relatives abused them and sold them as sex slaves, where the only hope of redemption is death, usually a violent one either by their pimps or their Johns. Every night I wake up with their cries of fake climax superimposed to their cries of fear and pain..."

"...Two girls died during the filming, beaten to death by their PCP crazed pimps..." she said sadly.

"...The worst thing, however is that I was a coward. I was intimidated by the togs not to seek Justice, official or otherwise..."

"...You would have been gang raped, castrated, tortured and impaled. You did what you could do at that moment to survive and you abandoned that world, which I am still a prisoner of after twenty years..." she said

"...I also abandoned you. I left the set the night of the second murder, just before dawn. I never looked back. I know I broke your heart, because I broke mine too...." he said looking away in shame.

"...That night while we loved each other off camera, you made promises of love. You made promises of a house in a farm on the Island at the other side of the world. Coffee and orange trees would have surrounded it. We will have beautiful children, running around the orchards, chasing German Shepard and their puppies. They would grow to be men and woman of principle and truth, protected from the sexual predators that roam the world, waiting for the right moment. We would have stopped the circle of violence. We would have happiness and love, but you abandoned both me and the dream that same night. You know you are the only man I have ever loved..."

"...I loved and still love you, and will until my last breath..." he said hugging her in his powerful arms. Both felt young again and in love.

"...You abandoning me hurt more than any breast augmentation or lipo-suction I ever had..."

He looked at her, straight in the eyes, kissed her tenderly in the forehead and said: "...I am truly sorry, and I loved you like the first night. Maybe we have a future after all these days are over..."

"...My love, I have no future. The Son of Satan will be nourished by these breasts and by my flesh. I will die. We still have some hours left, let's celebrate our love...."

"...I don't want to loose you, my love..."

"...We have no choice, in order to fulfill the prophecy I must die..." He turned towards José, who had given them some space; "...You have a mission, sir. Before you join us tonight at the lighthouse in Cabo Rojo, you must free my alternate. She is held, drugged and tied at the storage area behind the mirror in the surf shop. There are only two armed guards there. That should not be a challenge to a man of your talents. There is a reddish Jeep with the keys on the ignition. Take it to escape, drive to the Aguadilla airport, her father's private jet is there. She will be taken to safety. She will not be another victim on my conscience..."

José bowed, to each separately. He started walking and left the courtyard, running. When he was at the entrance of the compound, he waved back and smiled. Maybe Moreno will lay off his case, after a couple of hours of lovemaking. God knows well he needs it. Badly

Back in the courtyard, she took off her robe, grabbing him lovingly by the hand and guided him towards her bed. She turned off the lights and the cameras. She grabbed her favorite set of sheaths and redressed her bed, pouring fresh rose petals in the bed. By now he had undressed. She bent on her knees and washed his feet with a bassinet full with perfume.

He reciprocated. He cried; so did she. They embrace in an embrace they wished could last an eternity.
"...Twenty years lost, my love..." he said
"...I am sure that we can make up for them in a couple of hours..."

"...At least we can try. My only regret is that I will loose you, after finding you..."
"...Only the present exits, the past is gone, the future is to be lived..."

He raised her in his powerful arms, and gently deposited her in the bed. He went back to the door they came through and locked it shot. He ran, did a summer-salt jump, after doing a full rotation head down, landing at her side, after flying over her.
"...Quite impressive, my loved..."
"...Darling, you have seen nothing yet..."

Chapter 28
[[Swiss Guard Headquarters; Geneva, Switzerland]]

La Santa, came of the shower and look at herself in the mirror. She had been pregnant for less than a week and she already had the body of a seven-month mother to be....

She had never had any pregnancies in her youth, because of her husband's infertility. However this child, been conceived in consort with the Holly Spirit, grew faster every day. He also grew stronger by the seconds. She would swear that prodigy was able to communicate the most basic secrets to his mother. If it was at least the "Silver Child", the Lord's prophet. But who will bear the latest incarnation of the Lord himself? Suddenly she had Mary-envy.

At least the morning sickness was gone by now. She did wake up with bile taste in her mouth on a regular basis, but she seldom vomit anymore. Her body was almost perfect, more beautiful than ever. She suddenly envied Sophia Loren, whose body at seventy was as beautiful as ever without any plastic surgery: "…Every curve in my body, I owe to spaghetti…" Ms. Loren claimed.

The best thing about her new body is that it also matched her spiritual and mental youth. To her she was still the young girl, prior to been introduced by her own mother to prostitution and mutilated by her own father. The Spirit can heal all wounds. She heard the voice of her son within her.

"…Mother, now you can understand my thoughts. Please listen to me…!"

"…Yes dear, I am still, waiting for the prophet of the Lord to speak to me, His humble servant…"

"…Today Israel will rise again, signifying that the prophecy is to be fulfilled. The Devil worshipers that surround her had decided to destroy it. The Persian Empire has bowed to destroy her and her servants, blood thirsty jackals are aiming for her jugular…!"

"…Yes Lord, my ears are open, and I am still…"

"…Israel has the will and the Lord has anointed Her. She will rise and destroy her enemies. In the meantime we need to destroy the Son of the Devil. The Holly Warriors at the "Island at the other side of the world" are waiting to fulfill their destiny, but they will need some help, as the son of the Devil is an enemy full of trickery and power, by the time he get into battle, he will be a giant , requiring a concerted effort to destroy…"

"…I am still…!"

"…Israel's warrior is landing in Mallorca as we speak. He is going to Las Casas Monastery after a sacred vision instructed him to do so. I want you to wake up the Swiss guard and arrange for them to provide the warrior with transport to Las Casas and to the Island, they need him there before the great battle ensues'

She ran with her bathrobe on top, out of her room, yelling like a deranged mad woman.

"…Captain Ives, captain Ives…!"

The good captain ran in his thermal underwear towards her, wandering what was wrong with the pregnant saint-nun. Even in her present state she was a very desirable and beautiful woman.

"…Captain alert the Swiss Army. We need a escort at Palmas to transport the Wrath of Israel to the Island. I mean right now! His name is Eli and he will be there within the hour…" By this time her son has taken over and was giving the instructions directly. All erotic thoughts deflated in that instance and the good captain laid still, not wanting to miss anything.

"…His name is Eli, and he will be landing in forty five minutes, be sure he is in a plane within the next two hours, do you read me…?"

"…Loud and clear, it will be done…" and he disappeared, running down stairs, like if the Devil himself was steps behind.

"…I think that boy is in love with you…"

"…At least, "in lust", but perhaps we are progressing…"
"…You have my blessing, his soul is good and he truly loves you…"

"…Thanks for the info…"
"…Any time, mother, anytime .What is a prophet good for if the cannot read man's soul…"

Somewhere over the vicinity of Mallorca, Eli was deep meditation. Eli sat pensive, while he looked at the clouds outside. He hated this business. His curse was that he was so good at it. All the goals of his mission had been accomplished. Yet, he was getting too old for this crap! He had killed three men, which were not even his enemies!

He knew sooner or later he will make a fatal mistake. Nobody is perfect, one day I will miss subtleties in his environment and will finish with a bullets right between the eyes. The Iranians were rattling their sabers, militarizing the Lebanese border. At least he ha a truce with Osama, whatever that particular phrase meant. The body count kept piling up and he did not see any end to it. He was exhausted. At least he had slept a bit in this flight. It was always difficult to sleep. There were too many ghosts in his bed; too many bloody corpses claiming justice.

They finally landed at Palmas. He was walking towards ground transportation when he spotted the most peculiar man he has seen in his life. He was about five feet and eight inches, pear-like and with abundant hear, most of which was white. He dressed in Khakis and open white, long sleeve shirt, raised mid arm, and tennis hat. He was centrally bold but the peripheral hair compensated for the central boldness. His eyebrows were thicker than Graucho Marx and his chest hair was at least two inches long. He smelled of Brut. He had a sign "Vicen's Tours" with "ELI" written in mold, without running of the ink. Eli approached him.

"…Good morning Mr. Vicens…" said Eli tentatively.

"…Mr. Eli…? I am Fello Vicens III, here my last name is as common as Smith. So you will see many businesses with the name. How was your trip…?"

"…I slept most of it, who are you working for, Fello…?"

"…Right now I am working for you. If your question is who is paying me, now to help you the answer is quite complex. Please fallow me to my taxi and we will be on our way…"

"…Going back to the original question, which pays for you…?" he asked while fallowing him to another terminal.

"…For this trip, is going to be the Swiss Army and the Vatican who will foot the bill, but I have contracts from MOSSAD, Interpol, MI6 the CIA…" said the man counting with the two hands as he mentioned his different clients. He opened the door to the tarmac and in the private section of the hangars. There side by side were a Harrier jet and Sekorski helicopter.

"…Yours…?" asked Eli

"…Yes, these were payment for jobs well done in the past. I save the empire a couple of times. Israel owes me big, your compatriots sometimes confuse my peculiar anatomy with stupidity, and are not the most formal in keeping their payments up to date. I keep sending the bill to Uncle Middleman and it gets lost in cyberspace'

"…The Good uncle has a lot on his plate these days, my friend…"

"…Could you send him my bill when we finish this job…?"

"…Certainly, it would be my pleasure, if we finish this job…"

"…You mean, when we finish this job. I never miss and from what I have been reading about you in your record, neither do you…!" he said pointing towards a record with "Eli Goldman" written on top with the stamp "Top Secret" "…Put on the helmet is a two way microphone/receiver so we can talk…"

Eli did as instructed and they were off in the Sekorski.

"…How long is the trip to the monastery…?"

"…About thirty minutes, but will do in twenty as every other private is grounded. We are the only plane or helicopter airborne in Mallorca…"

"…How come you have my record, Fello,,,?"

"…I am chief intelligence officer for MOSSAD in Mallorca. I have all the records, I know every agent that operates in Europe and I have rescued them on more than one occasion…"

The humming of the helicopter, albeit deafening, was monotonous enough that Eli fell asleep.

Fello smiled and let him sleep. When you have killed as many people as this young man has, it is hard to sleep. Let him enjoy the ride. He telephoned the abbot to be ready for them when they landed, whom Swiss Guard the head of the Swiss Guard and the Swiss Army had previously notified.

After a few minutes they approached Las Casas. It was an old medieval castle, which had passed between the Jew, the Moors and the Christians. Wars and death had forced those transitions. However the castle now was a repository for the most valuable collection of saint relics in the world. The Collection of the Lord's relics was bigger than the Vatican's, where Pereira had been the caretaker for decades now. And they had tears, tears of every saint that ever lived, including the ones from the living Buddha . The abbot had prepared their shopping list, blood of Christ, tears of his brother(just in case he had picked John's tears and John the Baptist's in addition to the Buddha), one of the nails of the cross and pieces of the handle of the "spear of destiny", as the Vatican had the rest.

They landed, which waked up Eli. The abbot approached the helicopter and delivered the precious cargo. The exchange pleasantries and the abbot delivered the goods. He gave them a special blessing and left them for departure back to the airport.

Upon arriving to the airport, they dismounted from the helicopter, bag in hand. They approached the Harrier. In it a Sidewinder was open and the technicians were taking part of the explosives out, living about one third of the usual load behind and in their place, surrounded by foam, they place the precious cargo, the relics. He pushed several bottoms and the sidewinder closed.

"…It is not ready to shoot until we activate it, from the cabin…"

"…Are we ready to go…? I don't want to be late to our appointment, especially if we are plan B…"

"…Relax, we have hours to spare. I have to coordinate to get refueling four times, maybe five if the Americans cooperate. The Swiss are negotiating with National security and the CIA. We can not go until all this have secured, we don't want to fall in the Atlantic because we lost our fuel…."

"…Of course not…"

"…I am going to take a nap until the delay resolves, and so should you. We can do alternative napping when we are airborne…"

"…Sound like a plan to me, then to the Island at the end of the world…"

In the meantime, at the Island On the other side of the World, José's mission has been successful. José arrived at the Aguadilla airport. The rescue was easier than controlling this crazy child. Maybe it was not a bad idea after all for her to become the Son of Satan's wet nurse. Ever since he had rescued her from the two guards at the surf shop, she had not stopped talking about "their future". Maybe this was a form of imprinting, a reverse Stockholm's Syndrome, in which hostages will wall for their rescuers, instead of their kidnappers. Be as it may, this woman was clinging to him like a slug. It is very difficult to drive with have of your body immobilized, your right arm paralyzed and having your thighs caressed.

As he entered the designated hangar, two security officers were waiting for him. He handled them the girl , exchanged some pleasantries and turned around to leave.

"…Not so fast friend…" said one of the two men.

"…Now what…? You wanted her gift rapped..? José replied in dismay.

"…You are forgetting the ransom, don't you want your money…? The guard asked

"…I don't know what you are talking about. This girl was a prisoner. I rescued her. I was told to bring her to this hangar, I did. I was almost killed in the highway because she would not let off me. I don't want any money, I want to go back to my life and rest…"

"…So you had nothing to do with the kidnap…?" asked the second guard.

"…You finally got it, Sherlock. If there is a ransom, you can donate it to the ITKDF, so we can teach martial arts to under-privileged kids…"

He was interrupted, by clapping of several hands. Out of the shadows several members of the SWAT team came out of the shadows where they have been hiding, clapping.

Vicens approached him: "…I don't know whether to hug you or kick your ass…"

"…Is there any third option, like a coke and a Cuban Sandwich. I am starving…!" He smiled.

"…Ladies and gentleman of the SWAT team, I give you the killer of Mindanao…!"

The clapping went on crescendo and subsided. On of the policeman showed up with a coke and a freshly toasted Cuban Sandwich.

"…Vicens you really know how to run a joint…! What service…!"

"…You are welcome. I have some info for you. My uncle phoned me from Mallorca. He is a mercenary stationed there. A MOSSAD agent by the name of Eli is with him. They are flying tonight and hope to join you in the "festivities" tomorrow. He also passed a message to Mrs. Goldman, saying that Mr. Nascimento is dead…."

"...I got it..." said Jose in between chewing and swallowing his sandwich.

"...Furthermore, we will have a boat tonight, close to the Cabo Rojo lighthouse in case you need it to escape. We are evacuating Rincón, as to minimize civilian casualties..."

"...You think of everything, my friend..."

"...Well I don't want those two morons to get all the glory..."

"...You mean Garcia and Moreno, why do you all hate each other so much...?"

"... I have been always a straight shooter. These two were several points in IQ and behavior higher than a Neanderthal. However they raised themselves above the primordial ooze and made themselves man among men. In Iraq I could not aspire to be anything but their shadows. I resented that. But is stupid, every member of the team here owes their life to Moreno, every single one of them. We love him, but we also hate him. He force us to find the limits of pain and endurance, we became killing machines. Some of then could not take it and committed "suicide in the field". That is when you are so distracted that you are begging the snipers to take you off. We are alive today because he and Garcia kept us going. Passions are a stupid thing, the blind us from the blessings surrounding us, poison our harts and make love and friendship dirty words...."

"... You get a sandwich and a curse in philosophy. Do you have desserts here...?"

"...Marcos bring him the flan. Just kidding, you went to the well one time to often. We don't carry dessert, but we do have coffee..."

Marcos approached him with a coffee and a piece of pineapple flan.

"...I feel I am having my last supper here..."

"...I hope this is not the case. I like you very much. Furthermore I look forward to learn martial arts from you..."

"...I we survive to see the day after tomorrow I will teach you the basics of Accu-Ninja. You may not need to use a gun again in your life, I don't...."

"…We know Jose, but you turned Sampayo's compound into a killing field, without pulling the trigger ounce. That is impressive…"

"…Lets see how far my "impressive abilities" take me I the next two days. I hope is not straight to hell…"

"…I have been in hell and back. Is not pretty, especially when you have Moreno whipping you out through the nearest exit…"

"…Well I better go, I have given enough psychotherapy for today. See you tomorrow and thanks for the lunch…"

"…Next time, please order in advance. We are listed in the book under SWAT…"

Chapter 29
[[Route 413: Porn Star Mansion]]

Moreno waked up from his post-coital nap. Judging on the sunlight outside it was probably around mid afternoon. He shook his head in an attempt to focus on his situation... It was hard to focus when most of his attention was going to his visual cortex. He was enjoying the view of his lover, the porn star, and the re-constructed woman. All that was, of course, a chimera; a surgical construct. Nevertheless: quite an outstanding chimera.

He closed his eyes, in order to improve his chances of focusing.
"...José...!" Where in the world was that man. Hopefully he will be safe and sound, having accomplished his mission. It was imperative that his lover's sacrifice was not in vein and that the intended substitute sacrifice fled to safety. He hoped the other guys were still practicing their archery skills.
"...Hey, love, a penny for your thoughts...!" exclaimed his lover, while she played with his chest hair, absentminded and lovingly, making little swirls.
"...I was thinking about us, how it is not fair, that after all these years of yearning to be back with you, destiny will snatch you out of my arms..." he replied.
"...That sounds like bullshit, albeit beautiful one..."
'...There is plenty more where that came from. I was reviewing in my head the detail of the operation, there are so many weak spots, such a big margin of error, and it is very upsetting. In addition there are people that I don't trust in this group and that I despise. On the other hand I know I can trust Garcia with my life, and maybe Jose. You for sure, but you are not going to be there, regrettably it is not meant to be so..."He went silent, her lips had silenced him.

They heard a knock on the door. Instinctively Moreno covered them both with the sheaths and took his forty-five from under his pillow. She was not accustomed to the instruments of war, which made her extremely nervous. She was paradoxically aroused and repulsed by the situation at the same time. She made a mental note to make a military movie with torture, humiliation and bondage. Of course it will be a comedy, maybe a musical, maybe she could get the Rolling Stones to cameo, maybe Keith Richards, although he is already dead. Then she realized that there was not going to be any tomorrow and started whaling…"

"…Who is it…?" demanded Moreno gun in hand, safety off and caulked.

"…Its me, Garcia. Can I come in…?"

Moreno was actually happy to hear from his friend. He covered himself with a towel and jumped to the door. His revolver back on lock.

Garcia entered the room. Usually when he entered a room the big guy took the room over, by his shear size and his contagious "happy-go-lucky" personality and charm.

"…So you are the famous Garcia…! I heard good things about you. Have you ever considered working for the industry…?"

"…My wife will kill me, she wants exclusive management rights to all my assets, if you know what I mean. And to tell you the truth, if we survive this mess, I will be guarding Mr. Zola, which seems to be more than a full time job…!"

"…Garcia, why are you here…?" Moreno asked, genuinely intrigued.

"…The Llama send me, the Pope send me, and José sent me. The Llama gave me this mini digital web cam, that will connect to the cell phone and you can transmit the ceremony tonight live, we got even a nice flat screen at the Green House to watch it, we will have some lovely roasted avocado tacos that the monks are preparing for the occasion…"

"…Focus, Garcia…!" Both lovers said in unison.

"…The Pope sent the message that so far everything is going according to prophecy. Still expect about four to five thousand acolytes in the ceremony today. In addition do not let the Son of the Devil smell you, specially if you have been with her, as he will recognize you as lover of the lovely young lady, as you give me the impression you are…"

They both smiled.

"…He sent some heavy oils that may help you go undetected. Good luck on that…!"

"…Jose…?"

"…He will be back at dusk. You are not due in Cabo Rojo until 6:00 PM, so he had to do some errands, something to do with a parachute and life jackets. He mentioned that he met Vicens at the airport. He claims great admiration for you and that his uncle is flying tonight from Mallorca with reinforcements, including Eli, who will grace us with his presence in spite of previous engagements in Lebanon, Syria and Iran…."

"…Excellent report. Go back and put the troops to practice, specially that lazy son of a gun, Jerry…"

"…Well boss, he has practiced so much that his hands are bleeding, his wife is on his case, and his not the drugged-out gang-banger you met years ago. He has re-made himself. Is time you give him a break…"

"…Understood Sergeant, but you know first impressions are hard to forget…"

"…Give it a rest, sir. He deserves a second chance…"

"…I will consider it. You are a good judge of character, mostly…."

"…One last question, to your lady friend…"

"…Shoot Garcia…!" she said.

"…How big you have to be for the movies…? You know, just in case I widow some day…" he said sheepishly, almost embarrassed.

"…At least eight…" she answered, half jokingly.

"…No problem, there is more than enough…" he said as he left the room ,closing the door behind him.

They looked at each other an exclaimed in unison, laughing: "…More than enough…"

CHAPTER 30
[[Private Villa in Barcelona]]

"...Emptiness is the basis for everything, is like zero, without the emptiness of zero a billion could not exist. Everything that seems immaterial, actually is important, is part of the total..."

Omar was listening attentively to Osama, both sitting in a lotus-like position, facing each other, in a large Persian rug.

"...Furthermore..." Osama continued. "... The west is decadent and it will be eventually defeated, even with all its technology and gadgets. It will defeat itself, it will fall on its own weight. Like Rome, and Persia before, the British and French Empires they all imploded due to the weight of their own corruption and stupidity. So will the Great American Empire. So will the Great Chinese Empire. We will be the catalysts that push them to destroying themselves. They do not know the true nature of Allah. Only in the Saudi Dessert can you understand the nature of your creator. Only when you prostrate yourself nude in the sand and watch the sands of time surrounding your body and the firmament can you recites all the names of Allah and learn the secrets they posses. Allah is eternal, yet he shifts continuously, yet like the constellations in the heavenly vault, it has some predictable patterns..."

"...But Commander, what is our role in this life, if we are at the mercy of the will of a God who likes to test our faith and our commitment to him on a daily basis..." asked Omar.

"...Have you ever seen the great dessert serpent...?" asked Osama to his old friend. Ever since he had been with the Jews, his faith had become less passionate and more intellectual.

"...A pleasure to work with and spent nights with. If only woman had the capacity to do this, there would be nobody interested in Jihad. All Muslim men would be at home, talking and loving their wives all night long, and we could not find a single willing suicide bomber..." thought Osama

"...The desert serpent does the unimaginable, is designed like a worm, to penetrate the earth, to know its mysteries. In the desert, by the grace of Allah, it flies in the sad, like a bird, like a dragon. How does IT do it? It does it by the grace of Allah. He permits the serpent to use the sand as air and it flies. God does not violates its own laws, it adjusts the potential of each living creature to his Will..."

"...So, what you are saying, then is that with the blessing of God, we can accomplish anything. If we go against His Holly Will, even when the intentions are good, the results is disastrous, even the natural becomes unnatural..."

"...That is what happens to people when they consort with the Devil. Oh, the Devil is very real. It exists not only in the heart of man, but also in ever speck of sand in the desert. He has made himself invisible in the eyes of the non-believers, but he is very real, clouding the judgment of good man into doing atrocious acts..." said Osama.

"...That is what happened to our operatives in the Island. They made two grave mistakes. The consorted with the Devil Worshipers and Zarathrustans, disguised as Muslims. You can say they are the one and the same. I do not trust Iran; I think they want to impose on us their heretic form of Islam mixed with their impure primitive traditions. Their dreams of bringing back the Old Persian Empire, and forcing the return of the Seventh Imam is probably a concoction of the Devil Himself and nothing but the most horrible heresy. I don't want Iran with nukes, because they will only have enough power to dominate the Middle East. Instead of the American Economic Domination, we will suffer from a real slavery; the Persian Bastards will dominate Arabs for generations to come. Al our customs, traditions and faith will be in jeopardy..."

"...That is why you signed the contract with the Zionist pig. In addition we all owe our lives to him. Mr. Eli killed those assassins, and with the reinforcements they were organizing they could have destroyed us. Mr. Eli, a worshiper of THE BOOK, is on God's payroll. That is why he is still alive. Our agents in the Island, converted Zarathrustrans, lost a battle in which they grossly outnumbered their enemies, because Allah decided against them. Not a grain of sand moves in the dessert if is not his will...."

"...Have you any plans to destroy the Evil Empire of Persia, Commander...?"

"...As we speak we have planted explosives in all the major pipelines coming through Iran. In addition we have infiltrated the atomic development facilities..."

"...All these reactors were built by the Russians, but the casings, buildings and towers by the Ben Laden Corporation. With the cooperation of our old enemies, the Russians, we can sabotage every facility. The Russians trust the Iranian even less than they ever trusted the Americans. Putin needs the money that the Iranians can provide with their infinite pipe of petrodollars to finance growth. Afghanistan, Chechnya and Cuba almost bankrupt the treasure, The Hermitage has been looted and half the pieces there are reproductions. If the people of Russia knew this there would be the second revolution and they would have Putin's head at the Kremlin museum...."

"...So the Iranians would be destroyed no matter what, the Israeli plan is better because it will make them look like the idiots they are, the real paper tiger. They could not even beat Sadam, the most incompetent military leader the world has ever know, perhaps with the possible exception of Mussolini .."

"...And Mussolini had Libya..."

"...An Napoleon had Waterloo..."

"...And Hitler had Leningrad..."

"...And Hisbalah will have Lebanon. I am sending you there to coordinate the destruction of Hisbalah with your friend, Eli..."

"...So you want me to pack my bag and fly to Lebanon tomorrow…?"

"…Tonight, the Israeli offensive starts tomorrow. They will need you to mark the spot where the headquarters and the rockets will be located. You take a flight out of Barcelona to Turkey and our agents will help you land in the port of Lebanon. The Mediterranean is boiling with American and British ships to evacuate civilians. We have a safe passage signed by chief of ports in Lebanon, an old operative from the Afghan wars…"

"…And when we finish with Hisbalah and Israel destroys the nuclear capability of Iran, then I can turn around and destroy my wife…"

"…May Allah be with you my old friend, I know we will see each other again…"

"…The future of the middle east depends on that. With your blessings, I will leave for Lebanon…"

Osama looked at the west Mediterranean from his villa. He was still looking like Weisel, but in Arab cotton long pants, and long shirts. He did not wear headgear, as that will grab too much attention.

He watched as Omar as he walked down the pier into the parked hydroplane. Inside the plane was a very confused Omar? Yuri? The Zionists have brain washed him well. However the DNA that was sent to the Swiss lab will tell us the rest of the story. How much of a Jew his friend was genetically and how much of it was emotionally Jewish. He wanted revenge and he wanted it now, that behavior was universal. For now his mission will pacify both masters. If he was lucky he will be killed in Lebanon, in which case he will make it possible with the help of Mr. Eli to destroy Ms. Fatima, spiritually, psychologically, physically and ecumenically.

Ben Laden Construction Logo had been substituted by BLC, with the Mecca project in relieve and a big construction crane. By pushing the family name out of every logo, shirts, plane and boat that the family owned they have prevented themselves from becoming pariahs after 911. Instead they supported soccer teams all around the world, even the winner Italian team, "BLC -We Build The Future Together" He was still in the Board of Directors and he received twenty thousand dollars a day to his Swiss account. The Swiss were better at laundering than the Chinese, although the Chinese Red Army was catching up fast.

His organization of Holly Warriors, have deteriorated into common criminals, cut throats, degenerates, Zarathrustans. He was happy Zirkauwi had died as the bastard was out of control. From now on there was only one leader of Al Qaueda . If we base all or recruiting and actions on hate, we will only brew hate. Iran had to be neutralized. They had short-term goals. His goals were to bring the great Islam Empire from Spain to Turkey, from Turkey to Egypt. They will control billions of barrels of oil and that would fuel real development under Islamic law. But Mullahs should not have control, but a council of elders. Economic development, the armed forces and government should be in the hands of the elders. Mullahs will interpret Islamic Law only.

The "West" was not really the Great Satan. This title belongs to the Incubus to be born tonight in the Island. He will pray on the next three days to Allah for the destruction of Evil. He had no operatives in the Island, so will have to wait and pray for the best. He disrobed and laid in his prayer rug naked. It was going to be a long night, fasting except for water. He will have vision of heaven with Mohammed at his side. God, he needed a rest, badly

High above the clouds Yuri was watching his own image at the window. The sun was coming down and there were images of merchant ships and cruse ships bellow in the Mediterranean. Sooner or later he will have to destroy the man he had learned to love and respect. He owned his life to him many times over. That broke his heart. He hated his wife with the same passion she used to love her. She will pay for her greed and lack of compassion. A bullet between her eyes was just too good for her. She had to be humiliated, introduced to the real meaning of pain, and then executed like a common criminal.

He opened his luggage, there was a traditional Arab- Lebanese garment. A Laser- guided, a forty-five and ammunition. He knew the local languages, so he should be able to get free of most tight situations. In addition, a hundred thousand dollars in gold ingots, the currency of war.

Chapter 31
[[Friday Night, Rincón]]

José finally made it back to the house in route 413 towards the surf beach. The final details for tomorrow were been ironed out. Jerry was trying to insure that they would no mafia wars to destroy any efforts to defeat the Enemy.

Jose's wife had alerted the Macheteros regarding the heavy police surveillance of the area. Manuel was making an inventory of all weapons available. Garcia, Pereira and Ignacious were coordinating the preparation of the plaza in Rincon. The town has been evacuated, most to the disdain of the mayor who did all these "crazy things" to keep the Pope happy, because of fear of excommunication.

He feared the Pope more than his fear of losing the next election, which he feared greatly because the populace was annoyed at him because the never ending repair of the roads, sidewalks and buildings: The uncountable charges of corruption, the interminable public hearings in the local legislature. In addition the feds were after him for real and imagined federal charges. He needed real medication but feared that his multiple business deals will fall through if he did not continue to have the interminable energy that had pulled him out of the ghetto in New York to the serious contender for the governorship of the Island. Everybody wanted to kill him politically. He knew of at least ten people, including his ex-wife, who wanted him physically dead.

José arrived at the house and briefed Moreno about everything. Moreno was apprehensive, but seemed pleased. They had a chance of winning, and Mr. Eli was in the air somewhere over the Atlantic with a plan B. Hopefully the will make it in time. They have to be ready early and it was going to be 105 degrees tomorrow. It was going to be tears, blood and sweat; lots of sweat, indeed.

It was time to leave for the lighthouse in Cabo Rojo. They were already packed and ready to go. They wanted to get there by dusk, as to not be recognized by any known among the New Babylonians They were robed and ready to go.

The road to Cabo Rojo Lighthouse they reviewed the escape plan. If things would get too out of hand they can escape with most of their skin on.

"…Vicens claims that he and his boys from the SWAT team will give more that moral support

he will cover our retreat if necessary…" claimed José.

"…You know I don't trust that man, even with my grocery list. In Iraq he let us down on several occasions…" answered Moreno

"…Honey, listen to the man, the difference now is that there is a plan on the floor and if we have a little faith, lover…" said the Italian actress

"…For now, Mr. Jose I suggest a quick nap because will need are wits. I personally need a little rest from al the different activities I have been involved with lately…" he said as he hugged her.

Since it was a Friday, most of the infernal traffic Jam had subsided. The last fifteen minutes through the mangrove took them to the lighthouse. There was security everywhere. They parked behind the actual lighthouse. José discreetly threw the two large duffle bags behind their SUV.

"…Plan B, my friends. Courtesy of Captain Vicens…"

"…Hope we don't need it …"

"…If we do, there is enough space for all of us. We just need to activate the system ahead of time, each of us will have a remote. Press the blue button twice, immediately you will hear two explosions and tear gas plus a red smoke cloud. Run towards the center of the explosion, holding your breath. After that, go in the direction of the activity and run as if the son of the Devil was following you…"

"...Is that the best you can do...?" said Moreno.

"...Stop bitching, man and listen to what the man is telling us, for God's sake..."

"...Yes, bonehead, listen to your woman, you may learn to trust those who are trying to help you, moron...!"

"...You are the one that cause all these things, so if anybody is to be blame for our misfortunes is you..."

José jumped and smacked Moreno in the face, whip kick and roundhouse to each cheek before landing in his feet. Moreno was livid. He went for his gun.

"...For God's sake, what are you doing...?" cried the girlfriend while smacking him hard on the face.

"...Some habits are hard to brake..." he said apologizing to her, and bowing to him.

"...Its dark, they would not recognize us now, lets grab her by both arms and fake she is our unwilling prisoner. I think most of these people are drugged anyway..."

As they spoke a cadence mantra field the air, bringing the crowd into a climatic frenzy: "...Balzebuth, this is the time for you..." over and over again. They approached the stage and the woman between them started going into frenzy. The lights were blinding, spotlights pointed towards the two stages and others, which floated among the crowds. It had the feeling of a KISS concert, without the make-up. Suddenly, Sampayo appeared from under the stage with the very pregnant "Whore of Babylon". The whole place went into a higher level of frenzy. The poor woman, who was barely able to walk and went into a certified apoplectic fit, falling on the floor unconscious, In the presence of more than five thousand followers her contractions started and she crowned.

"...Come to us, Son of the Devil, your chosen people await you..." said Sampayo, the Pope of the Babylonians. The mob went into yet another frenzy. The watched the birth of the "forbidden child".

It was horrible. There was blood all over the place. In addition the baby was unnatural. It was very muscular in nature, a ram head over his shoulders and instead of baby cries, the heard these horrible low pitched sound, that scared the bravest, like a mixture between a rhino and a bear.

There was absolute silence in the five thousand. It crawled up its mother's leg her abdomen until it reached he ample bosom. Then the most horrible sound of horror and pain came out of "the Whore of Babylon." Then in the face of the five thousand she withered into dust while the monster grew about her size. It then pay attention to his wet nurse. However before breast-feeding he attempted to mount her. A horrible cry came out of his mouth, like the one he did at birth.

"…A mortal that loves this woman has made her his. I cannot mount her any more because I am too weak to fight true love. She is worthless to me, so throw her against the rocks. Who wants to give their eternal soul for me…?" A line started forming of crazed out women who wanted to be ravished and destroyed at the same time.

Jose and Moreno grabbed the woman and walked her in the general direction of the cliff, pretending to fallow the monster's orders.

Then it happened, the wind change and Moreno's odor reached the entity. He finished off another of his acolytes and stopped. He was now about eight feet tall and his body looked more like a bull than a ram.

"…Stop those with the Wet Nurse. They are enemies and the taller man loved my whore. They most be destroyed, or they will destroy all of you. Destroy the infidels…!" In unison two big explosions were heard and the area was filled with acrid smoke of tear gas. As they watch in astonishment two large plastic inflatable spheres appeared. The acolytes were gaining on them. Moreno took out his forty-five and killed the closest six and reloaded. From behind him ten shuriken flew and stopped ten more. Jose pushed her into one of the spheres, closed the door and pushed towards the cliff as soon as he could. The sphere closed. Six more shots and he threw another cloud of shuriken, while Moreno re-loaded and pushed José into the second sphere, which started rolling down hill. He emptied his third clip and ran as hard as he could. Jose pulled him in, just with enough time to close the sphere's hatchet. Some wounded fanatics attempted to stop the spheres and were run over by it.

They rolled into the abyss. Then they heard the helicopters and the coast guard boat before the felt the splash. They were pretty shaken but alive. Water had not penetrated the spheres. They could here the machine guns from the SWAT helicopter establishing the perimeter. By now the beast was ten feet tall:

"…Abandon the perimeter my children, tomorrow will face this enemy and we will prevail. They cannot win because they have no conviction. My father will stand behind us, he has made me indestructible. I will command his legions and we will destroy the sub-humans…"

Vicens himself fished the two sphere from the water with a smile and the boated out of there at full speed. The two men in the sphere were liberated. Jose thanked him, so did Moreno, with trepidation. The lady was most appreciative and kissed Vicens in the cheek.
"…Full speed ahead now! I want everybody in "terra firma" ASAP…"

At the distance they could here the horrible animal cries of the beast, which raged over the fact that they have escaped the most horrible of deaths. They will also be available to fight him tomorrow. However, for all practical purposes he was indestructible. There were few things he should fear but most of them were in museum as antiquities, out of harms way, in other continents. He will be in control of the Island in no time. These feeble minds could not stand his powers. He will send ambassadors around the world to conquer the world in his Father's name. Resistance will be futile. Those who resist him would be utterly destroyed, never to be remembered.

CHAPTER 32
[[Friday Night, Somewhere over the Atlantic]]

Eli awakened from his heavy sleep. There was the smell of combustible surrounding him. FelloVicens was at the helm. They were deep over the Atlantic. They have been recently re-fueled. This time by the Americans, which were not very happy about it. Eli had pulled all his strings, all the old debts were been paid...

"...My dear Eli. We got re-fuelled, but we were told that this will be the last. Unless you have another source; we barely have enough fuel to get to the Island..."

"...Nobody from "the tribes" in this area...?"

"...Nobody, the war in Lebanon has destroyed reserves ... the Brazilians and Argentineans refused us ,so did the Canadians ..."

"...We will deal with them at their time. Any British ships on maneuvers...?"

"...No..."

Eli looked out the cockpit window, he felt alone and helpless. He did not wanted to end in the middle of the Atlantic in an icy grave with this crazy Mallorcan.

"...Have you ever done anything for Mr. Chavez, Mr. Vicens...?"

"...No, or Castro for that matter...?"

"...Mr. Zola...?" He was running out of options.

"...Long time ago...Nothing recently...and beside I know as a fact that he does not control any tankers in the air..."

"...We are doomed..." said Eli.

"...Not necessarily..." said Vicens. "...Remember we don't need a landing strip with this machine and that we can probably land in the town square itself..."

"...I am more interested in getting there in time and losing my load than in landing anywhere, why I don't want is to have the Atlantic as my grave. What if they really need plan B and it does not get there in time...?"

"...Have faith, God do not abandon does who obey his plans and make life good for his children..."

"...How can I have faith, I only believe in technology, only believe in my Uzi, remote control and explosives..."

"...You are a sad man, Mr. Eli. So young and so sarcastic, so devoid of faith, and at the same time so effective and efficient...."

"...Self reliant, perhaps...?"

"...My friend, a man has to believe. If you don't believe, you are nothing..."

"...How many women had you loved in your life...?" asked Mr. Vicens.

"...About fourteen, give or take a few..." answered Eli.

"...Was your heart broken with each departure...?"

"...Yes. Of course..."

"...But in spite of the odds that you may get hurt, you went head on, and you are still here..."

"...So your point is? That we should jump in into God's hand and hope for the best...?"

"...Something like that! Is the realization, that unlike your many girl friends, God does not break your heart but fills it with love. Everything will fall in its place. That is why you and I are here at thirty thousand discussing metaphysics while the whole world goes to the shits..."

"...With our little grain of sand the whole world will not be wasted..."

"...I hope you are right, Mr. Vicens..."

"...I know I am. I know I am..." he said smiling with his Graucho Marx brows, behind the mask.

Meanwhile in Rincon, in the time square, in the Catholic Church the Pope, the Llama, Pereira and Ignacious officiated an ecumenical Buddhist/Catholic service. In the center of the altar was a five gallon golden jar full of holly water that the Pope had brought from Rome, blessed by John Paul I just before he died "for just an occasion like this". It was eleven thirty local time.

The Host had been consecrated and so was the wine. In the background monks intoned mantras, whose meaning had been lost in antiquity, the wine was reddish in color and was dumped into the Holly Water, turning the concoction pink. The tip of Spear of Destiny was dumped into the bowl, which turned the water bloody. It started boiling. The Llama started crying and dumped the silk handkerchief into the concoction turning the water pink again but it would not stop boiling.
"…Your holiness, do you have any tears from the original Buddha…?" asked Ignacious.
"…As a matter of fact I do have some…" he said as he opened a little bottle that hanged from his neck like a charm. He added about half the contents to the bowl and boiling subsided and the concoction was turned transparent again. The tip of the spear floated out of the bowl, with an incredible level of sharpness, like brand new. It floated to one of the Bo staff and incrusted itself in it, completing the weapon. Ounce it was completed it shined more the sun for a couple of minutes and collapsed in the hands of Ignacious, Pereira and the Llama.
"…According to the prophecy, those who receive the restored "Spear of Destiny" have to cooperate to kill the Son of the Devil' said the Pope. So you three gentlemen are bound to work together until the end, protect each other and you will succeed in your task. Separate and you will be destroyed…"said the Pope.

The ghost of Abuela entered the church, escorted by the ghost of Arthur Murray, both in formal dress. She looked at the scene and added: "…God have mercy! It was difficult to separate them before, now it will be impossible. Now the Pope gave them dispensation…!"
"…Evil woman…! I should have send you to hell when I could…" said Ignacious.
"…My friend, listen to the old witch, she may help us if you can

go beyond her constant homosexual taunting..." said Pereira.

"...I recommend two things: First: the monster by tomorrow will be about thirty feet high , pretty difficult to kill by one person ,so you have to develop a way of getting up there . Second: the way to kill this animal is by piercing its chest Spartan way, piercing down his lungs and his central vessels. Easier said than done, this time around, but certainly not impossible..." said Abuela Goya.

She left the place as she came, dancing the waltz out of the church, through the walls.

"...Anybody around with any great ideas...?" asked the Pope.

"...My people are acrobats and gymnasts by nature. We can probably train you to surpass this new obstacle..." added the Llama, while consulting in Vietnamese with several of his monks, all which started a lively discussion and took several suggestions. There was a consensus among them and they spoke among themselves for about ten minutes. They will attempt to train the occidentals on the way of balance on human columns and pyramids.

"...Then it is decided, our fate is in your hands, gentlemen. Do your best, make US proud...!" said the Pope

The pope picked up his cell phone and called Geneva. Yves answered:

"...You Holiness, what a surprise...! Yes, The Saint is here, she is about eight months, even though she has been pregnant for less than a week. The child, who calls himself "the prophet of the Lord", is able to communicate directly without the intervention of The Saint.

"...If we fail here you need to defend them with your life, plus you need to be sure that the election of the next Pope and maintaining the "purity" of the next election. That is, if you are up to the task..."

"...You know I will gladly give my life for Christ and his Church and his Vicar in Earth..."

"...Well the priority for now are those under your keep, right now. After that comes the Church and the next Pope. Under the circumstances, giving my age and health, there will be another Pope, either as a consequence of tomorrow or as a consequence of the natural law..."

"...Everybody here is excited about the birth of the prophet... "

"...Trust only those who had been under your service for more than ten years..."

"...I have not been under my service for more than seven, your Holiness, so I wound have to be under suspicion myself..."

"...Lets not get carried away...! There is an exception to every rule, son....! And besides, if there was any doubt about you, I know the prophet would have destroyed you by now. Furthermore in our last communication you asked me for permission to pursue the attentions of he Saint. Your intentions are as pure as you can imagine given the circumstances and very painful past...."

"...Please keep me posted..." said Yves.

"...Ditto, my son..." replied the Pope

The Llama took the floor:

"...We shall call the night. It's going to be a long day tomorrow. We should be awake early and prepare to defend the town. It not worth the effort, stop practicing anymore. The couples have been selected, the police have evacuated the town and they are bringing our two heroes back; sound and safe. So far we had the upper hand. However, they greatly outnumber us, plus the have the Monster in their corner..."The doors to the church opened up wide letting Jose, Moreno and Vicens enter the room.

They had sent the lady on her way to Rome, as she lacked any martial skills, she would only be balaster. Everybody looked exhausted. Jose spoke first: "... I ten to agree with the Llama, except that these people represent less of a risk to us than anything else. However to destroy the monster, we will have to destroy everybody else. The odds are getting somewhat better. At least everybody tonight was in a drugged stupor. Hopefully some of it will last until the morning, to our advantage…"

Moreno added: "…Lets rest tonight, we will need all our wits, to fight the enemy, even with the SWAT team and Maria throwing knives all over the place, we may still lose…"

Vicens added: "…We will guard the church tonight and guard the perimeter, croissants and coffee at 6:00 AM, courtesy of the Mayor and your friendly SWAT team. Go get some rest…"

At a distance Sampayo looked down the town from the mountain. Tomorrow will be the battles of all battles, the mother of all battles, to quote Sadam. They outnumbered these people five hundred to one. Plus the Son of the Devil was at their side. They could not lose.

Chapter 33
[[Rincón Town Square, Saturday Morning]]

Saturday morning was like any other in the town of Rincon, except for the total lack of activity. The four bakeries were closed. For the Islanders French Bread was the psychic cement that bounded their souls together...If you will, the Caribbean "dark matter" that bound their universe and brought meaning to their lives. Sharing the local French bread, from the shoe-shiners on the corner at the plaza to the millionaire industrialist, is part of the islander psyche.

The other unusual thing was the higher than usual police presence in the plaza for this time of the day. Such police presence was usual reserved for Friday and Saturday at the curfew call. This was usually, to get some rowdy drunk or stoned surfer, to cool in jail. The safest place on earth was that jail. The usually fed them with the local fare, and charged them like a local hotel. Rooms were clean and safe. Most American families were so relieved, when called by the local police, they pay the hotel fee, most believing that it was the bail.

The police had installed a bulletproof glass at the terrace of the City Hall. It dominated the plaza. Both the Pope and the Mayor will have a good view of the action from the safe heaven of the third floor. In addition four sharp shooters will be protecting them, posted in all the entrances to the terrace. Vicens was happy with himself. He reviewed the preparations with Moreno and the mayor, all of which were impressed and overwhelmed. Vicens apologized to Moreno from all damage he had tried to inflict both here and in Iraq:

"...My old friend, I owe you my life, so many times, indeed, that is not funny...! I apologize for arresting you in Iraq and sending you to Camp Pendleton, accused of war crimes. I apologize for trying to destroy both you and your reputation. I am not worth of your forgiveness, but if you will honor me with it I will be eternally grateful…"

"…I still hate your darn guts, but I forgive you. However do not give me any excuse to harm you because I will, with a vengeance…" said Garcia.

"…That is half ass forgiveness, which is worst than none at all. As a matter of fact we may be all be still alive because of your little trick , as our regiment was annihilated while we were on "vacation" in California…."said Moreno

"…I do apologize for that, my friend. God works in mysterious ways…" underlined Vicens.

"…You are all forgiven, I am forgiven, lets get ready, we do not have much time…" said the Llama arriving with his Tango assemble. "…Our group will go to the terrace, the electrical system has been connected and the tsunami warning alarm system and we will be amplified through the whole town…!" The monks, the Pope and the mayor were escorted to the terrace.

Mr. Manuel had placed barrels full of arrows in strategic places to complete the ying-yang circle with the help of Ms. Goldman. They place the sacred bowl with the spear of destiny in the middle of the town plaza. All the Zen-archery partners took their place in the circle. All the archers were ready the monks were already playing and the atmosphere was full of the eight beat cadence, calling them to get ready to shoot or dance.

After one hour of waiting, in anticipation, they heard it. The floor was trembling before they heard the footsteps. I felt like an earthquake. The heart of most, tremble along with the floor. Al their brains were filled with doubt. Then they heard a voice above all:

'…Concentrate…! Fools…! This is the confusion the Devil can bring to your hearts…! Listen to the beat, forget about anything else! Concentrate…!" that was the pope in his heavy German accent, shouting "concentrate "in all the languages of the people present. That broke the spell and the archers took their place, ready to fire.

Ignacious, Pereira and Jose were in the center with the sacred bowl

And then it happened. From the four corners of the plaza they came, looking like ants armed with swords and spears, eyes red and injected, ready for the kill. From every point of the sphere the arrows started flying in the direction of the crowds. The cadence of the tango was guiding them.

The battle cries of six thousand men were impossible to ignore. These cries, which previously made them tremble, were been changed to whales of agony. As the arrow pierced the flesh of the Babylonians, everything started quieting down. Soon the streets were filled with the stench of blood and guts.

So far they have been able to keep the perimeter. Mountains of cadavers were forming on the four corners of the plaza. These more than anything else had slowed down the attack considerably. The police was keeping from shooting, unless the lives of the warrior were at stake, as to save ammunition, to defend the Pope and the mayor, in a last desperate stance.

Then it happened: The Beast started approaching the plaza from the east, between the bank and one of the town's bakeries. By now he had turned into a twenty-foot colossus. The same agonizing and terrifying cry of his birth escaped its mouth. It scooped with his powerful arms the bodies of his followers out of the way. Sometimes he would eat from the flesh of the dead and the dying, in a diabolical form of communion. He opened that corner of the plaza and the attackers poured again through that corner. This was met with a barrage of arrows coming from all part of the sphere. Ten arrows every eight beats was taking heavy casualties on the enemy, who seemed make then more eager and determined to destroy the defenders.

The beast spoke clearly: "…You know you can not win, in shear numbers we still outnumber you three hundred to one. This is futile and it will decimate my followers and completely destroy you. If you surrender and join me and my Vicar we will spear your lives, provided of course, that you accept me as your new god, and renounce all the other ones, including, but not limited to the Carpenter, the crazy but enlighten Camel Herder, Buddha, Shiva etc, etc. Ounce we can establish my father's kingdom there would be no disease, no war for one thousand years. However those who oppose me will be dealt severely in the most horrible way. Of course, we will deal first with the Jews, who will be rounded and executed in mass, there is no place on Earth for the scum who invented the myth of monotheism and for five thousand years have shouted to the world that my father exists. It is all a big lie. Is the Jewish Lie, absolute evil does not exist and Hell is a figment of the Semitic imagination...."

An arrow flew and hit it in the left eye, penetrating its brain. The only Jew in the group, Ms. Goldman, had thrown it. She had tipped the arrow in the Holly Water concoction. No other arrow had penetrated the beast. She exclaimed: "...Never again, go to Hell...!"

"...Oh, we have a feisty Jew among the crowd...! I will make you mine and after that I will devour you alive...!" he said while taking the arrow out and repairing the eye back to normal.

Jose took his shuriken and immersed in the waters. They may become handy to distract the beast with pain, while the appropriate delivery system for the Holly Water had a chance to work.

The hoards of Babylonians were getting closer to the circle, so much so, that the snipers started to fire if they were getting too close to the sacred sphere. Of course you would get the occasional body with a bullet and an arrow piercing different parts of the body, but that was par for the course.

Then it happened. The Beast smell Moreno's smell and it went crazy. It realized that was the man that had prevented him from enjoying his wet nurse at birth. It sensed that she was long gone and that it would not have any second chances. That made it more than mad, blind with fury.

The center of the holly sphere realized that they would lose Moreno, if they did not act fast. They dipped all their arrows in sacred bowl and started shooting at the Beast while the rest of the archers and the snipers concentrated on the hordes. This slowed down the Beast, but it was able to kill one of Jose's disciples and it took time to devour it, while recovering from his wounds.

It was 7:00 am and the battle was in full swing. The Beast, gaining inches at the cost of lives of the defenders. The stench of blood and guts saturated everything. The Beast, without notice, ended the restless pursue of Moreno to pay attention to the terrace where the mayor and the Pope were. Realizing that the Pope was a bigger fish to fry it started running towards City Hall. A barrage of sniper fire, which was at the same time impressive, but ineffective, met him.

Garcia took out his gun. He ran to the sacred bowl and dip his clip on it. Without drying, he replaced the magazine and started firing. Every bullet hit the Beast in the head, making it lose the grip on the building and collapsing back first on the sidewalk. Now it was beyond furry it stood up, running towards the center of the sacred sphere.

The earth shook and the sonic wave which broke every window in the plaza. It knocked off most of the Babylonians, coming from the West side, unconcious. The Harrier was attempting a vertical landing using the last cubic centimeters of fuel left in the tank.
"…Do you have a target…?" asked Fello Vicens.
"…I have the Beast in range…" retorted Eli
"…Fire at will…!"

Eli pressed the fire button and the sidewinder hit the confused Beast in the center of the chest. Instead of blood, intense light, resembling the light coming from the sun emanated from the wound. The beast collapsed on its knees, mute. Its Chest was still twelve feet above the ground. The Harrier collapsed on its own weight devoid of any fuel to keep it afloat. The explosion of the tires in the landing gears waked up everybody from the stupor. The hoards of Babylonians quitted their task and started abandoning the plaza in all directions, some pursued by arrow from the remaining defenders.

Ignacious, Pereira and Jose ran towards the Beast, Spear of Destiny in hand. The Llama dangled himself from the terrace. The Beast was founded, but not totally incapacitated. Garcia emptied another clip of bullets sprayed by the Holly Water, at the back of the beast. Now every bullet, instead of blood, produced the intense light.

The Beast realized it had to re-incorporate in order to avoid destruction, but it was too late. When he pay attention back to its front, a human pyramid had been build with Jose at the top, and the two three priests at the bottom. Jose incrusted the spear of destiny, Spartan style, on the heart of the beast. Its body began to dissolve in a light and the small charge of the Sidewinder explode, finishing the job and pushing the pyramid ten feet back, knocking the four men out. They were a bloody mess, on fire and third degree burns on most of their bodies.

Garcia, who was closer to the sacred bowl, grabbed it instinctively, poring the remaining content on the four men. A great flash of light blinded everybody, fallowed by a severe headache that lasted about a minute. When they were able to open their eyes again, the three men were covered in the sacred light, standing nude. The sound of Jose's shuriken hitting the floor broke the trance. Slowly the light extinguished, leaving them nude, shaken, but completely healed.

"…God, even my appendectomy scar is gone…" declared Jose

half jokingly. They all looked about ten years younger.

The Plaza was deserted, except for the defenders. There was no trace that the Beast had ever been there. Eli and Vicens came out of the wreckage of Harrier. They were dazed and confused, but very much alive. The Pope and the Mayor had joined them at the plaza, so had the playing monks, exhausted from all the tango playing. Out of a pile of bodies Sampayo stood up with bow and arrow pointing at the Pope. Time froze. Out of nowhere a knife flew in the trajectory of Sampayo, hitting him in the heart, killing him instantly. There was a collective sign of relieve while they looked in the general direction of the knife firing when they saw Maria smiling at them sheepishly saying: "…Last Knife…"

Pereira picked the Spear of Destiny from the floor. Ignacious followed this development with interest. Pereira was about to return to its container, when the ghost of abuela appeared.

"…Boys you surpassed all my expectations, you have done very well. As of me, I have lived to fulfill my destiny and I am ready to walk towards the light…"

"…We will get you there…" said Pereira, and without giving it a second thought, speared the ghost right in the chest. The ghost, who had been an ethereal shadow, turned into a pure light form. This was fallowed by her disappearance.

"…May you go in peace, sister…" said the Pope, with a special Papal blessing.

"…I thought that we were not allowed to kill ghost anymore' said Ignacious sarcastically.

"…We did not kill her, my friend, said the Llama…" "…We directed her in the proper pathway to Nirvana. She had ascended to a higher level, thanks to our actions…"

"…We have a fighting chance, the anti-Christ will rise on the next fifty years. We have to prepare the men and woman of good will. He will be powerful, dominate by deceit, not brute force, unlike our Beast, which will make him much more dangerous. We need to get ready…" said the Pope

Zola was sitting in a corner of the square with the Vicens and Eli, sharing a Gallon of passion fruit juice that was liberated during the sonic explosion. Emma Goldman was embracing her brother, which she had not seen in more than five years.

"…Fello, how could you fly that infernal machine with all that noise…" asked Zola.

"…Well as long as Mr. Eli was quite, it was tolerable…"

"…Mr. Vicens, my pilot is retiring, as he is going to help prepare an underground network of distribution of goods in preparation to the arrival of the anti-Christ. Would you be interested in the job…? I will match your yearly earns and add ten percent…"

"…I will think about it, provided that you make my nephew chief of security…."

"…The job has been accepted by Mr. Moreno…"

Moreno approached the group: "… No matter, we are moving to Rome, to be close to my woman and the Vatican. The Pope has named me his special bodyguard. I am a "Swiss Citizen". So is Garcia, if he wants the Job of chief of police. All depends on his wife…"

José approached his wife. She was covered with sweat and blood, exhausted. He started:

"…Honey, is there any future for us…?"

"…I don't think so, dear. We have very little in common, other than sex…"

"…Should we divorce, and go our separate ways…?"

"…No, I like casual sex with you. You are the best male lover I ever had…"

"…Male lover…?"

"…Yes dear, I have been around…"

"…I guess so…!"

Ana Sampayo was sitting. She was melancholic with her husband's head resting on her skirt. They were both too exhausted to think. They had killed so many people that Ana had to puke in the corner, out of shear disgust. They were resting when the ghost of Ana's father appeared.

"…You both have done well, my grandsons should be darn proud of you two…"

"…Hello daddy, Mr. Nascimento is dead as you well know. I have an honor debt I have to pay. I need your help…"

"…I will tell you exactly where the ashes of Mr. Bohr and his family are entered so you can give them a hero's welcome back to Sweeden, and this ugly chapter of world history is completed. In the town of Makurdi, in the riviera of he Benue river, there is an old abandoned warehouse that used to store tobacco. Adjacent was a cigar factory. All that is left is the foundation, barely seen because of the undergrowth. Under that slab laid Bohr and his family, plus the spitfires. Bring the Bohrs home, dear..."

"…We will, Mr. Sampayo", said Jerry, "...You can count on both…!"

"…Ounce you had paid your debt honor, indeed there will be no reason for me to stay in this word and I will join my wife in heaven…"

EPILOGUE

Months had passed since the events of that fateful morning in the town of Rincon. Ana and Jerry had found the remains of the Bohr's clan, including the last three spitfires and transferred the bodies to Sweeden. Bohr's surviving son, Johansen, was a rich industrialist that been fighting with the Nigerian government for decades to exhume the bodies for proper burial back in Sweden.

The son was filled with emotions when the Sampayo's showed up with a eighteen-wheel truck full of memories stolen by unscrupulous despots in the past. When the slab covered the tomb and a likeness of Bohr surrounded by starving, but pot bellied children of decades ago, the whole word has forgotten, and whose lives were sacrificed in the altar of cheap petroleum decades ago. That had been first capitulation of the West against Wassail fundamentalism. This was fallowed by decades of internal abuse and terrorism, with extreme Islamic law. It was ironic that the very people betrayed Christian Biafra that decades after would be the victims of Islamic Terrorism.

In the meantime Lebanon was been reduced to ruble. The Switzerland of the Middle East was becoming its Monte Casino. Again the Zarathrustrans had underestimated the resolve of the Semitic tribes. Hizballah was the de facto government of South Lebanon. Under the misguided intelligence provided by Fatima's agents, they did not expected Israel's resolve to exist and to effectively cut all their links to Syria and Iran within the first thirty hours of the beginning of the war. Supplies could only come through the sea, very inefficient and slow. The Israeli air force was using the supply ships for target practice.

The Israeli army had arrived with three tank battalions. They were pounding Hizballah's headquarters around the clock. Yuri had been active in organizing both Osama's intelligence apparatus and providing the IDF with information and LASER tagging of targets, both at sea and land. Rocket launching site had been made ineffective in South Lebanon. The Palestinian uprising, other than the CNN propaganda reports, had become inconsequential. Hammas had been paralyzed, as their supplies route from Jordan and Egypt had been destroyed.

Yuri was sitting in a café in the capital awaiting a contact massager from Osama when his cell phone rang. It was Eli calling from the Bacca Valley.

"...Hello my friend, nice to hear your voice. Uncle is very happy with your work so far..."

"...One tries to be useful to his elders ounce in a while, how was your stint in the Island...?"

"...Was very educational, I even got a Papal blessing out of it. I also got a ticket for littering the plaza with a Harrier. I had to work on the Sabbath, but in our business, not a bad day..."

"...Is your sister in good health...?"

"...She also got a Papal blessing, and we may be married for all I know...! Yuri I am calling you to give you some information. We are attacking a scud missile depot in the valley, and there is a chance we might not make it alive..."

"...OK, to the point my friend, before we get too sentimental..."

"...Fatima, who has made basically impotent politically, is trying to make points by visiting the troops at the front tomorrow at 10:00am, minimal security. She will be an easy target at one thousand yards. I will e-mail you right now the coordinates, and the maps of the area, as for you to plan the escape route. One shot and you have to run like the Devil is behind you. Local commanders have orders to give you a five-minute handicap. That is all they could get from Uncle, the IDF does not want to give the appearance of being part of the conspiracy, and that would be the extent of the cooperation. Good luck...!"

"...Good Luck to you my friend..."

As he hanged the phone, a uniformed Lebanese army General approached him. His gun out was of the holster. He addressed him:
"…Are you Mr. Omar…?"
"…Yes I am..."

"…Fallow me..." he said pointing with the drawn gun towards a parked Mercedes.
Omar enter the car, and much to his surprise, Osama himself was there, e-mailing orders to several cells around the world. After his last message he addressed Omar.
"…By now, you should know about your wife been here in town tomorrow, so I brought you a present…"
He opened a box, and a dismantled, state of the art sniper rifle appeared.
"…It's German, it fires ten shots a minute. There is nothing more accurate at a thousand yards. Happy Birthday. Now go! Don't forget to keep me posted…"
Osama closed the attache case and push it in hands. The car sped away. The army General had disappeared. Omar picked up his wits, and started walking towards the café for another espresso, when the Israeli jets flew by, making the whole city tremble.

He decided instead to look for shelter in his basement apartment, almost a bunker, which was built during the civil war. A lonely, malnourished calico cat approached him.

"…Mr. Openheimer, how are you doing today…? Have you nuked any mice today…? Tomorrow I will kill my wife…" It is going to be the best day of my life…"

The cat, sensing no imminent treat, went back to its bed. Omar decided to fallow suit, after playing with his new toy, building and dismantling it.
"…Yes, Mr. Openheimer, a Jew-boy can celebrate Chanukah in

August..."

In Rome, García observed his old friend, Moreno, as he strode down one of the little street that made up the maze of neighbourhood around Vatican City. He was observing him from the balcony of his office, the office of the Chief of Police. Two Middle Eastern looking men had been fallowing him. They took two guns out, disarmed Moreno and pushed him into a waiting cab. They all sped away.

García entered his office. He sat on his desk. Across the desk, three men in ill-fitting suits waited for him. Eli, Dimitri Ustinov and Francesco Volare sat uncomfortably in very comfortable chairs. Volare was the Interpol attache in Rome. Ustinov was the KGB attache and personal friend of Putin. The phone then rang. It was Ratzinger:

"...García, I have thee cooperation of Turkish government, you have the green light...Good luck..."

The pope hanged the phone.

Garcia, placed the coat of the suit on, had the last sip of coffee and addressed the men:

"...The game is afoot...!"

Instinctively, all three caulked their guns, and place to the lock, placing them back in their holsters.

One by one they left the office. Outside, there was waiting an unmarked police car.

Eli was the last one to leave. He placed a bug in García's desk. This was on Middleman's direct orders, much to his regret.

Rincon Scuffle 299 Morell-Chardon

Cover Photo: © Ricardo Pacheco 2009

The Critics keep raving about <u>The Rincon Scuffle:</u>

".... A tale told by an idiot signifying nothing..." William Shakespeare
For *Elizabethan Times*

".... Definitively not part of *My Struggle...*" Adolph Hitler for *Paraguayan Dictator Monthly & The Hell Literary Journal*

"...As much joy to experience as my left arm amputation..." Miguel de Cervantes for La Mancha Gazette

"...Relatively speaking, this is a work of great gravity..." Albert Einstein for the *Swiss Patent Clerk Literary Gazette*

"...An obvious plagiarism from *One Hundred Years of Solitude...*" Garcia-Marquez for *Magic Realism International*

"... A unique *Metamorphosis...*" Kafka for *German Existentialist Monthly*

"...The whole Universe is in Chaos, but the situation is perfect..." Mao Tse Tung for the *Chinese Absolute Dictator Weekly*

"...*It* is time for another Literary Purge..." Joseph Stalin from the *Hell Literary Journal & The Gulag Review*

"...His work has been widely quoted, but grossly *miss-underestimated...*" President Bush for *The Beltway Gazette*

"...A Scream..." Edvard Munch for the *New Norwegian Expressionist*

"...As I originally read it in Swahili, the English version sounded like a very poor translation..." Borges for *The Ambassador*

www.ingramcontent.com/pod-product-compliance
Lightning Source LLC
Chambersburg PA
CBHW070724160426
43192CB00009B/1302